HIKING
TROPICAL
AUSTRALIA

Fan palms, Far North Queensland

HIKING
TROPICAL
AUSTRALIA

QUEENSLAND AND NORTHERN NEW SOUTH WALES

by

Lew Hinchman

Grass Tree Press

Published by
Grass Tree Press
P.O. Box 211
Potsdam, NY 13676

Manufacured in the United States of America

Edited by John N. Serio
Maps by Sandra Hinchman
Photographs by Sandra Hinchman unless otherwise noted
Designed and typeset by John N. Serio

Cover photograph by Tom Till, Elabana Falls, Lamington National
        Park, Queensland, Australia © Tom Till

Library of Congress Cataloging-in-Publication Data

Hinchman, Lewis P.
    Hiking tropical Australia: Queensland and northern New South
Wales / by Lew Hinchman; [edited by John N. Serio; maps by
Sandra Hinchman; photographs by Sandra Hinchman].
            p.   cm.
    Includes bibliographical references (p.   ) and index.
    ISBN 0-9648056-1-8 (pbk.)
    1. Hiking—Australia—Queensland—Guidebooks. 2. Hiking—
Australia—New South Wales—Guidebooks. 3. Queensland—
Guidebooks. 4. New South Wales—Guidebooks. I. Serio, John N.,
1943–   .
    II. Title.
    GV199.44.Q842H56   1999
    919.4304'66—dc21
                                                    99–19481
                                                        CIP

CONTENTS

Legend

Symbol	Label	Symbol	Label
———	road	⟧⟦	bridge
- - - -	jeeproad	⌂	cave
• • • •	trail or route	▣	overlook
-·-·-	boundary	◬	camping
⏚⏚	cliff	⌂	visitor center
𝓜	pinnacle	🜊	waterfall
⌂	dome	⊥	rock art
⌂	natural arch	⌁	reef
※	mountain	⣿	beach

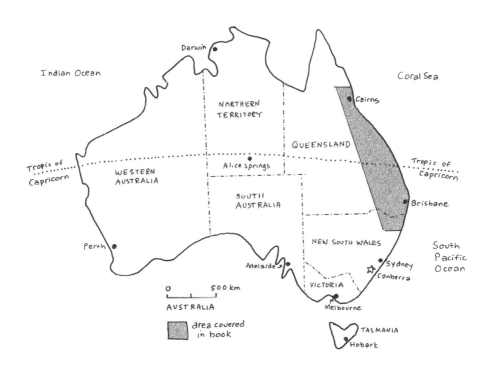

Darwin

Indian Ocean

Coral Sea

NORTHERN
TERRITORY

Cairns

QUEENSLAND

Tropic of
Capricorn

Tropic of
Capricorn

WESTERN
AUSTRALIA

Alice Springs

SOUTH
AUSTRALIA

Brisbane

Perth

NEW SOUTH WALES

South
Pacific
Ocean

Adelaide

0   500 km

AUSTRALIA

Sydney
Canberra

VICTORIA

Melbourne

area covered
in book

TASMANIA

Hobart

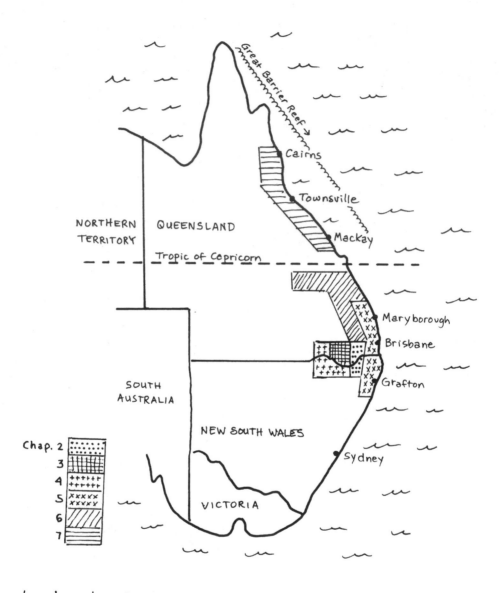

Great Barrier Reef

Cairns

Townsville

Mackay

NORTHERN
TERRITORY

QUEENSLAND

Tropic of Capricorn

Maryborough

Brisbane

Grafton

SOUTH
AUSTRALIA

NEW SOUTH WALES

Chap. 2
3
4
5
6
7

Sydney

VICTORIA

0   200   400   600 Km

EASTERN AUSTRALIA

PREFACE

This book grew out of both my love of hiking and a wonderful opportunity I enjoyed to live in and explore tropical Australia. As an American, my goal was to write a guidebook that would be useful to visitors from abroad who were considering an extended trip to Australia, but who did not have a clear idea about where they should go, how best to use their time, and what conditions they might expect to encounter. Thus, this book is written from the viewpoint of a foreign visitor, and will doubtless offer some information that Australians will not need. Nevertheless, Australians too should find this a handy resource, since it collects, in a single volume, trail descriptions that are otherwise scattered about in many guidebooks with a more local orientation. Ideally, all readers who intend to do some of these hikes should plan their trips well in advance, checking to see whether they will need to write away for permits or camping reservations. This book should help prevent the all-too-familiar scenario of hikers arriving at a spectacular national park, only to learn that they may not hike or camp in the places they wanted to, since all available sites or permits are already gone. By all means, be spontaneous and flexible, but plan ahead too, especially for the really popular parks and trails, which this guide will identify.

I would like to express gratitude to my wife, Sandy, and my son, Bryce, for hiking most of these many miles of trail with me, and helping me prepare the descriptions of them. Thanks also to Sandy for the countless hours she has put in reading and revising the manuscript, drawing the maps, taking the photographs, and giving me advice drawn from writing her own guidebook to the canyon country of the Southwest. This volume actually represents the combined efforts of the two of us. Thanks also go to Tom Till for providing the magnificent photograph that adorns the cover of the book. I am indebted as well to the authors of the many other excellent guidebooks to specific regions of Australia whose suggestions I used in planning my own itineraries. Their names and the titles of their books are listed in the bibliography, and I encourage my own readers to consult these works, as they often contain more detailed descriptions of particular regions than my own does. I wish to extend my appreciation to Elissa Clark for scanning the numerous photographs and maps and to Richard Austin for sharing his technical expertise. Finally, I want to thank my colleague and friend, John N. Serio, for laying out and editing the manuscript. Without his knowledge of desktop publishing, I could never have completed this project.

Chapter 1

INTRODUCTION

WHY AUSTRALIA?

During the past decade, North American hikers have begun to fan out across the globe, seeking the magnificent landscapes and exotic cultures of other countries. Of course, adventurous travelers had already long since "discovered" places like the Swiss Alps, Costa Rica, and even Nepal. But as our own parks and trails have grown overcrowded and the possibilities for solitude have dwindled, the trickle of American and Canadian outdoor enthusiasts traveling abroad has swelled to a flood. If we choose our destinations wisely, we can still enjoy the unhurried, uncrowded hiking and camping experiences that prevailed on our shores a generation ago.

This book recommends Australia, and specifically the subtropical and tropical region extending from northern New South Wales to Far North Queensland, as the sort of place that American and Canadian wilderness lovers would delight in exploring. Natural Australia—its plants and animals, landforms and evolutionary patterns—is wildly exotic. Yet Australia is a First World country, with a well-developed transportation system, high standards of health and safety, and an efficient, competent administration. Its citizens speak English, so visitors face no language problems in organizing trips or dealing with unforeseen mishaps. Best of all, the country has a vast and diverse system of national parks, one that compares favorably on many dimensions to U.S. and Canadian models. In short, Australia is easy to travel around and enjoy, yet utterly different from anything with which most North Americans are acquainted.

If there is any drawback in hiking and exploring the great island continent, it would be Australia's vast size—as large as the continental U.S. In fact, "Oz" (as Australians often call their country) feels even larger than the U.S., because the roads do not form a dense grid of high-speed interstates. Getting from Point A to Point B may involve circuitous routes and will surely take longer than expected. Indeed, the country cannot be "done" as a whole. Instead, you have to concentrate on a single region in order to limit time spent in planes, cars, and buses and to maximize trail time.

WHY TROPICAL AUSTRALIA?

The term "tropical" is used loosely here to characterize an arc of north-eastern Australia stretching from roughly 15° to 30° south latitude, but close enough to the coast to benefit from the South Pacific's moisture-laden winds and moderating climatic influence. In this book, you will get an introduction to the parks and hiking "tracks," as they are called, of the states of Queensland and northeastern New South Wales. The latter subregion is included because it has much in common with Queensland, geographically and biologically, and can be easily visited from Queensland's capital city of Brisbane. Strictly speaking, much of this area is not truly "tropical," since the Tropic of Capricorn passes through the city of Rockhampton, about a third of the way up the Queensland coast. Nevertheless, even the technically subtropical regions included in this guide will seem tropical enough to most North Americans who hike their rainforests and palm groves and drive past their banana and sugarcane plantations.

Prospective hikers should not think of Queensland or even New South Wales as "states" in the same sense as, say, Missouri or Montana, for both are far vaster than American states, though comparable to some Canadian provinces. Queensland alone stretches over 2100 kilometers (1300 miles) on the north/south axis and 1450 km (900 miles) from east to west at its widest point. If laid flat on a map of the United States, Queensland would extend from Maine to Florida and from New York to Illinois. Throw in the adjacent corner of New South Wales and you have a region that could occupy the most intrepid hiker for months or even years.

Australia's other states and territories, of course, have their own magnificent natural areas that visitors should by all means try to see, such as Uluru (Ayers Rock) and Kakadu in the Northern Territory, Cradle Mountain in Tasmania, or West Australia's Nambung and Bungle Bungle National Parks. But tropical Australia as defined here holds certain advantages that I want to highlight.

Extensive parklands. Queensland has set aside about 4% of its territory in nearly 100 national parks. Admittedly, some of these enclose only a few acres, but others rival in size some of the best known North American parks. Many of the parks in both Queensland and northern New South Wales that are featured in this book have been designated by the United Nations as "World Heritage Areas" for their biological and/or cultural uniqueness. By the time you visit Australia, both states will likely have added still more land to their park systems.

Year-round hiking. Most of tropical and subtropical Australia can be enjoyed all year round, unlike some other parts of the country. The region described in this book extends from about 900 km (550 miles) south of the Tropic of Capricorn to about 1300 km (800 miles) north of it. Hence, its climate ranges from temperate around the higher ranges and plateaus to the "endless summer" of the far north. Still, summers, at least in the southeast, rarely get unbearably hot; plus, they offer the opportunity to swim in stream-fed pools, lakes, and the ocean. Winter weather usually stays mild in the south and tropically warm throughout much of the north. A typical winter day in the mountain parks of northern New South Wales or southern Queensland might reach 15° C (60° F) at noon and fall to 5° C (40° F) by midnight. In the far north, you would frequently encounter winter days of 25–28° C (75–80° F), with mild evenings. Of course, these typical figures do conceal wide fluctuations. Because weather fronts move through and cause temperatures at different elevations to drop or climb dramatically, on any given day you might freeze or swelter. Yet no matter when you visit, you will surely find some parks, in some sections of the region, where you will be able to spend pleasant days hiking. This book will suggest the best times to visit the various parks and will caution readers in the few cases where inclement weather could cause serious problems.

The fine climate of the region has special importance for North Americans. Many of us tend to plan our hiking vacations for the northern hemisphere's summer. Hence, we often suffer from heat and insect pests, especially in our south and southwest. But Australia, where the seasons are reversed from ours, has its winter during June, July, and August. This means you can stroll through Lamington National Park or Fraser Island wearing a light sweater, under blue skies, with not a mosquito in sight, or swim in the Coral Sea without fear of stinging jellyfish.

Biological diversity. If you have a yen for exotic and unusual ecosystems, Queensland and northern New South Wales will not disappoint you. Most of the major parks described here support tropical or subtropical rainforests, environments not found north of Mexico on our own continent. Trails lead through sun-dappled palm groves, beneath towering tree ferns, and past enormous, liana-draped tropical hardwoods. The region's topography, with steep mountains thrusting up near the coast and precipitous rhyolite cliffs, has created countless cascades, some dropping hundreds of feet into idyllic pools. North America's parks are often austere, stern, and sublime; Australia's, by contrast, awaken echoes in the psyche of the Garden of Eden.

As if its lush forests and mountains were not enough, tropical Australia harbors many of the country's most intriguing and lovable creatures. You will certainly see plenty of kangaroos, wallabies, and other marsupials, as well as goannas (large lizards) and exotic birds such as parrots and cockatoos. With luck, you may also encounter koalas, wombats, possums, flying foxes, bandicoots, dingoes (wild dogs), crocodiles, and echidnas. For elaboration, see the section on wildlife, below.

Proximity of ocean. While many of America's finest wilderness reserves lie far from the ocean, tropical Australia's mostly fringe the coast. Thus, visitors rarely find themselves far from spectacular beaches, surfing, snorkeling, and scuba diving. The natural beauty of the state's mountains and forests finds its counterpart in coastal parks, islands, and the Great Barrier Reef, a World Heritage Area extending all the way from the latitude of Bundaberg in Queensland to the Torres Strait between Australia and Papua New Guinea. Where in the continental U.S. and Canada can you top off a long rainforest hike with a dive expedition to the world's largest coral reef?

PHYSICAL FEATURES

Geologists theorize that all the world's continents once formed a single great landmass called Pangaea. Roughly 100 million years ago, the southern section of that primordial supercontinent, Gondwana, broke away. It included present-day Australia, Antarctica, and South America. Apparently, dense rainforest covered much of Gondwana in those times. Then, about 50 million years ago, Australia and Antarctica broke away and soon after separated from one another, with Australia drifting northward toward the tropics (a process that still continues, at the rate of 4

Dunk Island from South Mission Beach

centimeters, or 1.5 inches, per year). Gradually, the continent grew drier, especially as the last ice age ended around 10,000 years ago.

The Great Dividing Range. Although Australia is now the world's driest and flattest continent, the area covered by this guidebook hardly fits that description. Queensland and northern New South Wales are defined, first, by a chain of mountains up to 1600 meters (5250 feet) high called the Great Dividing Range that runs parallel to Australia's eastern seaboard all along the continent's rim. The range meanders quite a bit, sometimes veering far inland; but—especially in the north—it often approaches the sea very closely. Most of the hikes described in this book lie in, or very close to, the Great Dividing Range. So the Australia described here will be one of the most mountainous and wettest parts. Indeed, some of the ancient rainforests of Gondwana have survived nearly unchanged in parts of Queensland, which alone has over 2 million acres of them.

Tablelands. Beyond the Great Dividing Range stretches a lonely, flat, desolate landscape, though in places marked by dramatic gorges or low hills. The region just west of the range forms high tablelands that have been by now mostly cleared for agriculture and livestock. Past the tablelands is the outback, where the terrain grows ever drier (except for isolated wet season cloudbursts) until it merges with the central deserts. The exception is far north Queensland, where reliable monsoonal rains in summer create a seasonally lush, wet environment ideal for crocodiles and barramundi but sometimes impassable for humans. Of the parks included in this book, only Sundown and Carnarvon display something of the outback character.

Volcanic landscapes. Volcanic activity has also left its signature on the landforms of Queensland and northern New South Wales. About 20 million years ago, a shield volcano, the forebear of today's Mt. Warning, stretched for nearly 100 km (62 miles) across the region. As will be explained later, ancestral Mt. Warning's caldera slopes created a series of mountain ranges around the border country that now harbor some of Australia's most beautiful national parks. Farther north, one encounters massive buttes—the dramatic remnants of ancient volcanoes—called the Glass House Mountains, as well as lesser volcanic peaks near the towns of Nambour and Gympie.

The Great Barrier Reef. Australia's most renowned natural feature, the Great Barrier Reef, belongs exclusively to Queensland, stretching around 2000 km (1240 miles) north from roughly the latitude of the city of Bundaberg to the Torres Strait separating Australia from Papua New Guinea. Almost all of it is protected as a national park and World Heritage Area. But the Reef lies disconcertingly far offshore: well over 160 km (100 miles) out, in fact, at its southern extremity.

Australia's ice age history accounts for the reef's remoteness. Up until about 12,000 years ago, the planet's ice sheets locked up so much water that sea level lay 100 meters (330 feet) below the current mark. The Australian coast stretched far east of its present-day boundary, and the reef was close by. But the glaciers melted, and the seas rose, inundating vast stretches of coastal plain and transforming mountain ranges into islands (such as the Whitsundays, Dunk, and Hinchinbrook). As the ocean level rose, the coral kept pace by adding new layers and eventually colonizing some of the drowned coastline.

Though we often think of the Great Barrier Reef as a single, long, continuous structure, it actually consists of around 3000 separate reefs, plus countless shoals, cays, and the complex of lagoons and passages that they enclose. In places the Great Barrier Reef may extend 50 km (over 30 miles) across. Although it obviously does not qualify as a hiker's destination (unless you count walking along the sand of a coral cay), the reef will doubtless lure many readers to explore it by boat or, better, with snorkel or scuba equipment. I have therefore included some information about getting out to it from Queensland coastal parks and towns.

Beaches and sand islands. South of the Great Barrier Reef, Australia boasts other fascinating variations on the interplay between land and water. The country has some of the world's longest and most magnificent beaches, many pounded by huge surf. Then too, several vast "sand islands" like Moreton and Fraser (the world's largest) front the mainland and offer hikers enticing journeys through diverse forests, across sprawling sand blows, and along the margin of freshwater lakes.

FLORA AND FAUNA

Australia's long isolation and its drift from ancient Gondwana toward Asia have bestowed upon it a wealth of strange, alluring flora and fauna. Some Australian trees, like the Antarctic beech, have living relatives today only in South America (formerly a component of Gondwana). Others, like the eucalyptus, acacia, and casuarina, have thrived and diversified on the island continent far more than anywhere else on earth. Taken as a whole, Australia's bush landscape strikes most North Americans as alien, unsettlingly different from any they have experienced. Australian trees and shrubs have little in common with the native species of our hemisphere. Grayish blues and olive greens predominate in the leafy crowns of forests, while the bark of eucalyptus, the most characteristic tree of the region, varies from gray-brown to mottled white and often peels. In every season of the year, there will be trees, bushes, or plants in bloom to delight the senses.

Yet surely, for most visitors, the animals of Australia will evoke even more wonder and curiosity. Nearly all of us have learned at least a bit about the continent's emblematic creatures: kangaroos, wallabies, platy-puses, dingoes, and koalas. All are well represented in tropical Austra-lia; in fact, Queensland alone tallied six million kangaroos in 1997, or nearly two for every one person. The commentaries on specific hikes and regions will suggest places where you may sight these often elusive animals and other lesser known beasts like the bandicoot and betong. Many of these creatures are, of course, marsupials: they sustain their tiny newborn young in pouches until they mature enough to step forth and live independently.

What visitors often don't expect from their trip to Australia is the marvelous profusion of birdlife. The continent harbors about 750 bird species, many more than the U.S. and Canada combined. Above all, the orders of avian life differ profoundly from those commonly seen in our homelands. Where the U.S. has a few vagrant parrots on its southern border, Australia counts 53 species, from enormous yellow-tailed black cockatoos to diminutive lorikeets. The parrot order includes some of the most colorful, fascinating, and exotic birds you will ever see. The gaudy rainbow lorikeet, eastern rosella, and king parrot all abound in Queens-land and should be easy to spot in certain areas. Honeyeaters, which don't occur at all in the continental U.S., fill 19 pages of the standard Aussie bird guide. As if these were not enough, visitors will undoubt-edly hear the maniacal laughter of the kookaburra on hikes and may even spot a giant emu or cassowary. If you are not a birder already, a trip to Australia may suffice to convert you.

In sum, the natural history of Australia contributes mightily to its appeal for hikers from overseas. The continent's long isolation and—even today—its relative wildness have left it a legacy of animals and plants unmatched anywhere except perhaps the most remote reaches of Africa or South America. While some countries, such as New Zealand, offer magnificent scenery, their native fauna and flora have been hard pressed by species substitution. Australia seems at first less majestic in its physical presence, but the longer one spends there and the keener one's knowledge of its evolutionary patterns, the greater the wonder at and appreciation of its natural treasures. This is a country that rewards the knowledgeable, inquisitive, and adventurous, so plan to polish your skills as an amateur naturalist.

MAKING ENDS MEET:
TRAVEL TO AND WITHIN TROPICAL AUSTRALIA

When my family announced that we would spend a year in Australia, many of our friends expressed shock that we would undertake such a costly trip. The majority of North Americans consider Australia a desti-

Sulphur-crested cockatoos

nation that is just too expensive to consider. Certainly, traveling halfway around the globe will cost a good bit, but for those who are willing to "rough it" (and most lovers of the outdoors are), expenses can be kept to manageable levels, costing not much more than, say, a trip to Europe.

Air tickets. Let's begin with airfares to Australia, a sticking point for many. Obtain copies of the Sunday edition of newspapers such as the *New York Times*, *Los Angeles Times*, or *Toronto Globe and Mail*, which carry a lot of ads for discount travel. Travel agents also often have connections to discounters. You should be able to secure round-trip fares from the West Coast for under U.S. $1000 (as of 1998). Fare levels depend on the months in which you want to travel. Ask the discounters about the times of year deemed "peak," "shoulder," and "low" seasons and the fare differences among them. Generally, low season arrives around May.

Although airfares will probably be your biggest expense, you must take into account what you get for your money. First, nearly all carriers allow free stopovers, both outbound and return, often at remote and exotic places. For example, you could spend a week in Fiji or Tahiti on the way to Australia and a week in New Zealand on the way home. Then imagine how much it would cost you to fly to those islands as destinations in themselves. In effect, you would have a chance to discover three different countries for the price of one.

Second, many of the airlines you might fly with either have frequent flier programs of their own, or else (like Qantas) they are partners of U.S. and Canadian airlines that have such programs. Suppose that you flew on Qantas to Brisbane and back from New York, and assigned the roughly 28,000 miles earned to your favorite American carrier. You would then qualify for a free ticket to any destination in the continental United States or be within reach of a 35,000 mile award to Mexico or the Carribean. And if you also have credit cards that earn you frequent flier miles for each dollar spent, putting the tickets on your credit card would get you even closer to the "magic number." If you are not a member of a frequent flier plan, by all means enroll before you go, remembering that new members usually start with a bonus of 4000 or 5000 miles. In short, your ticket will buy you a round trip to Australia, stopovers at Pacific islands, and valuable air awards for your next trip.

Finally, some carriers will convey you on to your destination city (say, Brisbane or Mackay) at no extra charge from the international arrival capital of Sydney. Buying a separate ticket for that leg would otherwise cost several hundred dollars. Thus, when you add up all the benefits of a ticket to Australia, it seems almost cheap.

Transportation within Australia. Once you land in Brisbane, Cairns, or another gateway city, what can you expect to pay for a traveler's necessities? Outdoor enthusiasts will probably need a car for many of the hikes outlined in this book, although some can be reached by bus, via shuttles arranged by "backpacker" hostels, or in organized tours. I would strongly recommend renting a car for at least part of your stay in Australia, since it simplifies and speeds up travel. Rental (or "hire") cars do not come cheap. However, visitors can find bargains if they shop around and check out the smaller, local companies, rather than reserving in advance from multinational giants such as Hertz or Avis. Some of these local companies offer somewhat older, but still perfectly good, vehicles at reduced rates. As of 1998, it was possible to find a compact car with 200 free km (120 miles) per day for a rate of U.S. $30, though that figure may change significantly and represents only a guideline. Four-wheel drive vehicles are also available to rent, but since they are quite expensive, I have deliberately included in this book only hikes that can be accessed by conventional automobiles (though sometimes on rather bumpy roads). Gasoline ("petrol") in 1998 cost the equivalent of about U.S. $1.75 per gallon, higher than in the U.S. but far less than in Europe.

The decision about whether and when to rent a car will depend somewhat on the itinerary you have mapped out. You must determine the most efficient way to travel around within the parts of the vast Queensland/northern New South Wales region that you wish to see. You could certainly rent a car at your gateway city and drive it everywhere you want to visit. But if all that driving seems too daunting, consider taking trains or buses up and down the coast. Since most of the national parks featured in this book lie very near the main coastal transportation routes, visitors can easily divide their trip into subregions and rent cars in each "hub" city, then fan out to desired locations in the area.

For example, a reasonable itinerary could include arrival in Brisbane, a bus trip north to Mackay, then another bus trip to Cairns, renting vehicles in each city.

However, if you plan to travel beyond the coastal strip—for example, to Tasmania or to the Northern Territory—you may want to purchase airline "coupons" in advance for these more remote destinations. Qantas, for instance, will sell you "short haul" coupons for U.S. $170 each and "long haul" coupons for $220 each (1997 prices). The catch is that you must buy at least four before you enter Australia. If you subsequently decide to purchase more of them, you need only to go to a Qantas ticket office, present your international ticket at the counter, and buy up to six additional coupons. In that case, you might want to forget about buses and trains and simply fly between Queensland venues with short haul coupons. There is some question, though, about whether airline coupons will always save you money. Sometimes, Qantas or Ansett offer discounted round-trip fares on popular routes, usually advertised in newspapers, that cost less than the total of your two coupons. So, if you can build some flexibility into your schedule, such ordinary discount fares might prove a bargain.

Food. Food expenses obviously vary dramatically depending upon one's tastes. But you will find prices to be a bit higher for some grocery items (such as milk, chicken, and beer) and much lower for others (such as lamb chops and many fresh fruits). The quality of food, especially fruits and vegetables, is excellent. On the whole, expect to pay a little more than you would at home. Remember, however, that you will pay no sales tax on any item, since taxes have already been factored into the marked price. Restaurants, too, are not exorbitantly expensive; many establishments have a BYOB policy, and tips (though welcome) are not expected. Australia has the array of fast food restaurants familiar to North Americans, as well as inexpensive fish and chips places, so you can eat cheaply there as well.

Lodging. Lodging represents the one item of the travel budget where flexibility reigns. You can save big if you are willing to do a lot of camping and/or staying in hostels. Australians call the latter "backpacker" hostels, not in our sense of the word, but because such lodgings appeal to low-budget, youthful travelers who carry their belongings in backpacks or rucksacks. They will rent you a bed in a dormitory-style room, or else—sometimes—a private room of your own, though without private bath facilities. A few of these hostels offer pleasant, inexpensive accommodations with amenities such as pools, kitchens, and shuttle services; others, unfortunately, are dumps. Costs tend to run about U.S. $10 to $15 per person, per night. You can consult guidebooks such as the *Lonely Planet* series for details. For camping you can expect to pay anywhere from Au. $3 to Au. $12 per person depending on the type of campground and the level of amenities. The bottom line is that, for a month-long camping/hiking trip, staying mostly (but not exclusively) in park service campgrounds, the costs would run about Au. $100–$200, or U.S. $63–$125. It would be difficult to camp and lodge this cheaply in North America.

Other costs. Besides the indispensable costs of any trip—transportation, food, lodging—you may have some other expenses to bear, depending upon where you go and how long you stay. Australia requires visas for tourists from the U.S. Charges vary depending on length of stay. The Australian consulate nearest you can supply further details, as can most travel agents. Furthermore, a few exceptionally beautiful island parks, such as Fraser, Moreton, Hinchinbrook, and Dunk, can only be reached by boat and may levy trail-use fees as well. On the other hand, you will never have to pay the sorts of hut or guide fees that are common in some other countries.

PLANNING YOUR TRIP

Assuming that the reader is committed to visiting tropical Australia, and feels that he or she can afford it, the next questions that arise are: where should I go and how do I plan the excursions? The main body of this book should suggest answers to the first question, and the second will be tackled here.

Timing. After reading the hike descriptions, try to formulate a tentative itinerary, with dates in mind. Then check to see what advance work needs to be done, if any. At some parks (such as Gibraltar and Washpool in New South Wales) one simply shows up, selects a campsite, and starts hiking. Few people seem to go there, and in any event all campsites get assigned by a self-registration system. But at other parks, such as Bundjalung, Lamington, and especially Carnarvon, Hinchinbrook, and Dunk Island, advance reservations ("bookings") may be necessary, especially on weekends and school holidays. For Hinchinbrook you may have to arrange permits months in advance. And that may entail a phone call or two to Australia to adjust your desired dates to the ones that the Queensland National Parks and Wildlife Service (QNPWS) has available. Of course, last minute cancellations may develop, so you should never give up hope. Generally speaking, the busiest times for camping and permits are late June to mid-July, late September and early October, mid-December to late January, and the Easter season, as these are roughly the school holiday periods.

Nevertheless, aside from a very few popular parks, you can usually count on showing up at a Queensland or New South Wales national park

Strangler fig, Daintree National Park

at almost any time (and certainly on weekdays), finding a campsite, and going hiking. Several times, we have been the only party (or almost the only one) in the campground of a park that would be overflowing with visitors if it were in the U.S.

If and when you call local park headquarters, note that many are staffed only between 1 P.M. and 3 P.M. You will have to calculate the appropriate time lag between the east coast of Australia and your time zone in North America. It ranges from 15 hours earlier in Australia (for Eastern Standard Time) to 18 hours earlier (for Pacific Standard Time). Shifts in Daylight Savings Time will affect the differential in various ways, since New South Wales goes on daylight time in the southern hemisphere summer, while Queensland does not.

Climate and seasons. As noted earlier most parks in tropical Australia have a mild climate year round. Still, some seasons will afford more pleasant hiking than others. I have given detailed advice about when to visit certain areas in the descriptions below, but will offer a few general suggestions here. Many regions of Australia, including those covered in this guidebook, have wet and dry seasons. Rainfall is normally heaviest between December and March, the southern summer, and tapers off markedly between June and August. However, the wet and dry pattern varies with latitude, the southern areas showing less extreme fluctuations in rainfall than those farther north. Thus, for example, a visitor to the national parks around Brisbane could expect at least some dry, sunny weather even in summer. But far north Queensland often experiences showers every day for weeks on end during the wet season in addition to extremes of temperature and humidity. Of course, these wet and dry patterns represent only climatic averages. In unusual years the wet season may generate relatively little rainfall, while autumn or spring could usher in ceaseless downpours. In short, there are no guarantees about the weather in Australia any more than in other parts of the world. My best advice would be to visit tropical Australia in the period from April through November, and certainly to avoid far north Queensland during its summer rainy season. If you do come during the Australian summer, stick to the southern part of the region and create a flexible itinerary so you can quickly change plans if bad weather impends.

CAMPING

Provided you have a car, camping will turn out to be the least expensive and most convenient way to spend your nights in Australia. Since you have come to this island continent to see its natural beauty and wondrous wildlife, campgrounds put you in the right place. Many of the most fascinating of Australia's animals frequent campgrounds and have become used to the presence of human beings. In fact many are downright tame and will pester you for food or steal unsupervised morsels.

You will encounter three kinds of campgrounds in the region described here. First, you will usually have the opportunity to stay in a national park campground at or near your hiking destination. Obviously these campgrounds offer lots of advantages. They put you right where you want to be, amid the natural splendor of rainforests, gorges, or islands. And they don't cost much, usually only Au. $3 per person in Queensland parks. The amenities, though far from luxurious, exceed what many North American parks offer. Usually you get flush toilets, showers, clean rest rooms, grills, and free firewood. The one thing North Americans will miss are the picnic tables that our parks routinely provide. In Australia these are a rare find.

Second, in a few places like Lamington's Binna Burra section, private inholders manage the campgrounds, usually charging higher rates than the QNPWS but offering more amenities. Fundamentally, though, they don't differ that much from park service campgrounds. Then, too, state forests sometimes provide nice campgrounds such as the ones near Conondale National Park. New South Wales parks are fairly similar to those in Queensland, though often better equipped. A few even provide shelters with fireplaces in case of inclement weather. Some of the parks in both states have specifically designated sites, so that only a certain number of people can camp there at any one time. Others have expansive, grassy lawns upon which any number of tents may be pitched. Be sure to check which kind of campground your chosen parks have, because at the second type you will never be turned away, while at the first you might be. All in all, most public or quasi-public campgrounds in the region provide pleasant, uncrowded accommodation.

When public campgrounds are full or not available, you may need to opt for the commercial version, which Aussies call a "caravan park." Expect to pay more for the dubious privilege of pitching your tent in these places—up to Au. $25 per night. On the other hand, some also rent trailers ("on-site vans") or cabins, Spartan boxes with beds but no linens. Often these will cost only a bit more than a tent site and will supply a stove, refrigerator, and electricity. These private operations often cater to people with RVs ("caravans"), and many of their customers may be permanent or semipermanent residents, as in North American trailer parks. They will rent you a tent site, but it may be little more than a tiny rectangle wedged in between the metal sides of adjacent trailers, devoid of picnic tables, grills, and privacy. To be sure, you get to use the communal kitchens, showers, TV and game rooms, and (sometimes) swimming pool. Yet camping in caravan parks frequently proves a depressing experience. In these pages, I will mention some of the better commercial operations near parks that lack public campgrounds. Doubtless, you could find other good ones on your own.

Besides camping in park service and commercial campgrounds, one can sometimes also stay overnight in the backcountry. Here, however, we encounter one of the major differences between Australian and North American hiking. The U.S. and Canada both have thousands of miles of trails through the backcountry of their parks and wilderness areas. Hikers can easily embark on multi-day trips, camping and perhaps fishing along the way, carrying gear in big, American-style packs. Not so in Australia. Most national parks have few trails, and many of these can be walked in an hour or an afternoon. Consequently, hikers won't have many opportunities for extended hikes and backcountry camping. Australia is preeminently a land for day-hiking, unless hikers are prepared to do some heavy-duty bushwhacking. One reason for the paucity of hiking trails (called "walking tracks" in Australia) may be sought in the continent's terrain. In Australia's east, most of the reasonably level land has been cleared; what remains are rugged rainforested mountains and escarpments. Building trails across such terrain involves Herculean efforts, what with stinging trees, leeches, thorny vines, and poisonous snakes all around (see below on these hazards). And maintaining them would also be difficult and costly. Trails can disappear under jungle, mud, and landslides in just a few years. Second, Australia has a small tax base (about 18 million citizens) and millions of acres of parklands to support. The QNPWS and other state park services face a severe budget crisis; indeed, many visitor centers are unstaffed, or open only a few hours at a time. Australia simply does not have the resources to build and maintain an elaborate network of trails such as one finds in a place like Yosemite or Banff. Thus, opportunities for long backpacking trips and remote site camping are limited.

Noosa coast headlands, Noosa National Park

Still, a few parks do offer such possibilities, notably Lamington, Carnarvon, Hinchinbrook, and Cooloola. If you want to camp out overnight in any backcountry site, you must make a reservation in advance and pay a fee. Given the popularity of some of these sites, you really need to obtain permits well in advance by contacting the park and sending in the required fee. I will offer specific advice on doing so in the appropriate sections.

TRAILS AND GEAR

Trail categories. Australians like to classify trails into several categories. The best trails qualify as "graded tracks," meaning that their builders designed them not to be too steep, usually by putting in switchbacks, smoothing out rough spots, and constructing good drainage systems. Examples abound, but surely the finest are in Lamington National Park in southeast Queensland. These graded tracks should please all but the most dour and spartan outdoorspersons. Their smoothness makes it unnecessary to monitor each step (to avoid roots, rocks, or vines), so you can enjoy the views, look for wildlife, and take it easy. Making 3 or 4 km (2–2.5 miles) per hour on such trails will not overwhelm most people, so a 20 km walk can be completed in under a day, and often without breaking a sweat.

Besides graded tracks, Australia's parks also have secondary, ungraded trails. Though usually well-marked by blazes, disks, or cairns, these trails can be rough and very steep. Overhanging brush or downed trees may impede your progress, and you may have to scramble up and down hills. The Thorsborne Trail on Hinchinbrook Island and the track to the summit of Mt. Bartle Frere, Queensland's highest peak, come to mind as examples. This guidebook will describe such trails carefully and offer advice about how difficult they are.

Apart from these established trails, Queensland's parks also have numerous hiker-made trails and cross-country routes. Other guidebooks give excellent insight into these latter. Here, you will find reference only to a few of the easier ones, such as the side-canyons of Carnarvon Gorge. On a short vacation in Australia, the trails will keep you busy enough. Sometimes there will be evidence of controlled burns along trails, designed to prevent major fires from devastating the land. Before embarking on a backpacking trip, it is wise to ask the authorities whether this practice is currently going on, or has recently occurred, since hiking through a charred forest is unlikely to please many travelers.

Maps. For most of the hikes described here, the maps provided in the book should suffice. However, I would strongly advise topos or good park maps for a few places, as noted in the text. Obviously, any off-track hiking will require not only a topo but also a compass and knowledge of how to use it. You may obtain maps from park information centers or from the Queensland Department of Natural Resources, Land Service Center, Map Sales Counter, G.P.O. Box 1401, Brisbane, Qld. 4001.

Water. Amazingly, most of the national parks described between these covers have extremely pure water—at least at this writing—that you can drink unfiltered right from the stream. Giardiasis has not yet become the scourge in Australia that it is in the U.S., despite a recent outbreak in Sydney. However, one must take precautions in some locales, such as around Carnarvon National Park, and wherever feral pigs might contaminate upstream sources. Also, a few hikes described here will have long, waterless stretches, so you will need adequate capacity to carry water between fill-up points. To be on the safe side, bring along a small filter or some purification tablets.

Stoves and lanterns. Many American hikers have stoves or lanterns that run on Coleman fuel or butane. If you have both, bring the butane type, as "gaz" cartridges can be purchased in any camping store. Coleman fuel seems to be scarce to nonexistent, though possibly it can be found in big-city emporiums. Australians use a lot of kerosene-fueled devices, so if you own one of those, you will be in luck. You will need a stove, since some parks ban campfires altogether, while others forbid them in the backcountry.

HAZARDS AND NUISANCES

Australia has its share of exotic dangers and pests. Yet probably you will have less trouble with them than with some of their North American counterparts.

Poisonous snakes. Australia boasts the world's most venomous serpent, as gauged by the toxicity of its venom: the western taipan snake. But several other species come close to it, including the tiger snake, king brown, and death adder. We have seen a few of these along trails and especially on rocks, but have had no close calls. Most snakes appear to be fairly shy, and tend to slither away when they encounter humans, although taipans will strike repeatedly if surprised or cornered. My impression is that snakes would pose the greatest threat in dense underbrush and grassland where you can't easily see them. On trails and bare slopes, you and the snake should spot each other early enough to avoid a confrontation. But if you choose to go bushwhacking in dense undergrowth, wear appropriate clothing and footwear and exercise extreme caution. In the event of a snakebite, immobilize the area of the bite, wrap a pressure bandage around it, and seek immediate medical attention. You may also run into some of the common carpet pythons lying on trails, specimens of which can grow to twenty feet or more. These enormous serpents have no venom but appear formidable enough to most people.

Dangerous plants. Hikers should avoid contact with several types of rainforest plants. Lantana (a non-native invader) and lawyer vine (also called the wait-awhile) have sharp spines that can inflict painful wounds. Lawyer vines, especially, can "grab" you as you walk along the trail and stop you cold until you remove them. They are actually a species of vinelike palm that climbs by hooking onto trees and shrubs. They often form dense, impenetrable spiky thickets that force cross-country "bush-walkers" to wear gloves and other protective clothing. While lantana and lawyer vines can only cause scrapes and puncture wounds, the far-worse gympie or stinging tree actually poisons its victim. Tiny hairs in the leaves, especially of younger trees, secrete a toxin that burns the skin. Typically, when you brush against a gympie leaf, the hairs will adhere to your skin and continue to cause pain for weeks or even months. No treatment succeeds entirely in banishing the pain, but rainforest hands recommend pouring alcohol on affected skin to neutralize the poison, and "lifting" the hairs out by applying and pulling off strips of adhesive tape. Gympies usually grow in forest clearings, in disturbed areas, and around logging roads. Fortunately, their leaves are unmistakable: very large and heart-shaped, and perforated by numerous insect holes. Learn to recognize them, and avoid them by all means.

Jellyfish. Australia has several kinds of jellyfish to beware of, most notably the dreaded box jellyfish, found in tropical waters only. Because of the ocean's proximity to the hiking trails outlined here, walkers will inevitably be drawn to the Pacific. But before you plunge into those blue waters, consider carefully. Between roughly October and April (the times vary depending on location), box jellyfish abound from about Rockhampton northward, tending to be most common in relatively muddy, shallow estuaries and river mouths. If you visit northern Queensland during these months, do not swim in the ocean unless the beach has been roped off and is signed as "stinger free." Usually, where stingers are present, warning signs will be posted. This marine menace can kill or cause horrible pain and permanent scarring. Fortunately, if you go offshore—for example, to the Great Barrier Reef—you need not worry, since box jellyfish do not float out that far. Immediate medical attention is needed for all jellyfish stings. Lifeguards often have a supply of vinegar on hand with which to douse swimmers stung by bluebottles and other non-deadly species.

Crocodiles. These fearsome saurians fall into two categories: "freshies" (the freshwater species) and "salties" (the saltwater or estuarine species). The salties are the ones to beware of. They have made quite a comeback in northern Queensland, though they are not found below the Tropic of Capricorn. Heavier and with wider snouts than the freshies, they haunt rivers and bays near the coast, and range fairly far inland in brackish, tidal creeks. Each year they attack and kill a few people, usually those who wade or swim in waters where the crocs hunt. Their M.O. is to pull the victim underwater until drowning occurs. Salties should not bother hikers on most of the trails listed here, though they could pose a threat in certain parts of Hinchinbrook Island. Signs are generally posted to remind people to avoid the places where salties hang out. In the extremely unlikely event of an attack, you have nothing to lose by fighting back, perhaps poking the animal in a tender spot such as its eyes.

Sharks. Two kinds of dangerous sharks inhabit the oceans off Australia. First, there is the great white shark of *Jaws* fame, a true monster of the deep, which prefers cold water and does not often turn up in the tropical and subtropical area covered in this book. Second, there is the tiger shark, which has been implicated in an increasing number of attacks on swimmers and surfers in recent years, as the oceans have been overfished. It is highly unlikely, however, that you will encounter a shark.

Insects. Eastern Australia has its share of insect pests. The notorious bush flies can drive hikers crazy by buzzing around and landing on them constantly. They seem worse the closer one gets to the outback, where they are especially prolific in rainy years; in contrast, they rarely bother anyone in rainforests or around beaches.

Box jellyfish warning sign

Mosquitoes ("mozzies") can become a nuisance in some habitats, such as marshy "wallum" landscapes, and wet, muddy forests. Still, we have found them much less bothersome in Australia than in the mountains of North America, where snowmelt pools and soggy tundra allow billions to flourish. Australian mosquitoes are smaller than their North American counterparts, and they make little if any noise, so that they are often gone before you know they have bitten you. Repellent works well against them. Occasionally they carry Ross River Fever, a debilitating illness.

Ticks and leeches are a bigger problem. Ticks live in open forest and grassland, while leeches abound in the rainforest, especially during the wet season. We have played host to both. Clothing deters ticks somewhat, while bare skin gives them easy pickings. Periodically check all over your body for these pests. They vary in size, and there is one species that is somewhat dangerous; still, Australian ticks do not carry serious illnesses such as Lyme disease or Rocky Mountain spotted fever. Ticks can be removed by applying insect repellent or methylated spirits to them with a cotton ball, and tugging with tweezers. Be sure that the head has not been left in. The bite, and its scar, may be visible for a long time.

Leeches like to crawl up your legs, drop down into your socks, and turn your feet into a bloody mess. They inject an anticoagulant, so even after they drop off, the wound bleeds heavily for a long time. Pressure from a bandage or cloth helps to stop the blood flow. Deter leeches by rubbing footwear with a strong, ointment-type repellent, and watching where you step. You will sometimes see leeches balancing on end, mouth in the air, looking for a host. Their bites remain quite itchy for up to a week. To remove them, just flick them off, or apply salt or heat to their bodies.

Other bothersome creatures. Besides these potential threats, or nuisances, hikers should watch out for a few other creatures. Dingoes, or wild dogs, have been known to destroy tents and sleeping bags on Fraser Island, presumably while searching for food. Bush rats will leave your gear alone, provided that food is hung securely in a tree or stowed in a "rat box"; they are common on Hinchinbrook Island. Cassowaries—rare, tall, flightless birds that live in the northern rainforest—can behave very aggressively toward humans, but they see poorly, so your best defense is to slip behind a tree and remain motionless. Magpies, satin bower birds, currawongs, and brush-turkeys will all steal any food left unattended, and even break into coolers to get at it. Magpies will also dive-bomb people during the mating and nesting season; they are partial to sneak attacks, but cause no injury. For the most part, however, hikers who exercise caution and common sense, know their environment, and take proper precautions should have few problems with any of the creatures in this rogue's gallery.

BUSH ETHICS

In recent years, Australians have become much more aware of the fragility of their natural environment and concerned about preserving it. In fact, the continent has witnessed epic battles between developers and "greens," some of them in places where readers of this book may hike (such as Protestors Falls in New South Wales, Noosa National Park, the rainforest of Cape Tribulation, and the coastal town of Cardwell, on the Hinchinbrook channel). So remember that you are a guest in Australia, and that others have waged difficult campaigns, often at significant personal cost, to preserve the wilderness you enjoy. I have included a list of currently accepted hiking and camping practices which, for the most part, does not diverge much from similar outdoor ethics in North America and Europe. I urge you to observe these strictures, both for the sake of Australia's unique environment and to forestall the need for more stringent bureaucratic controls on park users.

- Carry out all the supplies you have brought into the backcountry. Leave nothing behind, particularly items that are non-biodegradable such as aluminum foil, cans, and plastic. If you see any trash in the backcountry, pack it out with you. In campgrounds, dispose of rubbish in designated containers or, if these are unavailable, take it to the nearest public waste bin. Use trash bags so that rangers will not face the unappetizing task of picking up individual bits of refuse.

- In the backcountry, choose places for your wilderness toilet that are well away from water and cleared campsites. There are not many cleared campsites in the rainforest, so don't spoil them for others. Bury all waste 6 inches deep with a trowel, and either pack out your toilet paper or burn it, if allowed, except where fire danger exists.

- Don't take plants, rocks, live shells, or other enticing "souvenirs" from national parks. Leave them for others to enjoy.

- Remember that, however tempting it may be to feed wild birds and animals, this practice is to be resisted. "People food" is often bad for the health of other creatures. Feeding animals causes them to become overly dependent on human largesse, and to become overly bold, even aggressive. It also leads to the proliferation of some species at the expense of others, disturbing the balance of nature.

- Observe strictly all rules limiting campfires. Some parks, such as Lamington and Hinchinbrook, forbid them entirely in the backcountry, but occasionally visitors make them anyway, risking destructive wildfires for the sake of cooking their hot dogs. In response, rangers feel compelled to close campsites that have become unpleasant, charred clearings filled with blackened rocks and half-burned logs. The Binna Burra section of Lamington National Park has lost three of its former six backcountry sites for that reason. If you do make campfires where they are allowed, use existing fire rings or, better yet, a firepan, and burn only dead, downed timber.

- Stay on the trail instead of cutting across switchbacks in an attempt to shorten your hike. The new paths that this practice creates quickly erode and damage the main track.

- Do not pollute water sources with soap or dish detergent. You can get by without these conveniences for a couple of days. All washing should be done 200 meters (650 feet) from standing or flowing water.

- Camp at existing sites; don't create new ones. And refrain from cutting down vegetation to make tent poles or bedding.

USING THIS BOOK

Although this volume theoretically takes in the whole territory of Queensland and northern New South Wales—a vast region—in practice I have limited trail descriptions to those within roughly 320 km (200 miles) of the coast. The endless stretches of outback Australia harbor some interesting parks, but for most visitors, getting to and touring them would prove difficult. Some of them prohibit entry to all but scientific researchers. Others have no access roads or constructed trails. A few can be reached only by 4-WD roads, which would entail spending a fortune for vehicle rental. Several, like Lawn Hill National Park, do have trails and decent access, but lie so far off the beaten track that it could take days to reach them.

The list of parks and trails compiled in this book makes possible a compact, focused itinerary. You can see and do a lot with a minimum of driving around between hikes and other activities.

For the sake of clarity and ease of planning, I have divided the parks and hikes into six subsections, derived either from geography or ecology. Ideally, your trip would include destinations in several of these regions. They are as follows:

- **The Eastern Scenic Rim**, that is, the Mt. Warning caldera, which takes in the mountain itself as well as the ranges and parks formed by the ancient caldera rim that straddles the Queensland/New South Wales border. This section has perhaps the finest subtropical rainforest left in Australia.

- **The Western Scenic Rim**, including the ranges that sweep north and west from the remnants of the caldera, forming a segment of the Great Dividing Range in these parts. This extension of the Scenic Rim boasts the highest peaks in southeastern Queensland and some very rugged terrain.

- **The Granite Belt**, comprising border parks like Girraween and Sundown but also reaching far into New South Wales to take in the Washpool and Gibraltar Ranges. Most of the parks in this section display striking granite landscapes: bare summits with balanced rocks, plunging waterfalls, and fairly open forests, all in a relatively cool climate.

- **Sand, Sea, and Islands**, reaching all the way from Bundjalung National Park in New South Wales to Burrum Coast National Park north of Hervey Bay, Queensland. This demarcation covers many of the region's most popular and well-known parks, like Noosa, Fraser Island, and Cooloola.

- **Escarpment and Range**, encompassing inland parks stretching from Carnarvon and Blackdown in the north to the Bunyas and Conondales in the south. They vary from rainforest-clad ridges to canyon-carved tablelands with a faintly "Southwestern" feel.

- **The Far North**, featuring tropical rainforest topography from roughly Mackay to Cape Tribulation. Here visitors discover the region's highest peaks and its true tropical rainforests, most protected in World Heritage-listed reserves.

In the comfort of your home, decide how much time and money you can afford to spend, read the regional and trail descriptions, consult the relevant maps, and plot out a workable itinerary. Be sure to leave adequate time for driving, shopping and other practicalities, and just plain relaxing. Many hiking trips have suffered from emotional stresses caused by unreasonably ambitious schedules. Also, don't forget that Australia offers other attractions besides "bushwalking." Scuba diving, rock climbing, cultural encounters, local architecture and history, and nightlife and shopping may bid for a share of your time. This volume will mention some of these possibilities, but you will need to consult a general-purpose guidebook in order to review them all.

Within each subregion, hikes will be arranged under the park or state forest (if any) in which they are located. I have not described every trail in every park, but only those I have walked and deemed worthwhile. Each park description is introduced with a brief overview of essential information concerning such matters as trailhead access and camping availability. Then the individual hikes contain further prefaces summarizing trail distances, walking times, levels of difficulty, main attractions, and miscellaneous notes. Clearly, the difficulty of a hike depends on one's judgment and experience. I myself am a fiftyish, far-from-fit college professor, though with many years of North American hiking under my belt. Moreover, my wife and our then ten-year-old son accompanied me on most of the hikes described here. You may find some hikes easier than we did, and if you yearn for more of a challenge, you could pick up one of the guidebooks listed in the bibliography that specialize in rugged, off-trail walks.

In any case, I consider an "easy" trail one that is well-surfaced and graded, short and fairly level. A "moderate" trail would feature fairly stiff climbs, a long walk, rough, uneven surface, or some combination of the above. A "difficult" hike involves long distances coupled with considerable elevation change, and trails bad enough that you might either lose them occasionally or have to scramble on them. Difficult hikes entail a bit of risk, so do not undertake them without forethought. For example, it would verge on the suicidal to attempt Mt. Bartle Frere, Queensland's highest peak, in bad weather, when the steep, root-gnarled track would be wet and slick. To refine the system, I have also dubbed some trails "moderately easy" or "moderately difficult." The qualifiers should speak for themselves.

Finally, I have calculated most hiking distances and other important figures in both metric and U.S. measurements, rounding them off to the nearest 0.25 except where more precision seemed necessary. Australia uses the metric system almost exclusively. Bear in mind that a meter is slightly more than a yard, and that one kilometer (1000 meters) equals 0.62 of a mile.

Chapter 2

SCENIC RIM, EAST

Topographic relief maps of the border region between southeast Queensland and northeast New South Wales bear witness to the ancient cataclysmic events that shaped its geology. An immense shield volcano, the ancestor of today's Mt. Warning, gradually thrust up to about 2000 meters (6560 feet) during the Tertiary Period. It last erupted about 23 million years ago, leaving behind a huge caldera plus subsidiary lava vents at places like Egg Rock (Queensland) and Nimbin Rocks (New

South Wales). The Tweed Volcano, as it is called, formed not only the present-day peak of Mt. Warning—now worn down to a stump of 1157 meters (3800 feet)—but also the slopes of its vast caldera.

The slopes ring Mt. Warning on three sides (the remaining side of the caldera having been mostly removed by the Pacific Ocean) and go by the names of the McPherson, Tweed, and Nightcap Ranges. These ranges form the eastern part of what is known as the Scenic Rim which officially extends over 100 km (62 miles) from Mt. Mistake to Point Danger near Coolangatta, Queensland. Unofficially, it also takes in Mt. Warning itself and the Nightcap Range. If you stand on Mt. Warning today, you can readily grasp the geologic history of the region: cliffs and escarpments mark the surrounding caldera-slope ranges, while the broken lowlands at the mountain's base manifest the erosive power of the Tweed River and its tributaries, which have carved a fertile valley nearly all the way around the mountain.

These geologic features translate into a hiker's paradise. The basalt lavas of the ancestral volcano have helped to create rich soils that sustain magnificent rainforests in all the ranges. Rhyolite lavas, by contrast, have encouraged more open eucalypt woodlands and have eroded into steep cliffs and long escarpments over which tumble impressive waterfalls. Creeks flowing across these volcanic ranges have created some deep gorges as well. Thus, parks like Lamington, Springbrook, and Border Ranges have it all: the enclosed, muted green world of the rainforest; immense vistas that open out from clifftop lookouts; and shaded pools beneath rapids and cascades.

Fortunately, the state and federal governments of Australia have set aside much of the region as national parks or forest reserves. Though logging has made some inroads, especially in the Nightcap Range, the upper reaches of the ranges, as well as Mt. Warning itself, remain relatively pristine. In 1994 these parks were designated a World Heritage Area. You will find developed public campgrounds and a few back-country sites everywhere except on Mt. Warning itself. Above all, the border region offers a network of excellent trails. Lamington National Park alone has about 150 km (90 miles) of primary tracks and many more secondary routes. Unquestionably, the parks in this region have more miles of maintained trails than exist in any of the other regions covered in this book. Visitors to Australia could easily spend all their time here and still not see everything.

The border region can be reached easily by car. From Brisbane airport, one simply follows signs for the Gold Coast, taking the Pacific Highway (Route 1) south to the appropriate exit, as described below in the heading for each park. Hikers will find abundant, good-quality water in all the parks of the Eastern Scenic Rim, though a few hikes may involve dry, waterless stretches, so it is wise to carry a canteen or two.

LAMINGTON NATIONAL PARK

Lamington, the largest national park in southeast Queensland, has an elaborate and beautifully maintained system of trails, superb and varied scenery, backcountry campsites for multi-night trips, a mild climate most of the time, abundant wildlife, and few insect pests. Even my son, who favors TV and computer games, loved our hikes there. Because of its many walks, the Lamington section will necessarily take up a significant portion of the book. But that is as it should be. Lamington is such a spectacular place, with its gorges, hundreds of waterfalls, and stunning vistas, that every hiker should plan to spend at least a couple of days there.

The geologic history of the park has already been sketched out above. Lamington preserves a wall of the ancient Tweed Volcano caldera. The park's southwest rim features a sheer cliff that meanders for miles along an irregular course that defines the Queensland–New South Wales border, punctuated by "mountains" like Mounts Hobwee and Bithongabel and numerous lookouts from the clifftop trails. Toward the north, Lamington tilts gradually down, although its slopes are cut by several swiftly flowing rivers that form deep gorges and countless cascades. These streams often have trails running alongside them. To the east, the Lamington Plateau drops precipitously down into the Numinbah Valley, a gap separating it from the Springbrook Plateau. To the south and southwest, the park extends for many kilometers, though it is almost all remote wilderness in that direction, devoid of any maintained trails.

The most popular trails fan out from two locations: Green Mountains (O'Reilly's) and Binna Burra. These are small settlements within the park that offer visitor services. All hike descriptions will be arranged under one or the other of these jumping-off points.

Road access. To Green Mountains: From Brisbane, take the Pacific Highway (Route 1) south to Oxenford. Exit here and follow the first sign toward Tamborine Mountain (off a roundabout). This will take you out of town. After 2 km (1.25 miles) or so, look for signs to Maudsland. Turn left and follow this road until it reaches a T-intersection. Go right at the T, following all signs to Canungra (the same direction as Beaudesert). Once in the hamlet of Canungra, turn left, following the signs for Lamington National Park, Green Mountains, or O'Reilly's. You will head up a long, twisting road, one lane in many places, that takes 45 minutes to an hour to cover only 37 km (23 miles). Use caution here, especially at night, when kangaroos and other animals frequently cross the road.

To Binna Burra: Take the Pacific Highway as above, but exit at Nerang. Follow all signs to Beechmont and then to Binna Burra.

Camping. In Green Mountains: The campground here is run by the Queensland National Park and Wildlife Service (QNPWS). You normally need to call ahead and reserve a spot, especially for weekends. Sometimes all sites are booked up a month in advance, in which case your only hope is that there will be a late cancellation. The campground is situated to the right of the road just before you reach the main parking area and the O'Reilly's guest house complex. The sites are pretty basic, merely flattened tent pads. There are no tables; however, water is supplied, as well as hot showers.

You can pay and obtain camping permits at the park's information center opposite O'Reilly's Inn. Here too you can request permits for backcountry camping at Echo Point and Mt. Bithongabel. Across the road, O'Reilly's runs a store and cafeteria-style restaurant (boasting fine views). Birdseed for feeding king parrots and crimson rosellas, both regular visi-

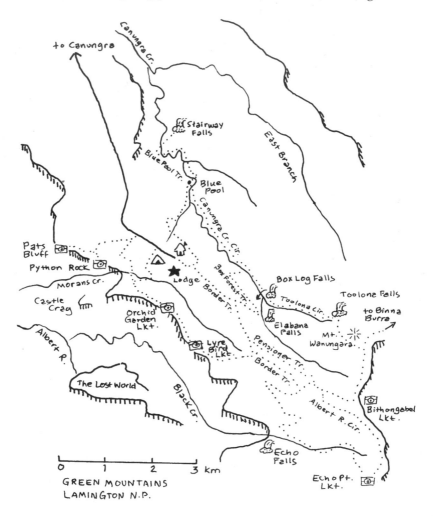

GREEN MOUNTAINS
LAMINGTON N.P.

tors to the area, is available for purchase. The campground proper has no grills, so if you want to barbecue, you must use the picnic facilities to the left of the main parking area. To reserve QNPWS campsites, including backcountry sites, dial (07) 5544-0634 from 1 to 3:30 P.M.

In Binna Burra: The Binna Burra Lodge operates this campground. They have an assortment of options: basic campsites under the trees, pre setup 4-person tents, and even some rustic cabins, all at much higher cost than the QNPWS campground at Green Mountains. But you do get hot showers, plus a shelter with picnic tables and gas-fired, coin-operated grills and burners (great in inclement weather). The Binna Burra store sells a few grocery items and light meals. To reserve backcountry campsites at Mt. Hobwee, Illinbah Clearing, and Nagarigoon, you need to go back down the main road to the visitor center, or call (07) 5533-3584 between 12:30 and 3 P.M. For campsites at Binna Burra proper, phone (07) 5533-3622.

Season. Any, but it can get quite cold here, especially in the winter months, and trails can become unpleasantly muddy after extended rains.

HIKES FROM GREEN MOUNTAINS

1. *Tree Top Walk*

> **Distance: 1 km (0.62 mile) round trip**
> **Time: 30 minutes, including stops at observation platforms**
> **Difficulty: easy**
> **Attractions: views, birdlife, informative displays**

The Tree Top Walk, the first of its kind in Australia, consists of a series of connected suspension bridges that offer views of the rainforest canopy and its inhabitants. It can be combined with a visit to the Botanical Garden. Pick up the trail off the narrow road that extends past O'Reilly's. (Alternatively, access it at its junction with the Border Track, 0.7 km/750 yards from the information kiosk, for a slightly longer walk.) The trail must be walked in a counterclockwise direction to avoid traffic congestion. The elevated boardwalk is up to 15 meters (50 feet) above the forest floor. It is possible to get even higher by climbing ladders to two platforms. From the upper deck, 30 meters (100 feet) above the ground, you are treated to excellent 360 degree views of the park. Note that there are limits to the number of persons allowed on one deck, or one bridge segment, at the same time. Interpretive signs assist visitors in tree identification. Just past the official exit of the Tree Top Walk is the Botanical Garden, which is especially beautiful in springtime. Follow signs to return to the parking area.

2. Python Rock/Pats Bluff

> **Distance: 5.6 km (3.5 miles) round trip**
> **Time: 2 hours**
> **Difficulty: easy**
> **Attractions: informative plaques, views**

This short walk offers delightful rainforest scenery, informative displays, and a superb lookout platform at Python Rock.

You begin at the same pullout from which the Morans Falls track takes off, about 1 km (0.62 mile) north of the Green Mountains car park, on the east side of the main road. The track is level and has a gravel surface (suitable for wheelchairs).

Displays along the way illuminate many forest mysteries, such as how strangler figs grow. Just past the 1 km mark, you reach a junction. Veer left; Python Rock lies 500 meters (0.3 mile) ahead, through brush box trees and, finally, open grass tree habitat. The wide platform yields vistas back to Morans Falls and across to Castle Crag and the Lost World plateau. In the distance, you will discern the outlines of Mt. Lindesay, Mt. Barney, and the Main Range.

Return to the junction and, if you like, turn left and walk another 1.25 km (0.75 mile) out to Pats Bluff. Notice the well-buttressed black booyong trees near the junction. Eventually, the trail meets a rutted 4-WD road running alongside power lines, so the feeling of wilderness evaporates here. Still, Pats Bluff, slightly downhill and across the road, bestows views even more panoramic and extensive than did Python Rock. You can appreciate the remote character of the upper forks of the Albert River and its lofty neighbors, the Lost World and Mt. Widgee. Return the way you came.

3. Morans Falls

> **Distance: 4.5 km (2.75 miles) round trip**
> **Time: 1.5 hours**
> **Difficulty: moderately easy**
> **Attractions: waterfalls, views, rainforest**

This short, popular trail leaves from a small carpark 1 km north of O'Reilly's. It descends 180 meters on switchbacks through eucalyptus and rain forest to a lovely, 80 meter high waterfall. Morans Falls is visible from a lookout about 100 meters (330 feet) before you cross Morans Creek. From the creek, ascend to a picnic area at km 2.25 (mile 1.5). Here you enjoy terrific views to the west that include Mt. Lindesay and the McPherson Range. Once, you could continue down to the base of the falls on stairs, but for now that part of the trail is blocked off. There are three options for the return trip. You can double back the way you came, or try the steep shortcut that ascends along Morans Creek. Alternatively, hardy souls can continue, via the "Red Road," to Castle Crag and Lyre-bird Lookout to make a loop ending at O'Reilly's (see description, be-low, for details).

4. Box Forest Circuit

Distance: 10.75 km (6.75 miles) round trip
Time: 4–5 hours
Difficulty: moderately easy
Attractions: Elabana and Box Log Falls, gargantuan brush box
trees, palm groves

The trailhead is at the kiosk across from O'Reilly's. Begin the loop on the Border Track, the main route between Green Mountains and Binna Burra, which is blacktopped for the first 0.7 km (750 yards). Several trails branch off this track. Views occasionally open up to the opposite ridge, but most of the time you are surrounded by tree ferns, strangler figs, epiphytes, and huge lianas that hang down from the canopy in tangled masses. Tree identification is facilitated by interpretive signs.

Turn left onto the Box Forest Circuit at km 1.75 (mile 1.0). Your path descends gently through the rainforest toward the valley of Canungra Creek.

At about km 2.75 (mile 1.75), there is another marked junction. The left fork heads down past a grove of gigantic brush box trees, the "gi-ants' garden," while the right fork leads to Picnic Rock and Elabana Falls. Although these forks comprise a loop that can be done in either direc-tion, it is recommended that you proceed clockwise, taking the left fork. This fork gradually switchbacks down past gigantic brush box trees, with their distinctive pink bark, and several small but enchanting waterfalls. The brush boxes can be identified not only by their bark, but also by their bare, pale pink branch tips and burled, gnarled bases. Before long you arrive at Canungra Creek, at km 5.25 (mile 3.25), and nearby Yanbacoochie Falls. This small waterfall is difficult to reach, but if you continue south (upstream), you will find other cascades, easily accessed by short spurs. Note that the trail crosses from the west bank, where you have been walking, over to the east side just above another small water-fall, Wajinya. The crossing is marked by an arrow mounted on a post on the opposite bank. Probably you can cross on rocks, but you may have to wade, depending on the water level.

At the arrow, go left (uphill) to pick up the trail. Shortly thereafter you cross the creek again on boulders, regaining the west bank. Here you leave Canungra Creek and ascend along one of its tributaries, Toolona Creek. In the next 1 km, locate side trails to two beautiful falls set in Eden-like gorges: Box Log Falls (spur length = 50 meters) and Elabana Falls (spur length = 100 meters). After these detours, you ascend to Pic-nic Rock, at the top of Elabana Falls. This is a nice place to stop and relax.

From here the trail climbs the slopes of Canungra Valley, through spectacular rainforest. At km 9 (mile 5.5) it rejoins the Border Track connecting Green Mountains and Binna Burra. Turn right here and return to the parking area.

5. *Albert River Circuit*

Distance: 21 km (13 miles) round trip
Time: 1 long day (8 hours) or overnight
Difficulty: moderate
Attractions: over a dozen waterfalls, scenic lookouts

This loop can be done as a long dayhike or (preferably) an overnight backpack, with a camp at Echo Point Lookout. Campers must reserve a backcountry site in advance with park rangers. Since the hike involves many stream crossings, you may want to avoid it at high water levels.

From O'Reilly's, cross the street to the information kiosk, and set off on the Border Track. Pass junctions with the Tree Top Walk (km 0.75), Box Forest Trail (km 1.75), and the Pensioners Track (km 2.5). Very shortly after the Border Track and Pensioners Track rejoin each other at km 5 (mile 3), the Albert River Circuit begins on the right. Plan to walk the loop in a counterclockwise direction.

The trail first crosses a pass into the Albert River drainage. It then descends on switchbacks along the right bank of Lightning Creek, a tributary of the Albert River. Many waterfalls, typically small and unnamed, grace this portion of the hike, and are accessible via short spurs. The trail finally crosses Lightning Creek at km 9.5 (mile 6), near Lightning Falls. Descending farther, it soon meets the Albert River, just above Black Canyon, a remote defile below you gouged out by the Albert.

Here the trail starts a 2.5 km (1.5 mile) climb, following the Albert River, at this point scarcely more than a creek. You will be crossing the river repeatedly over the next few kilometers. Several beautiful waterfalls appear in rapid succession: Echo Falls at km 9.75, Gurrgunngulli at km 10, Mirror at km 10.25, Joolbahla at 10.5, Gwahlahla at 10.75, and finally Bithongabel at km 11 (mile 6.5). Now you cross the river for the final time, and begin an ascent. Fill up all canteens here in preparation for a long waterless stretch, especially if you are backpacking.

The primitive campsite is near a sign about 160 meters (175 yards) short of Echo Point Lookout, at km 12.25 (mile 7.5). The Lookout, adorned by some healthy grass trees, offers superb views of the Pacific coast, Mt. Warning, and the McPherson Range, as does a small break in the rainforest about 500 meters (0.3 mile) farther on. At these overlooks, you are on the border of Queensland and New South Wales. For some distance, the trail remains near the edge of the cliff-bound Lamington plateau. It continues to climb for a while before leveling off on its way to close the loop and rejoin the Border Track at km 15.75 (mile 9.75). You intersect the Pensioners Track on the right at km 16, and since that trail parallels the Border Track, you can take it if you wish as an alternate route back to O'Reilly's. The routes are of equal length and both are downhill, though the Pensioners Track, as its name suggests, is slightly easier.

6. Toolona Circuit

Distance: 17.5 km (10.75 miles) round trip
Time: 1 day (5 to 7 hours) or overnight
Difficulty: moderate
Attractions: outstanding rainforest, Antarctic beech trees,
   exceptionally beautiful falls

This hike is arguably the best in Lamington National Park, one that all well conditioned "bushwalkers" will want to undertake. It resembles the other waterfall circuits—Coomera and Albert River—in its progression from gorge to high tableland to easy returns on the Border Track, but has even more spectacular falls and forests. It is possible to organize this hike as a 2-day outing, camping at Mt. Bithongabel and seeing more of the high country on the Queensland/New South Wales border; be sure to reserve a campsite in advance if you intend to do this.

Begin at the upper end of the Green Mountains picnic area, just past the park kiosk with its displays. Walk about 1.75 km/1 mile, following signs for the Border Track, until the turnoff left toward Elabana Falls, Picnic Rock, and the Toolona Circuit. Take this turnoff. After another 1 km you reach the junction for the Box Forest Circuit; here take the right fork toward Elabana Falls and Toolona. Having visited these much photographed cascades on a short spur trail, continue on uphill at the next junction, following signs for the Toolona Circuit. You have come about 3.75 km (2.25 miles) so far.

Liana, Lamington National Park

Passing a remarkable strangler fig growing almost horizontally from trailside, you quickly reach the first in a series of dazzling cascades: Triple Falls. Cross Toolona Creek here and continue uphill, after investigating the downhill spur, which leads to a photographer's vantage point.

From here on, waterfalls tumble down the creek one after another. You must frequently detour onto rough spur trails to see them all. Don't fail to check out Gwongurai Falls, but the loveliest, I believe, are Chalaba (Rainbow) and Toolona Falls, both right on the trail. By the time you reach the latter, you will have made several stream crossings, all on rocks (no wading, except at high water levels).

Above Toolona Falls, you climb steadily past small, picturesque rapids into the higher Antarctic Beech zone. After 9.5 km (6 miles), you arrive at the Border Track junction. Here you should detour left 100 meters to spectacular Wanungara Lookout and enjoy the panorama over New South Wales.

Back on the Border Track, follow signs to Green Mountains, past moss-covered, hoary Antarctic beeches, surely among the largest specimens of that species in the park. At the junction with the track to Mt. Bithongabel, go right, continuing on the Border Track toward Green Mountains. On the way, you can follow either the Border Track itself or the (somewhat easier) Pensioners Track, both of which boast beautiful tree ferns. Eventually these tracks link back up for the return to the parking area near O'Reilly's.

7. Blue Pool/Stairway Falls

Distance: 9.75 km (6 miles) round trip to Blue Pool; or 13.25 km
(8.25 miles) round trip for full circuit to Stairway Falls
Time: 3 hours round-trip for Blue Pool; 6 or 7 hours for full
circuit
Difficulty: moderate
Attractions: beautiful rainforest, swimming hole, remote waterfall

Though not as enticing as some other Lamington trails, this hike down Canungra Creek has much to offer: ancient red cedars, shady cascades, a chilly swimming hole (the Blue Pool), and lovely Stairway Falls.

The time and difficulty ratings for the hike are variable, depending upon water levels in Canungra Creek. Since many stream crossings are required, and wading may be necessary, wear old boots or sneakers that you do not mind getting wet, and consider using a walking stick. The distance is also variable, depending on whether you decide to go only to Blue Pool or all the way to Stairway Falls.

Begin at the kiosk opposite O'Reilly's Guest House. After about 250 meters (800 feet) on the Border Track take the marked path on the left toward the Blue Pool. The trail follows Darraboola Creek for several kilometers, crossing its tributaries at intervals. Stairs assist hikers on potentially steep descents. In the sunny clearings beware of stinging (gympie) trees, described in chapter 1. About halfway down the trail you encounter the once-prized red cedars—tall, scaly-barked trees with buttress roots. The trail is often lined by philodendrons, and it boasts a root "arch." Look for Lamington's renowned spiny crayfish in the creeks; they are candy-striped crustaceans with a reputation for aggressiveness. After passing a couple of small falls and some impressive brush box trees, you arrive at the Blue Pool. Sometimes people spot eels swimming here.

At the pool, the trail you have hiked converges with the ones up and down Canungra Creek. The trail on the left goes to Stairway Falls, crossing the creek 6 times in the space of 1.75 km (1 mile). At the crossings look for red arrows painted on the rocks indicating the best fords and the trail's continuation. After about 0.5 km, you need to pick your way across some rock ledges on the right bank of the creek. Don't cross here; the next crossing is about 200 meters farther downstream.

Eventually you arrive at Stairway Falls, plunging over two levels into a large, cool pool. The track continues on past the falls, but most people stop here. You can either retrace your steps all the way to Green Mountains, or proceed upstream from the Blue Pool on a much longer loop called the Canungra Circuit, not described here. Be advised that the longer loop requires many additional stream crossings.

8. Moonlight Crag/Lyrebird Lookout Loop

Distance: 8 km (5 miles) round trip
Time: 4 hours
Difficulty: moderate
Attractions: solitude, remote lookouts

If you want to escape crowds and try something a little more adventurous, consider this circuit. About half of it follows secondary trails not often maintained, so it is overgrown and occasionally hard to follow. In compensation, you will get to enjoy seldom-visited lookouts and dense, remote forest which harbors a wealth of bird life.

Begin on the "Red Road," a 4-WD road that departs to the left (west) as you walk down the main park road from O'Reilly's, about 75 meters north of the campground access. Follow all signs to Balanced Rock until you reach a sign to the left of the road (after a stiff uphill climb) pointing the way to Moonlight Crag. Leaving the road here, follow the trail into the forest. Soon you emerge at the crag, one of the finest lookouts in Lamington. You can almost reach out and touch the Lost World plateau, and you perceive how deep the Albert River gorge really is.

From here, go left, and follow a faint trail up a few switchbacks. If confused, look for an old fence line. The trail parallels the fence for a few

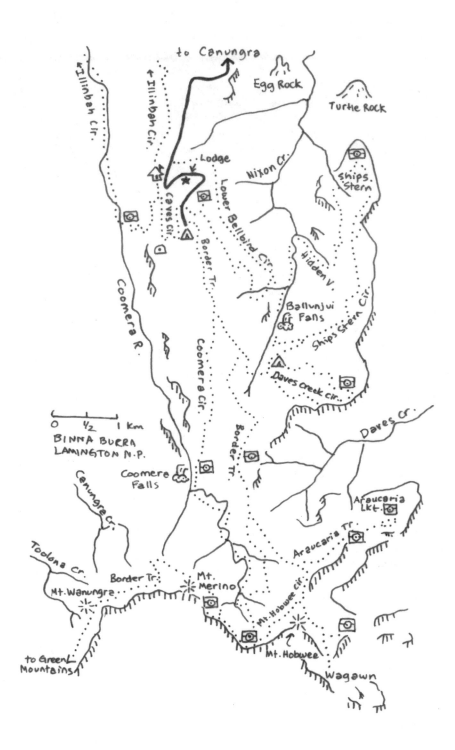

hundred meters before veering off to the right. Eventually, you reach a place called the Orchid Grotto. Dense vegetation obscures your views here, but the arrangement of trees, boulders, ferns, and orchids has great aesthetic appeal. Continue on for about another 20 minutes to Lyrebird Lookout, which gives close-up looks at the high peaks of the McPherson Range and the upper reaches of the Albert River Valley.

Follow the somewhat obscure trail back eastward from Lyrebird Lookout. It drops down to a small creek, then forks, with the left branch heading to O'Reilly's and the right branch leading to the Border Track. Go right here, toward the Border Track. The trail in this vicinity may be difficult to follow, and you need to be careful not to lose it. However, it quickly improves and intersects the Border Track at an acute angle. The intersection is not marked, but since the Border Track is far better maintained than the trail you were just on, you should have little trouble recognizing it. Turn left onto the Border Track to complete the loop back to O'Reilly's.

HIKES FROM BINNA BURRA

1. Senses Trail

> **Distance: 1 km (0.62 mile) round trip**
> **Time: 30 minutes**
> **Difficulty: easy**
> **Attractions: learning to use senses other than sight**

This unusual circuit begins along the main park road below the campground, near the turnoff for Binna Burra Lodge. Designed especially for the blind, it has ropes to hang onto and interpretive signs in Braille. People with sight sometimes choose to walk this loop wearing blindfolds, but be careful of steps if you do this. The trail allows you to enjoy the smells, sounds, and textures of the rainforest, things sometimes missed by persons who are not visually impaired.

2. Caves Circuit

> **Distance: 4.75 km (2.75 miles) round trip**
> **Time: 1 or 1.5 hours**
> **Difficulty: moderately easy**
> **Attractions: caves, views**

Starting from the grassy saddle below the campground near the driveway to Binna Burra Lodge, this "circuit" requires a steep 1.5 km (1 mile) road walk from the visitor information center at the trail's end. Alternatively, you can finish the trip with a 3.25 km (2 mile) backtrack.

The trail descends steadily on switchbacks. At about km 2 (mile 1.25) you come to a waterfall next to a vegetation-covered cliff face. Rounding a bend, you see the first of the circuit's caves: Kweebani, or "Cooking" Cave, a large, shallow amphitheater gouged out of volcanic tuff. Paper wasps have built nests here, and water sometimes trickles down from the cliffs above to form gossamer falls.

The trail descends on steps, then contours around to another large but even shallower alcove. You climb to a point near the top of this alcove on a flight of stairs, and then pass through an arch blasted out of the cliffs by the park service. The black volcanic rock here is perlite, a type of obsidian. The archway is about 1 km from the information center.

From here on, you are treated to excellent views of the valley of the Coomera River, as rainforest gives way to drier, sparser vegetation. You pass a bench on which you can rest and enjoy the scenery. Within just a few minutes, there is a 40 meter spur on the left that descends steeply on steps to Talangai ("White") Cave, which is also formed of tuff. Back on the main trail, it is only about 250 meters (800 feet) to the park road. Walk the road to the campground or retrace your steps.

3. Lower Ballunjui Falls

Distance: 11.25 km (7 miles) round trip
Time: 4 hours
Difficulty: moderate
Attractions: superb rainforest, some good lookouts, a high waterfall

Although mostly part of the Ships Stern Circuit, the Lower Ballunjui Falls track makes an attractive, shorter alternative for those having less time or energy. Start by walking down the main road from the campground a short distance to the grassy area opposite the driveway to Binna Burra Lodge. Locate the sign for Bellbird Lookout/Lower Ballunjui Falls and follow the trail downhill. The trail quickly veers right and enters soaring rainforest. It switchbacks past an enormous, gnarly white mahogany tree and then to the turnoff for Bellbird Lookout about 500 meters (0.3 mile) from the start, a short detour of moderate interest.

Continue on to the right and out onto a steeply sloping ridge. Here the trail offers unusual glimpses of rainforest canopy growing up to hiker-level from the lower slopes. You may catch sight of upper-story rainforest birds as well as loads of epiphytes (air plants) growing on the higher trunks of the trees.

After about 2.5 km (1.5 miles) you arrive at a spur to Yangahla or Picnic Rock (not to be confused with a place of the same name in the Green Mountains section of the park). This is a slab projecting into space from which you enjoy a panoramic look at the upper reaches of the valley carved out by Nixon Creek. Note the rhyolite monolith of Egg Rock, once a volcanic vent, off to the south, as well as the Ships Stern across the way. With luck you may be able to spot some sulphur-crested cockatoos—snow white birds with golden crowns—swooping over the valley below; their harsh shrieks often echo through the quiet woods.

The trail passes some cliffs and descends some steep slopes on stairs. After meandering through the split Kong Gong Rock, you soon encounter a trail heading off to the left, the Lower Bellbird Circuit. It takes about 1.5 hours of walking to reach this point. Go right here, entering some of the lushest rainforest in Lamington: green glades of stately piccabeen palms studded here and there by huge brush box and flooded gums. Take note of a strange grotto to the right of the trail. The cliffs support an amazing latticework of roots extending from the trees above to the soil below the cliff. In wet times, a waterfall forms here.

After bypassing the Ships Stern Circuit, you head right. Lower Ballunjui Falls of Nixon Creek lies 0.5 km (0.3 mile) ahead. From the trail's end, both Upper and Lower Ballunjui Falls are visible, spilling down nearly 150 meters (500 feet) from the heights above. The Lower Falls makes a fine picture, as the tumbling water sparkles against black basaltic cliffs.

The return trip—a double back—requires an ascent of almost 300 meters (1000 feet), yet it seems easy given the superb grading and immaculate manicuring of Lamington's trails. Still, be sure to carry enough water, since even an easy ascent costs some perspiration.

4. Lower Bellbird Circuit

> **Distance: 12 km (7.5 miles) round trip**
> **Time: 3 hours**
> **Difficulty: moderate**
> **Attractions: waterfalls, rainforest**

Like the Ships Stern Circuit, the Lower Bellbird Circuit coincides initially with the trail to Lower Ballunjui Falls (see above). Since the trail ends along the park road over 1.5 km (1 mile) below the campground, completing a loop requires either a road walk or a return along the Caves Circuit. The latter is somewhat longer but much less steep, and well worth doing in its own right.

The signed trailhead is just off the main park road below the campground, opposite the turnoff to Binna Burra Lodge. After about an hour of downhill walking, you reach the Lower Bellbird turnoff on the left at km 3.75 (mile 2.25). Within 10 to 15 minutes you come to a small cascade and, shortly thereafter, descend a low cliff on steps. It is a beautiful spot, with a little cave in the cliff and a freestanding, isolated rock wall that is covered with epiphytes. Little sunlight penetrates the dense, palm-dominated rainforest here, so this part of the trail can be soggy (and leech-infested) after a rain.

Some gentle ups and downs follow as you wend your way through moss-covered boulders and luxuriant ferns carpeting the forest floor. About halfway into the hike the trail goes under an "arch" formed by an enormous fallen tree. Within 10 minutes you pass below high cliffs; there is a beautiful waterfall here. Rounding a corner, you enjoy views (temporarily) across Nixon Creek to the Ships Stern Range. A kilometer later, you leave the rainforest behind. Your trail now becomes a mowed grass path, lined by lantanas, which ascends steeply to the park road. At the road, turn left and go uphill 500 meters to the visitor information center. From here, return to the campground via either the road (1.5 km/1 mile) or the Caves Circuit (3.25 km/2 miles), described above.

5. Ships Stern Circuit

Distance: 18.75 km (11.5 miles) round trip, plus detours
Time: 1 day
Difficulty: moderately difficult
Attractions: overlooks, waterfalls

The Ships Stern Range is a high promontory that divides the Numinbah Valley and its tributary stream, Nixon Creek. Bring water with you, for much of the trail is dry. The trip can be lengthened by opting for one or more worthwhile detours to special attractions.

The trailhead is located in the grassy area below the campground, opposite the driveway to Binna Burra Lodge. Initially the track is the same one you take for the Lower Bellbird Circuit and Lower Ballunjui Falls (described above). The Lower Bellbird Circuit splits off to the left at km 3.75 (mile 2.5), while the Lower Ballunjui Falls spur is a right turn at km 4.75. A visit to this spectacular waterfall adds slightly more than 1 km (0.62 mile) round-trip to your hike.

Back on the main Ships Stern Circuit, continue straight ahead, following the left bank of Nixon Creek through a beautiful grove of piccabeen palms. The trail levels out considerably. At km 5.5 (mile 3.5) you cross Chiminya Creek; then the trail descends on steps to cross Nixon Creek, 0.25 km (275 yards) later. It is usually possible to rock hop here, except at high water levels, but be careful, since the rocks may be slippery. Fill water bottles here before proceeding.

Past Nixon Creek, the trail begins a long climb of several kilometers. You pass beneath an undulating gray cliff fronted with piccabeen palms, a picturesque spot. After crossing a small stream and climbing some stairs, you enter an area rich with tree ferns. As you approach the top of the plateau, there is a steep side trail that ascends on steps to Charaboomba Rock at km 8.0 (mile 5). This detour of 675 meters (0.4 mile) round trip passes by banksias, scribbly gums, and grass trees to a lookout from which Upper and Lower Ballunjui Falls and Egg Rock are in view. It is a lovely place for a picnic lunch.

Just past here, off the main trail, is Moonjaroora Lookout, which offers views across the valley to Binna Burra. At km 9.75 (mile 6), atop the Ships Stern plateau, is a third lookout, Kooloobano Point, only 100 meters off the trail. You are very close to both Egg Rock and Turtle Rock here, and can see all the way to the Gold Coast. Vistas are spectacular, since you are no longer in dense forest.

Return to the main trail, heading in the direction "Binna Burra via Upper Ballunjui Falls." As the trail contours around the promontory, still more overlooks offer views of the Springbrook plateau, Numinbah Valley, and Mt. Warning. There is a junction at km 10.75, near the end of the promontory. Take your pick of trails here, since the routes rejoin within 500 meters (0.3 mile). The left fork goes to more lookouts on the eastern side, while the right fork clings to the western rim.

Once the trails reunite, you descend from the Ships Stern and enter the woods. The trail crosses a low pass, and soon starts a slow, easy climb as the vegetation gradually shifts back to rainforest.

At km 14 (mile 8.75) there is a spur to Upper Ballunjui Falls, under 2.5 km (1.5 miles) return. The spur takes about an hour, round trip, to complete. It descends through a grove of tree ferns first to the impressive Ballunjui Cascades at km 0.5 (mile 0.3), and then to the bottom of Booboora Falls at the 1 km (0.62 mile) mark. Still descending, it crosses and recrosses Nixon Creek just above the lip of Lower Ballunjui Falls. Steep steps lead downhill for a few meters past the second crossing, permitting you to contemplate the top part of the waterfall. Grass trees add to the charm of this area. Backtrack to the main trail.

In the next kilometer or so are several trail junctions. Short spurs on the right lead to the top of Ballunjui Cascade and the bottom of gemlike Nagarigoon Falls. Immediately past this latter spur is a toilet and camping area, on the left. Your trail bears right here, and also bears right at the two signed junctions with the Daves Creek Circuit. At km 16, you intersect the Border Track. Take the right fork of the Border Track, and walk the final 2.25 km (1.5 miles) downhill, past junctions with the Coomera and Rainforest Circuits, to Binna Burra. The trail terminates at a kiosk near the end of the park road, above the campground.

6. Daves Creek Circuit

Distance: 12 km (7.5 miles) round trip
Time: 5 hours
Difficulty: moderate
Attractions: views, transition from rainforest to open country

Hikers wax enthusiastic about this trail because it offers so much variety for a fairly short loop walk. It begins at a kiosk at the end of the parking area near the campground and tea house. After beautiful rainforest walking on the Border Track, you pass the Coomera Circuit turnoff, and then reach another fork in the trail. Here, 2.25 km (1.5 miles) out, you select the lefthand trail toward Ships Stern and Daves Creek.

By now the altitude has increased to over 900 meters/3000 feet; the rainforest has begun to thin out a little, and tree ferns have become more common. At the next junction, after 3.5 km, the first leg of the Daves Creek loop departs from the Ships Stern/Upper Ballunjui Tracks, so you turn right here. You will return to this point after a counterclockwise walk. This part of the loop will head off toward the west and descend into the upper end of the Nixon Creek drainage. Along the way, you will walk atop some rather precipitous dropoffs, but the excellent condition of the track makes hiking perfectly safe.

As you cross several feeder rivulets of Nixon Creek, notice how the vegetation has changed again. The forest opens up and new trees—especially coachwood (straight, whitish-gray trunks), the huge, rough-barked New England blackbutts, and casuarinas (or she-oaks)—have taken over. This is because you have crossed the boundary from fertile, basalt-derived soil to less fertile, rhyolite-based terrain.

Shortly after you cross this geologic frontier, you encounter a junction. Take the right (Daves Creek) fork, quickly emerging from the forest into "heath," dominated by low-growing plants like banksia, wattle, and small casuarinas, that allows sweeping vistas of the surrounding country. At various lookouts, and really from anywhere on the trail, you can survey the well-cultivated Numinbah Valley across to the Springbrook plateau and southward to higher overlooks in Lamington, all bounded by rhyolite cliffs. At km 5 (mile 3), take the detour to Molongolee Cave; it's nothing special in itself, but has an interesting dripping spring and viewpoint nearby.

Within the next 15 or 20 minutes, you cross a small creek, climb a low, wooded knoll, and reach Numinbah Lookout at about the halfway point (km 6/mile 3.75). From here, you notice a deeply incised gorge to the right that opens into the Numinbah Valley below. This is called Woggunba Valley, and encloses the trail's namesake, Daves Creek.

On the return leg, after 1 km or so, you pass a rough, unmarked trail heading off to the left and then climbing steeply up some rocks. This short spur leads to the summit of Surprise Rock, a good viewpoint. The surprise is that, at the end of the rock, you need to scramble down a tree trunk to descend and continue (or else just retrace your steps).

After another kilometer, you arrive at an important junction. The right fork leads on out to the Ships Stern, pausing to admire Nagarigoon Falls, only 200 meters/650 feet down the track. Don't miss this unusual cascade flowing over masses of reddish moss.

Returning to the main Daves Creek loop, continue on for another few yards and you regain the junction previously described. Follow the signs back to Binna Burra. If you wish, you can make a short detour along the way: at the Coomera Seat, look for a trail leading to the Tullawall

Circuit. It is actually an alternative branch of the Border Track with a short in-and-out trail up to a stand of Antarctic beech trees. If you have not seen Antarctic beeches elsewhere, it is worth a look.

7. Coomera Circuit/Mt. Hobwee

Distance: 22.5 km (14 miles) round trip
Time: 1 day or overnight
Difficulty: moderately difficult
Attractions: waterfalls, Antarctic beeches, remote country

The Coomera River, one of Lamington's major drainages, cuts the deepest, most rugged gorge in the park. The Coomera Circuit leads hikers on a precipitous trail high above the gorge, past many falls, and then on up to the river's headwaters before rejoining the Border Track. At that point, one can either return directly or go on to a backcountry campsite at Mt. Hobwee, from which other attractions can be visited.

Begin the hike at the upper end of the Binna Burra parking lot, where the Border Track heads off toward Green Mountains. After 2 km (1.25 miles), at a bench called the Coomera Seat, the trail branches in three directions. Here you leave the Border Track and take the middle trail, following signs for the Coomera Circuit. You travel through dense, lush rainforest, before crossing over into somewhat more open woodland as the trail begins its gradual descent toward Coomera gorge. This declivity, more than 150 meters/500 feet deep in places, is so difficult of passage that it was only descended for the first time (by abseilers) in the 1970s. Abseiling in the gorge is now forbidden.

The Coomera Circuit winds along on the gorge's east side. There are precipitous drops to the right of the trail. Formerly, hikers could descend on stairs to a platform suspended above the abyss, from which they enjoyed stunning views of Coomera Falls (65 meters high) and Yarrabilgong Falls (150 meters high), which plummet into a pool far below. For safety reasons, this platform is now closed, and until it reopens visitors must (cautiously!) find their own viewpoint. A short distance uptrail from the platform, more waterfalls come into view both down in the gorge and on the opposite cliff wall. At this point you will be glimpsing the depths of the Coomera Crevice, a very narrow and dark upper section of the main gorge.

Leaving the gorge at about km 5.75 (mile 3.5), hikers must first cross and soon recross the river on rocks (easy, at normal water levels). After passing several more cascades, major and minor, walkers reach Gwongarragong Falls, at km 7.5/mile 4.75. This waterfall, with its Shangri-la setting, may be the circuit's finest. After roughly 2 more kms (1.25 miles) and still more falls, cross the river for the sixth and last time. Fill up canteens here, especially if you are camping, and hope that the huge spear lilies all around you are in bloom. Past the river crossing, at

Spear lily in bloom, Coomera River

the Border Track junction, turn right, in the direction of Green Mountains, if you plan to spend the night at the Mt. Hobwee camp; otherwise,
turn left toward Binna Burra to complete your loop.

Hikers proceeding toward Mt. Hobwee reach another junction in
about 1 km (0.62 mile). Here go left, following signs for the Mt. Hobwee
Circuit. The trail may be a bit overgrown in places, but the Antarctic
beeches and glimpses of great space beyond will make up for it. Do not
miss the Dacelo Lookout, about a 15 minute roundtrip walk on a spur
trail on the right; it offers outstanding views of Mt. Warning and its environs in northern New South Wales. After you have walked about 1.5
kms/1 mile from the Mt. Hobwee Circuit/Border Track junction, another junction appears, with a sign directing walkers to Mt. Hobwee's
summit, at km 13.5 (mile 8.5). This track winds around the mountain
like a corkscrew, passing under an "arch" formed by the trunk of an
ancient Antarctic beech, and up to the top (elevation 1,140 meters/3760
feet). The views from here will probably disappoint most visitors, as
will the small, unlevel campsite. Still, it is one of the few backcountry
campsites in the Binna Burra section of the park.

From Mt. Hobwee, hikers with two hours to spare may take a highly
recommended side trip to Mt. Wagawn. Descend Mt. Hobwee and turn
right at the first junction, which is not signposted. Walk about 1 km (0.62
mile) and then bear right again at the Mt. Wagawn turnoff. From there, a
5.5 km (3.5 mile) roundtrip hike awaits you. In just a few minutes, you
will pass a beautiful little spring, trickling pure, cool water into a rock
bowl. Continue on, taking the spur trail out to the Garragoolba Lookout

(an additional 1.25 km / 0.75 mile round trip) if you like, though views from Mt. Wagawn itself prove to be much better. After some beautiful forest scenery, the trees thin out and the Wagawn Lookout looms below. Dropping down to the lookout, hikers are greeted by a truly exceptional panorama that includes the south-facing cliffs of the Springbrook Plateau, Mounts Cougal and Warning, the Numinbah Valley, and the walls of the volcanic caldera that is now called the McPherson Range. You may either backtrack to a camp on Mt. Hobwee, if you planned an overnight hike, or follow signs toward Binna Burra for the return journey.

From Mt. Hobwee, the most direct route back to Binna Burra, 10.5 km / 6.5 miles distant, leads past this same Mt. Wagawn turnoff. About 1 km past that turnoff, there will be a spur to Araucaria Lookout, and then another 1 km past that, you rejoin the Border Track. From here it is about 5.5 km (3.5 miles) to the Binna Burra parking lot. The trip from Mt. Hobwee to Binna Burra is unchallenging and average hikers can expect to complete it in about 3 hours. Pause at the Joalah Lookout on the right to enjoy distant, enticing views of the Numinbah Valley and its side-canyon, the Woggunba Valley, the source of Daves Creek. After more outstanding rainforest scenery, including enormous epiphytes, hikers reach the trail's end.

SPRINGBROOK NATIONAL PARK

The Springbrook Plateau, across the Numinbah Valley from Lamington National Park, looms above the densely settled Gold Coast, a lush, forested backdrop to the region's sybaritic surf culture and high-rise apartments. Although the plateau top has been settled and lightly developed (pottery shops, guest houses, small restaurants, etc.), it retains a bucolic ambience. The scattered sections of Springbrook National Park lie mostly below the plateau rim, reaching down into its wooded valleys and canyons. The precipitous rhyolite lava cliffs that hem in the plateau top have formed dozens of waterfalls, ranging from minor rivulets to majestic cascades plunging hundreds of feet. Springbrook will not offer the pristine solitude of some other places in the region, but it will afford truly spectacular scenery and uncomplicated, pleasant walking. Various overlooks give visitors only a taste of the park's attractions. To experience the power and grace of the waterfalls, it is necessary to hit the trail.

Road access. To reach the various sections of Springbrook National Park, take the Pacific Highway (Route 1) to the town of Mudgereeba, about 30 km (18.5 miles) north of Coolangatta and the New South Wales border. Here, turn off at the exit that indicates Springbrook and Hinze Dam. Cross over the highway on an overpass, and then follow all signs for Springbrook National Park, 29 km (18 miles) distant. The road leads out of town and up a fairly steep, narrow road onto the Springbrook Plateau. After passing Apple Tree Park, you start seeing signs for the national park's various features. Soon you come to the visitor center, which has some worthwhile displays and helpful brochures. Alternate access is via Numinbah Valley Road (aka Nerang-Murwillumbah Road) from the town of Nerang. This route is not quite so steep.

Camping. The Queensland National Park and Wildlife Service (QNPWS) provides a site near Gwongorella Picnic Area, one of the first sections of the national park that you will pass.

Season. Any, but since summer rains increase the falls' volume significantly, December to February may be the ideal time to visit.

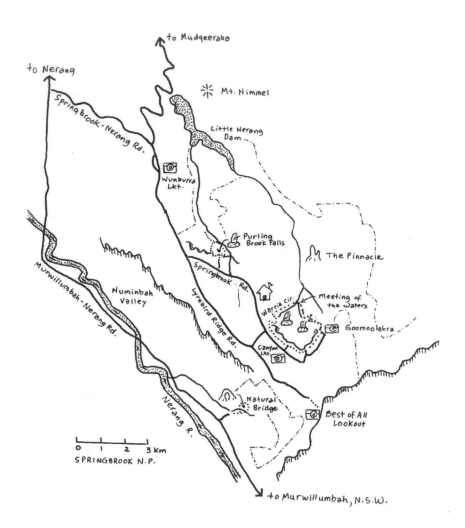

1. Best of All Lookout

Distance: 700 meters round trip
Time: 15 minutes
Difficulty: easy
Attractions: views, trees

This short but scenic hike begins at the end of Lyrebird Range Road. To get there, take the first right turn off the main park road after the information center, following signs. Then turn left onto Lyrebird Range Road, which dead-ends near the plateau rim. Park here.

The paved path descends slightly through intensely green rainforest on its way to the overlook. Just 50 meters from the end of the trail is a magnificent stand of Antarctic beech trees, a relict species found only in selected areas that once belonged to the ancient supercontinent of Gondwana. Although no waterfalls are visible from the lookout, the sublime views extend all the way from Mt. Warning to the Pacific Ocean. Go back the way you came.

2. Purling Brook Falls/Waringa Pool

Distance: 6 km (3.75 miles) round trip
Time: 1.5 or 2 hours
Difficulty: moderate
Attractions: waterfalls, cliffs, swimming hole

Shortly after you enter the park, turn left off the main road, following signs that direct you to the parking area for Purling Brook Falls, Springbrook's most famous feature. Plan to do the hike in a clockwise direction in order to avoid a brutally steep ascent on the return. The trip can be shortened by 2 km (1.25 miles) if you decide to forgo the spur trail to Waringa Pool.

Only 100 meters into the hike you gain your first view of the falls, from a lookout platform. No other overlook in the park can rival this vantage point on a waterfall, since you can see the entire vertical plunge of Purling Brook from here. Past the lookout, the trail is no longer paved but is still wide and immaculately maintained. It descends slightly as it hugs the rim of the plateau. You cross a tributary creek on a bridge, at the top of a waterfall. An unofficial, rather precipitous overlook allows you to see a small portion of the waterfall's drop.

Meanwhile, the trail beyond the bridge plummets on switchbacks and countless stairs. As you descend, the vegetation changes from woodlands to rainforest with piccabeen palms, tree ferns, strangler figs, vines, and epiphytes. Soon you see, from below, the first tier of the same waterfall that you earlier encountered above. Another bridge crosses the stream here. Continue to descend on the lantana-lined path, which now becomes less steep as it traverses toward Purling Brook Falls. At the 2 km (1.25

Purling Brook Falls, Springbrook N. P.

mile) mark from the trailhead, with Purling Brook Falls dead ahead, you reach the junction with the spur to Waringa Pool. There is a bench here.

Turn left to visit Waringa Pool, 1 km (0.62 mile) downstream. The shady trail follows Purling Brook's left bank. It again crosses the tributary stream, near its final cascade, before descending on switchbacks to Waringa Pool. There is another cascade just above the large swimming hole. The spur trail ends here.

Return to the junction with the main trail. The trail passes directly behind the waterfall, which has a pool surrounded by luxuriant vegetation at its base. The cliffs are buff colored, but stained red and black from minerals carried in the water. Expect to get a bit wet here from the spray of the falls. If you are lucky, you may see a rainbow. There is another bench on the far side of the falls on which you can relax and take in the scene.

Now you start your ascent back to the rim of the plateau. Thankfully, it is much more gentle and gradual than the downhill trail, having longer switchbacks and fewer stairs. Once you reach the top, you enjoy good views of both waterfalls. Immediately before the trail crosses Purling Brook on a bridge above the falls, a short spur trail on the right leads to another overlook. The views here, however, are inferior to the ones you had earlier on the trail. It is about 300 meters/1000 feet from here to the carpark, on a paved pathway.

3. Warrie Circuit

> **Distance: 17 km (10.5 miles) round trip**
> **Time: 4 hours**
> **Difficulty: moderate**
> **Attractions: possibly the top waterfall circuit in Queensland;**
> **rainforest, scenic views**

The premier hike in Springbrook National Park is surely the Warrie Circuit, a loop trail through the upper reaches of the Little Nerang River Valley. Though it can be accessed at several points along the plateau rim, the recommended starting point is Canyon Lookout, 1 km (0.62 mile) past the information center on the park road.

At the Lookout, turn right, proceeding around the loop in a counterclockwise direction. Just to the right you will spot a sign for the trailhead. Across the canyon you can already discern powerful Goomoolahra Falls, a feature you'll soon reach by foot. The trail descends gradually past several other major waterfalls, including Twin and Rainbow Falls. The former requires a short detour to be fully appreciated.

After about 5 km (3 miles) of spectacular walking on a narrow, cliffside track, you arrive at Goomoolahra Falls. Beyond here, the hiking population thins out, since the picnic area above the falls offers casual walkers their last opportunity for a long while to get down off the rim onto the trail system.

Now the track describes a long, switchbacking descent, past several impressive cascades, toward a rendezvous with the "meeting of the waters," where two of Little Nerang Creek's chief tributaries converge. The meeting marks the lowest point on the trail and comes about 11 km (6.75 miles) into the hike. It is a lovely spot, featuring vine-hung pools and swift rapids.

From here on, the hike takes you inexorably uphill. But more rewards await you; as you get closer to the rim, you will pass—and once pass in back of—more outstanding waterfalls. And, again, as the trail nears the rhyolite cliff zone, vegetation thins and superb vistas open out over the Little Nerang Canyon and across to the cliffs opposite. A restaurant right by the carpark might also entice a few hikers at trail's end.

4. Natural Bridge

> **Distance: 1 km (0.62 mile) round trip**
> **Time: 30 minutes**
> **Difficulty: easy**
> **Attractions: an unusual, highly photogenic natural span in a
>   rainforest setting**

This short, paved trail leads to one of tropical Australia's unique beauty spots: a rock cavern with a waterfall pouring through a hole in its ceiling. However, it begins in a different section of Springbrook than the other featured hikes, so you will have to drive a bit to reach it. From the main part of the park you drive back down to a fork in the road at which one branch goes to Mudgeeraba and the other to Nerang. Follow the Nerang branch until it meets the Murwillumbah-Nerang road. There turn left in the direction of Murwillumbah and continue about 17 km (10.5 miles) to the well marked turnoff to the Natural Bridge.

Walk the circuit in a clockwise direction. You descend on steps through a magnificent rainforest to a scenic viewpoint from which the falls and cave are visible. Not far past here is a spur trail leading into the cavern itself. Glow worms can sometimes be seen inside. A cold plunge pool is at the base of the waterfall, which probably formed when the creek undercut an old lava flow, then scoured out a hole in its roof. Beyond the cave, the trail climbs a bit to an overlook near the top of the falls. Crossing the creek, the trail returns to the parking lot.

MT. WARNING NATIONAL PARK

This park protects the remnants of the ancient Tweed Volcano that shaped so much of the eastern Scenic Rim. Mt. Warning, although about the same height as other peaks in the area, attracts far more hikers because of its solitary grandeur, steep profile, and proximity to the sea. Captain Cook named it over two centuries ago because it stood out so starkly against the surrounding landscape that it could warn mariners away from dangerous rocks. But today, many visitors climb it so that they can be the first in mainland Australia to watch the sun rise over the Pacific.

Road access. From the town of Murwillumbah, N.S.W., near the Pacific Highway (Route 1), take the road marked for Kyogle. After about 12 km (7.5 miles), turn onto a spur road heading to the national park, another 5 km (3 miles) distant. The road dead-ends at a parking lot where the trail begins.

Camping. The national park does not allow camping, but there is a pleasant commercial campground on the park road just before the boundary.

Season. Any, but winter could be cold at the summit.

1. Mt. Warning Ascent

> **Distance: 8.75 km (5.5 miles) round trip**
> **Time: 3 to 4 hours**
> **Difficulty: moderate**
> **Attractions: rainforest; panoramas from the summit**

Hikers will not find this 1157 meter (3795 feet) ascent to be a terribly difficult challenge. The trail to the summit is so expertly engineered that it rarely becomes tiring. Only in the last 100 meters or so, where the mountain becomes quite steep, will climbers have to exert themselves. Most of the year, water may be found at several points along the trail as springs and freshets pour forth from the mountain's slopes. Bring a sweater or jacket in cool weather, since winds on top can be fierce.

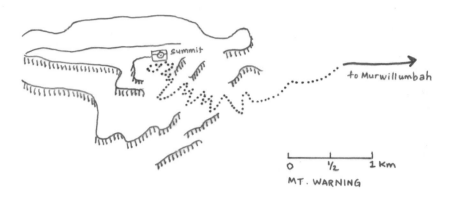

MT. WARNING

The first few kilometers lead through spectacular, old growth rainforest, with many of the tree species identified by signs. At higher elevations, views of the countryside become more frequent as the lush rainforest gives way to more stunted specimens, especially the blue mountain ash, actually a kind of eucalyptus. About 15 minutes from the summit, hikers face a hand-over-hand scramble up rock slabs, aided by chains installed by the park service. The slabs have so many hand- and footholds that some hikers will find the chains to be unnecessary. Though a bit tiring, this part of the climb is not really dangerous; young and old can complete it with no problem.

The summit rewards hikers with a 360° panorama enjoyed from four separate but interconnected viewing platforms. Plaques bearing etched-on maps show the most prominent natural features in all directions. Eastward vistas extend from Broken Head, south of Byron Bay, clear up to Surfers Paradise and beyond. To the north, west, and south, the walls of the caldera of Mt. Warning rise up prominently, their crests and valleys now protected in several national parks. But don't expect solitude up here. The trail is a busy highway, and the summit a veritable photographers' studio.

NIGHTCAP NATIONAL PARK

The southern rim of ancestral Mt. Warning has been partially protected within the confines of Nightcap National Park and adjacent state forest reserves, but only after tense confrontations between loggers and environmentalists led to creation of the park in 1983. Though much of the Nightcap Range has been cut over, plenty of undisturbed or only partially logged forest remains.

These mountains are lower by an average of 200 meters (650 feet) or so than their counterparts to the north and west. The eastern section of the range is still managed predominantly for commercial forestry; however, it has some nice hiking trails, especially the one to renowned Minyon Falls in Whian Whian State Forest. The National Park itself mostly preserves the higher, western reaches of the Nightcap Range, although even there, incursions like TV transmission towers and old logging roads inject a discordant note. On the whole hikers may find this range less inspiring than its neighbors. Still, the northern New South Wales region has a unique appeal—at least for some people—because the counterculture has colonized much of it. In these parts you will still come across vestiges of the hippie movement of the late 1960s and the back-to-the-land groundswell of the 1970s. So a trip to northern New South Wales soon evolves into a journey of cultural as well as natural discovery.

There are other walking tracks in the Nightcap Range aside from those featured here. Unfortunately, however, they tend to be overgrown and difficult to follow.

Road access. Described for each individual hike. See below.

Camping. There are two widely separated camping areas described below under hikes #1 and #2.

Season. Any, although summer rains could make the region's many dirt roads slippery.

In the area. The village of Nimbin is fun to visit, both for its beautiful, upland setting and its "hippie" ambience.

1. Protesters Falls

> **Distance: 1.5 km (1 mile) round trip**
> **Time: 30 minutes**
> **Difficulty: easy**
> **Attractions: a lovely and historically important waterfall**

Road access. From the Brisbane area take the Pacific Highway (Route 1) to the town of Bangalow, about 55 km (35 miles) south of Murwillumbah, New South Wales. At Bangalow follow signs west to Lismore, and thence north to The Channon, reached by a secondary road off the Nimbin-Lismore highway. In The Channon you will see signs for the Terania Creek picnic and camping area, about 15 km (9.25 miles) up a partly gravel road. The latter is narrow and often rough, but above all it can be closed by heavy rain which would inundate several creek fords. So don't drive up there if rain threatens.

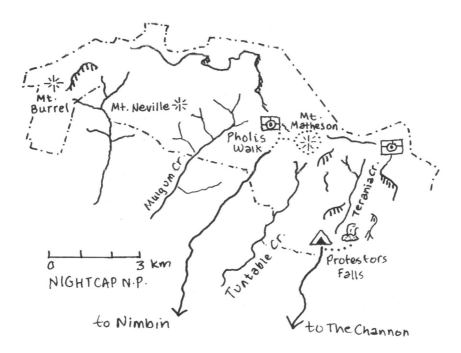

Camping. The campground at the end of the Terania Creek road offers pleasant surroundings and a shelter, but no water except that flowing in the creek. You are supposed to limit your stay to one night.

Charming Protestors Falls derives its name from a successful 1979 protest by environmentalists—the first of its kind in Australia—to prevent logging companies from clearcutting local forests. The trailhead lies immediately south of the Terania Creek camping and picnic area, on the right side of the road. After crossing Waterfall Creek, a Terania Creek tributary, on a bridge, the trail passes through a palm grove and ascends via steps to a large amphitheater. Protestors Falls is located here, tumbling down from the rhyolite cliffs above. A rock-lined pool at the base of the falls looks inviting, but may be rather dirty for swimming. Return the way you came.

2. Minyon Falls /Quondong Falls Loop

> **Distance: 8.5 km (5.25 miles) round trip**
> **Time: 3 or 4 hours**
> **Difficulty: moderately easy except near lower falls**
> **Attractions: magnificent palm groves, rainforest, two high falls**

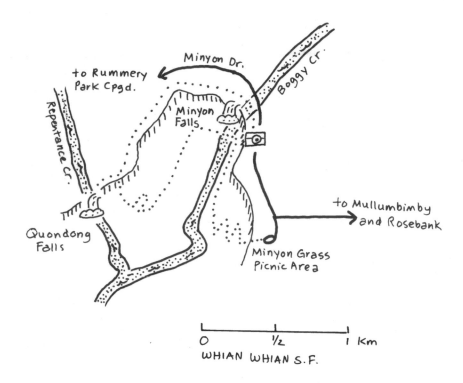

WHIAN WHIAN S.F.

Road access. From the Brisbane area drive south on the Pacific Highway (Route 1) about 30 km (18.5 miles) past Murwillumbah until you arrive at the turnoff for Mullumbimby, 4 km (2.5 miles) off the main highway. Once you come into town, proceed to the second main cross street and turn left there. No signs help you find the turn, but look for the post office at the intersection. Drive out of town on a narrow road for about 4.5 km (2.75 miles) until you see a sign indicating Minyon Falls 16 kms to the right. Turn and follow this road for another few kilometers waiting for a small sign for Minyon Falls, again to the right, near a church. This is the Repentance Creek Road, which you will follow for another 3 km (1.75 miles) or so, mostly on gravel, until just before you reach the creek itself, where a prominent sign stating "Minyon Falls: 5" directs you to the right. Continue on up the grade, bearing left after 3 km as signs direct, until you enter Whian Whian State Forest and soon hit a T-intersection. Turn left into the Minyon Grass picnic area and parking lot.

Camping. About 3 km (1.75 miles) past Minyon Grass there is a camping area called Rummery Park, run by the local shire. To reach it, turn right at the T-intersection mentioned in the road access description above and continue up Minyon Drive until you see signs for the campground.

Begin the hiking loop at the Minyon Grass picnic area. Walk past the display panel, and you will catch a first glimpse of the falls in the distance, framed by eucalypts. Start down the trail past the display; you'll soon perceive the rapid transition from the rim's eucalypt forest to rainforest. Here you enter the aptly named Valley of Palms, a verdant gorge overtopped by tall, straight piccabeen (aka bangalow) palms growing in unbroken groves. You will appreciate them best when the trail nears Repentance Creek and the wall of green all around you opens up a bit. Be careful crossing an extensive deadfall across the trail near here, if rangers have not yet cleared it away.

After about a half hour you come in sight of the falls. A sign invites you to cross the creek to the left on the trail to Quondong (usually spelled Quandong) Falls and the top of Minyon Falls. But for now forge ahead up the rocks to the right. The trail soon peters out, so you must scramble and improvise in order to get a clear view of Minyon Falls. The absolutely sheer, multihued cliff behind this 100 meter (330 foot) high cascade creates a beautiful backdrop for the tableau of tumbling waters and deep plunge pool.

Finishing your sojourn at the falls, retreat to the creek crossing and follow the sign toward Quondong Falls (3 km/1.75 miles) and upper Minyon Falls (5 km/3 miles). The walking becomes easier now as you pass through extensive stands of palm and other rainforest trees along a fairly level, unobstructed trail. You will even note a few large red cedars that the loggers missed. At one point an inattentive hiker might lose the trail as it seems to disappear under a mat of dead palm fronds littering the forest floor. But your walking track actually makes a U-turn around a huge fallen log and soon reemerges.

After a long traverse below the escarpment, the trail climbs toward the rim and its characteristic open eucalypt forest. About 30 or 40 minutes past Lower Minyon, Quondong Falls comes into view spilling over the cliff into an alcove below. A few minutes more walking brings you to a spur leading to the top of Quondong, 500 meters (0.3 mile) away. The entire detour only takes about 15 minutes, but disappoints, because you can't see much of the waterfall from directly above it.

Returning to the main trail you have 2 more km (1.25 miles) of mostly uphill walking. In late autumn, golden-flowered banksias bloom in profusion along the way. As you approach the falls don't miss Loorahn Lookout, which provides the best vantage point for photographing the cascade's entire drop. After perhaps 2 hours and 15 minutes, you reach and cross Repentance Creek, and then emerge into a picnic area. Another lookout atop Minyon Falls reveals the dense jungle canopy of the valley of palms below you.

From here stroll up to the dirt road (Minyon Drive) and turn right. You can roadwalk back to the picnic area in under 20 minutes, thus completing the loop.

3. Pholis Gap/Mt. Matheson

Distance: 4.75 km (3 miles) round trip
Time: 1.5 or 2 hours
Difficulty: moderately easy
Attractions: rainforest, some unusual views

Road access. Locate the New South Wales village of Nimbin on your road map and drive there, most likely from the town of Lismore. In Nimbin look for a sign to Rainbow Power Company. Coming in from the south, you will readily spot the sign directing you onto the right prong of a Y-intersection. Drive past Rainbow Power, continuing about 1 km (0.62 mile) to the Tuntable Creek Road. Turn right there and follow all signs to Mt. Nardi, 11 km (6.75 miles) distant. When you reach the top of this peak, obvious from the TV transmitters, look for a spur road signed for Mt. Nardi Lookout. Turn right there and park almost immediately, just across from a display kiosk.

Camping. There is no official campground anywhere near these trails, only a picnic area atop Mt. Nardi. Thus, you will have to do the walks en route to another destination, or perhaps as a leisurely daytrip from either Nimbin or Terania Creek campground.

Because the Mt. Matheson Track forms a subsidiary loop off the Pholis Gap Track, hikers can conveniently walk both during the same outing. Be sure to carry water, since the hike involves a tiring climb. To begin, find the sign for both trails behind the kiosk. You plunge into tall, shady rainforest right away, as the trail starts a gradual descent. If you have a brochure along, you can stop at numbered posts along the way and learn more about the forest. Otherwise just enjoy the filtered light, vines, tree ferns, and buttress-rooted trees. After 600 meters (650 yards), the Mt. Matheson track departs to the right. Follow it out around the mountain as it passes through a series of distinct ecosystems. At one point you enter a transition zone in which tree ferns, a rainforest denizen, grow alongside the grass trees typical of open eucalypt forests. The trail has some ups and downs, and occasionally gets overgrown, but mostly it is easy walking. After about a half hour you rejoin the Pholis Gap Track and head right. Officially you have only 900 meters (0.5 mile) left to trail's end, but that figure underestimates the true distance.

Beyond the Mt. Matheson turnoff your trail starts to descend in earnest, often on steps, through a forest slowly changing to the drier eucalypt type. Overgrowing trailside vegetation hinders progress and scratches unprotected skin. Still, views improve as the forest canopy thins out. You will enjoy glimpses into the Doon Doon Valley from a lookout about 5 minutes from the trail's end. Notice the very large blackbutt trees and the exceptionally tall grass trees growing out here. The trail culminates in an inspiring vista that takes in Mt. Warning and its satellite peaks as well as distant escarpments on the state border. Return by the Pholis Gap Track, an ascent of nearly 250 meters (825 feet).

BORDER RANGES NATIONAL PARK

One could describe Border Ranges as the New South Wales extension of Queensland's Lamington National Park. The two parks together, both World Heritage listed, include most of the western and northwestern remnants of ancestral Mt. Warning's caldera. Their geology, flora, and fauna differ little. However, the parks have distinct virtues. While Lamington, with its superb trail network, appeals most to hikers, Border Ranges will please motorists who seek to enjoy excellent views of the region from roadside lookouts. The Border Ranges scenic drive mean-

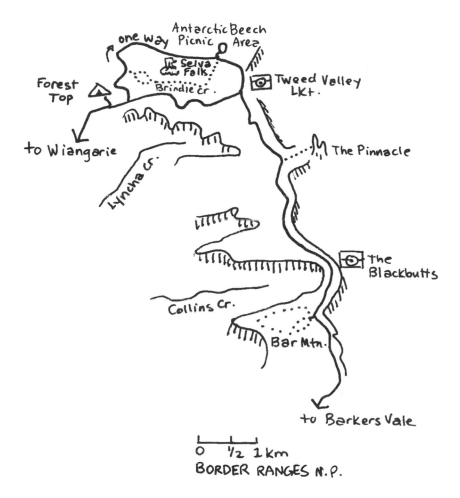

ders for many kilometers along the rim, before dropping back down to lower country through some fine rainforest. En route, short trails lead out to various overlooks or connect camping and picnic areas. Though more accessible to motorized tourism, Border Ranges does not attract nearly as many visitors as Lamington and has a more remote, undiscovered feel. While its small trail system cannot match the amazing beauty and diversity of Lamington, it does offer many scenic spots.

Road access. You definitely need a map to find your way to this park. Locate the road between Kyogle and Murwillumbah (just off Route 1), New South Wales. Follow it in either direction, keeping watch for a small sign directing motorists northward onto a spur road into Border Ranges. From Murwillumbah the turnoff should come up in about 44 km (27.25 miles). Take this good gravel road through the park to arrive at the trailheads described here. It would require about a 1.5 hour drive to the Forest Tops Campground, not including the many stops you will take. Near the summit of the road, you come to a one-way (clockwise) loop drive. The scenic drive heads downhill from Forest Tops Campground and eventually meets the Lions Road connecting Kyogle, New South Wales, with Rathdowney, Queensland. This road, now mostly paved, gives access to many parks in southeast Queensland via the Mt. Lindesay Highway. Top off your fuel tank before attempting this journey, because the Border Ranges scenic drive alone runs for 102 km (63 miles) without any service stations.

Camping. Border Ranges National Park provides two campgrounds, both on the scenic drive. Forest Tops, a grassy clearing high up in the range, has a few tables, a shelter, and grills with firewood provided. The lower elevation Sheep Station Creek campground is much larger and offers individual sites, but would be very warm in summer.

Season. Any, but the unpaved, steep loop drive could prove tricky to ascend in summer downpours.

1. Booyong Trail/Rosewood Circuit

> **Distance: 9.25 km (5.75 miles) round trip, plus 1.5 km (1 mile) for the optional Rosewood Circuit**
> **Time: 3 to 4 hours**
> **Difficulty: moderately easy**
> **Attractions: solitude, unusual trees, a lovely waterfall**

The Booyong Trail leads from the Forest Tops Campground down to the campground at Sheep Station Creek. It skirts the upper end of the creek and then drops down to cross one of its tributaries several times, passing dramatic Brushbox Falls (via a detour circuit) before reaching its destination. Along the way, hikers may want to traverse a side loop, the Rosewood Circuit, which adds about 35 or 40 minutes to the journey.

The hike should be done in a downhill direction, since the elevation difference runs to some 550 meters (1800 feet).

The Booyong Trail lacks the splendor and mystery of some other rainforest walks, because it passes through logged-over terrain. Instead of experiencing the towering "great cathedral" effect, walkers will wander through long stretches of medium-height, second growth forest, interspersed with a few huge strangler figs (not logged, because they lack commercial value). In such a disturbed, high-sunlight environment, forest floor scrub grows luxuriantly, as do the poisonous stinging trees (gympies), lawyer vines, and other hiker-unfriendly species. Nevertheless, the trail has its moments: the Rosewood detour offers some impressive old forest giants, including the trail's namesake tree; Brushbox Falls cascades mightily into a huge, deep pool; and—generally—one can expect solitude on this track.

The hike begins at the back end of Forest Tops Campground. Take the track through forest for about 0.5 km (0.3 mile), until you come to an old logging road. Go right on this road, following it until it again reverts to trail. Along the road, watch for open-forest bird species such as the red-backed black wren.

After a long descent, about 75 minutes into the trip, a tiny spring trickles out of the rock beside the trail. This is your first water. A map on a plaque beside it marks your progress. Not long after the spring, hikers encounter a large, disturbed area, probably a blow-down. Notice the many stinging trees growing up in the bright sunlight of the clearing, being careful not to brush against their leaves.

Two hours from the trailhead, you come to a bridge over Sheep Station Creek's main tributary. Just across it, the Rosewood Circuit commences, with a steep

Lawyer vine

uphill stretch. This circuit returns you to the main trail within about 40 minutes of walking. Flooded gum trees now begin to appear, tall eucalypti with "socks" of dark bark at the bottom of their trunks.

Rejoining the main trail, you cross a low ridge, and then detour onto the short loop that passes dramatic Brushbox Falls. The signage is confusing here. Basically, you follow the trail past an overlook, down to some old loggers' graffiti. Cross a bridge and go up the hill. Although the trail forks here, the two branches soon reconverge. In a few minutes, you arrive at Sheep Station Creek Campground. This lower section of the hike can be hot in summer, so be sure to carry water.

2. Bar Mountain Loop

> Distance: 3.5 km (2.25 miles) round trip
> Time: 1.25 to 1.5 hours
> Difficulty: moderate
> Attractions: unusual views to the west, Antarctic beeches

When you have driven up to the top of the range and entered the rainforest zone, look for the Bar Mountain picnic area on the left side of the road. From here a recently developed loop hike takes off toward a lookout over Collins Creek basin. The trail is fairly new, and you may find that infrequent maintenance allows a lot of overhanging branches above and accumulated deadfall below. Be sure to lock your car and take all valuables with you, since there have been reports of car-clouting here.

Walking the circuit in a clockwise direction, you descend through both old growth and second-growth forest to a fenced overlook. On the way look for moss-covered Antarctic beeches with their multiple trunks. In other parks you often need to walk many kilometers to inspect these patriarchs of the woods; here, they grow only a short walk from the parking lot. From the overlook, which is past the trail's halfway point, you enjoy vistas toward the west, unusual for Border Ranges. In season the flame trees in the valley far below fairly glow amid the deep green rainforest. On the return trip, pause to enjoy a dramatic cliff face decorated with spring-fed vegetation. Stairs allow you to ascend the cliff easily as you make your way back to the parking area.

3. Pinnacle Overlook

> Distance: 400 meters (0.25 mile) round trip
> Time: 15 minutes to the platform
> Difficulty: easy
> Attractions: impressive monolith, views of the Tweed Valley

This trail begins at a designated carpark along the main road about 11 km (6.75 miles) past the Bar Mountain picnic area. It winds through rainforest vegetation, passing by tall, healthy specimens of grass trees, to ascend slightly to a viewing platform. The overlook offers a wonderful vantage point on the Pinnacle, a rock monolith. Return the way you came.

Goanna

It is possible to open the gate of the fence around the platform to gain access to an unofficial route that beelines out to the Pinnacle. This non-maintained route—shadeless and very steep—descends a few hundred feet before tiptoeing across a razorback and climbing to the Pinnacle. From the formation you enjoy 360° views, but the route, rated moderately difficult, is not for the faint of heart. It takes 2 to 3 hours, round trip, and is best attempted in early morning. Be sure to bring water if you decide to give it a try.

4. Brindle Creek

Distance: 5.25 km (3.25 miles), one way
Time: 2 to 2.5 hours
Difficulty: moderate
Attractions: rainforest, Selva Falls

Because this is not a loop trail, you will either need to set up a car shuttle or plan to road-walk back to your car. Those with two vehicles can leave one at the Antarctic Beech Picnic Area, where the trail begins, and the other at Brindle Creek Picnic Area. An alternative plan is simply to start at the Brindle Creek Picnic Area, hike to picturesque Selva Falls, and double back.

From the Antarctic Beech Picnic Area, the trail descends steeply through one of the most diverse rainforests in Australia. It can be somewhat hard to follow at times, especially when it makes an abrupt change of direction. Part of the way it is marked either by small stakes or aluminum disks. At about the halfway point, there is a short spur to Selva Falls, certainly one of the most beautiful anywhere, not because of its height or volume of water, but because of its remote, pristine, Garden of Eden-like setting. Eels and crayfish inhabit the plunge pool at its base.

Past Selva Falls, the trail continues to descend, but more gradually now. Several creek crossings are required. Helmholtzia lilies line the creek, and there are magnificent Antarctic beech trees, two of which have formed arches along the trail. The lower end of the trail is exceptionally scenic on its way to the Brindle Creek parking lot.

Chapter 3

SCENIC RIM, WEST

The western section of the Scenic Rim extends roughly from Mt. Mistake in the northern Main Range down to Mts. Barney and Lindesay, where the McPherson Range and Border Ranges National Park begin. This region has a lower profile than its eastern counterpart. While Gold Coast vacationers arrive by the busload at Lamington and Springbrook, western parks like Mt. Barney host relatively few visitors, and campgrounds rarely fill up.

In spite of its lower key atmosphere, the western Scenic Rim boasts some of the most rugged and photogenic terrain in tropical Australia. The highest mountains in southern Queensland are all here, including Mt. Barney (1351 meters / 4550 feet) and Mt. Superbus (1371 meters / 4625

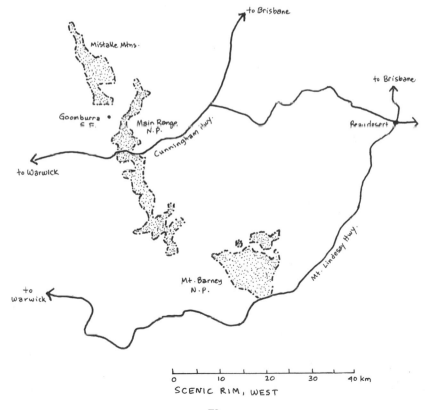

SCENIC RIM, WEST

feet). The east-facing escarpment of the Main Range forms an almost solid wall rising as much as 1000 meters (3300 feet) above the plains. And all of the parks described here boast verdant rainforests, waterfalls, and impressive outcrops of exposed rock. It would be difficult to find a more spectacular landscape anywhere in tropical Australia.

Geologically and biologically, the western Scenic Rim shares much with its eastern counterpart. Volcanic rock, especially rhyolite, predominates, except at Mt. Barney, which is composed of a granitelike rock. Often the local rhyolite forms nearly sheer, banded cliffs resembling sedimentary layers. The "wedding cake" profile of Mt. Lindesay and the pyramidal top of Mt. Mitchell both illustrate that phenomenon. One encounters rather less rainforest and more eucalypt woodland in the western Scenic Rim, especially around Mt. Barney. Overall, the western ranges seem more rugged, less accessible, and less developed than their eastern neighbors. Certainly they have fewer constructed, well-maintained trails. However, if you are willing to strike out along rougher, less distinct paths, and drive on some bumpy dirt roads, you will find ways to explore even some of the more remote sections of the western Scenic Rim. The following suggestions mark only a brief introduction to the region, concentrating mostly on the easier and better-known walking tracks. Intrepid Aussie bushwalkers have created many other faint cross-country routes that you may eventually want to try.

MAIN RANGE NATIONAL PARK

Main Range National Park protects a far-western outlier of the Scenic Rim that forms the divide between eastward-flowing rivers and the Condamine River drainage, which empties west into the Murray River and flows all the way to the Southern Ocean in South Australia. Of the park's four sections, the Cunninghams Gap area offers the easiest access and the most hiking trails. Some of these tracks offer marvelous scenery. However, the park's allure for hikers diminishes somewhat because of the busy highway that routes truck traffic through Cunninghams Gap, a pass in the range. As a result, it is difficult for hikers to escape noise pollution on the trails. Still, sublime views along the nearly sheer wall of the Main Range and abundant birdlife (especially bellbirds) may outweigh, for many visitors, the disturbances caused by heavy traffic. Other sections of the park, especially the Mistake Mountains (see below), offer far more solitude.

Road access. From Brisbane, follow Route 15, the Cunningham Highway, southwest for about 100 km (62 miles). As you approach the range, the highway climbs up toward Cunninghams Gap. Just past the summit, look for a parking lot on the right, to the north of the road. From here, several trails fan out.

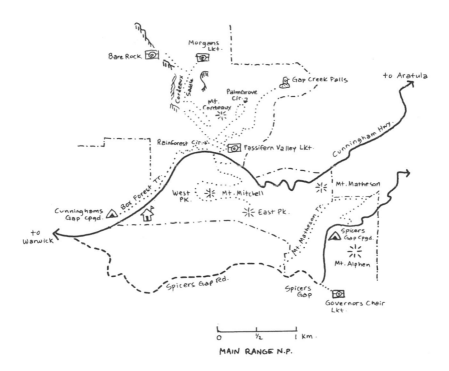

MAIN RANGE N.P.

The turnoff for the Spicers Gap section of the park, the next pass south of Cunninghams Gap, is about 5 km (3 miles) southwest of Aratula on Route 15. Turn at the sign for Moogerah Dam and Spicers Gap. About 6 km (3.75 miles) down this road, turn right at an intersection marked for Spicers Gap, following signs to the campground and picnic area. You will have to drive about 4 km (2.5 miles) on a steep, rutted dirt road that becomes impassable when wet.

Camping. The Cunninghams Gap section of the park has a well-appointed campground, 4 km (2.5 miles) west of Cunninghams Gap just off Route 15, opposite a service station. It offers a convenient stopping point on the way to Girraween National Park and other Granite Belt locales. The campground, though plagued by highway noise, is rarely crowded and has shady sites, picnic tables, flush toilets, and firewood for its grills.

The QNPWS also maintains a campground at Spicers Gap which is reached by the road directions detailed above.

Season. You can visit the park at almost any time of year, but the high peaks often attract clouds and rain in the December to May period. Also, high winds and exposed trails could occasionally make winter hiking very chilly.

1. Mt. Cordeaux/Bare Rock Trail

Distance: 6.75 km (4.25 miles) round trip to Mt. Cordeaux
    Lookout; 12.25 km (7.5 miles) round trip to Bare Rock
Time: 4 to 5 hours round trip to Bare Rock
Difficulty: moderate
Attractions: outstanding views, unusual rock formations,
    rainforest

The track to Mt. Cordeaux/Bare Rock should delight visitors on account of its many unobstructed views up and down the range and out toward the plains west of Ipswich. Park at the Cunninghams Gap rest area, located on your right if you are traveling west, just beyond the top of the pass. The trail commences near the east end of the parking lot. Passing by a monument, it climbs steadily, but not very steeply, through a shady forest. Before long you arrive at a short loop trail, the Rainforest Circuit. Go right here, pausing to enjoy the view from Fassifern Valley Lookout. You may see lyrebirds here. The Rainforest Circuit soon rejoins the main track. Where the loop closes, about 1 km (0.62 mile) from the parking lot, there are intersections with the Gap Creek Falls and Palm Circuit Trails.

At about km 3.5 (mile 2.25) you reach an old "open cut" gold mine, visible from a fenced platform. Just past here, take the 65 meter (70 yard) spur trail to the Mt. Cordeaux Lookout, lined with grass trees. From the lookout, a rough path winds up toward the summit, but only well-equipped rock climbers should attempt this dangerous route. The view from the lookout extends for many miles to the south, taking in the Main Range's rugged east face, Mt. Mitchell, and even faraway Mt. Barney National Park.

Returning to the main trail, you walk on a narrow ridge called Cordeaux Saddle linking Mt. Cordeaux's needlelike promontory to the rest of the range. Wild views greet you here. Between this ridge and the Bare Rock spur, the well-graded trail continues its ascent. Within 2 km (1.25 miles) you encounter signs pointing toward Mt. Morgan, 350 meters distant, and Bare Rock, 680 meters away. Mt. Morgan can be skipped in favor of Bare Rock, which affords better, more extensive views of the northern reaches of the park. Out here, you finally escape the rumble of heavy trucks and bask in the solitude and beauty of this magnificent range.

Retrace your steps to your car. Near the bottom, when you intersect the Rainforest Loop, you can turn right for variety if you wish.

2. Palm Grove Circuit

Distance: 4.5 km (2.75 miles) round trip
Time: 1 to 1.5 hours
Difficulty: easy
Attractions: piccabeen palms, a variety of forest types

This pleasant trail branches off the trail to Mt. Cordeaux, about 1 km (0.62 mile) from the Cunninghams Gap parking area.

The trail has very gentle grades and is shaded in the afternoon. It contours through the forest below Mt. Cordeaux, offering occasional views of Mounts Cordeaux and Mitchell, and eventually arrives at a 1 km loop. The loop features both palm groves and, on drier slopes, grass trees. Return the way you came.

3. Box Forest Track

> **Distance: 4.25 km (2.75 miles) one way**
> **Time: 1.25 hours**
> **Difficulty: easy**
> **Attractions: nice rainforest, bellbirds**

At the west end of the Cunninghams Gap rest area, described above, a trail leads southward, via a picnic area, to the main campground. Since it follows Gap Creek, the highway's route, it does not offer much relief from traffic noise. However, the bird and plant life along the way will make many people forget such distractions.

The first half of the track winds past numerous brush box trees, gnarly and bark-clad below, but smooth and barkless in their upper reaches. Once you arrive at the picnic area, note the chorus of bellbird calls resounding in the forest all around you. This area seems to be a colony for them, and you will hear their melodious chirps for many a meter beyond. Toward its end, the trail passes near the creek, offering opportunities to swim or to soak tired feet. The scenery has gradually shifted; tall eucalypti predominate now, and the rainforest has been left behind. At one point, the trail forks, with the lefthand branch leading to an old stone bridge across the creek. Don't take this path, unless you want to plunge into the swimming hole nearby. Instead, follow the right fork. Cross the private road leading to Kamp Stacey and pick up the trail on its other side. A few more minutes of walking bring you back to the campground.

4. Mt. Matheson Loop

> **Distance: 8.5 km (5.25 miles) round trip**
> **Time: 2.25 hours**
> **Difficulty: moderately easy**
> **Attractions: some of the best views in the Main Range, a historic old road**

The Mt. Matheson "loop" involves considerable roadwalking to close the circuit. However, one of the roads included in the route has historic interest, having been constructed by convict labor in the mid-nineteenth century.

The trail takes off opposite the parking lot for Spicers Gap picnic area and climbs gradually through open eucalypt forest. After 1.75 km (1 mile) or about 30 minutes of climbing, the trail tops out on the lightly wooded summit of Mt. Matheson (sometimes spelled Mathieson). Here, and all along the next 1 km of trail, you'll look right across to the "layered" face of Mt. Mitchell and north to Mt. Cordeaux and the Mistake Range. Unfortunately, you will also hear traffic rumbling up the busy Cunningham Highway.

From Mt. Matheson, the trail bears slightly left and downhill onto a ridge that supports luxuriant grass tree stands. Listen for the chorus of bellbirds all around you in the forest. After another 10 minutes or so, the trail runs into an outcrop of boulders and seems to disappear. Continue straight over or past them, keeping the same heading rather than descending from the ridge on either side. Beyond the outcrop, the trail reappears and then meanders to a lofty lookout pinnacle on a flank of Mt. Mitchell. Enjoy the view from here, for soon the trail veers back into the forest, passing some magnificent strangler figs, and finally emerges into an open, grassy meadow shaded by eucalypti.

In the meadow, 1.75 km (1 mile) beyond Mt. Matheson, a bit over an hour from the start, you pass a rusty contraption called a "timber jinker" and gradually descend to the historic road mentioned earlier. Now nothing more than a rutted 4-WD track, this road was once an engineering marvel, and has therefore been declared a "heritage trail." Plaques explain details of the construction technology employed in the 1840s and '50s. Meanwhile, you enjoy occasional views up to Spicers Peak to the south of the road.

About 1.75 km (1 mile) farther, or 20 more minutes later, the heritage road meets the Spicers Gap road at a spacious parking area. On its far side look for signs to Governors Chair Lookout, 150 meters away atop a sheer cliff. It rewards hikers with vistas clear down to the McPherson and Border Ranges and far to the east over the Moogerah Peaks. Returning from the lookout, follow signs to Spicers Gap Campground, about 2 km (1.25 miles) distant. All this roadwalking goes fast, so you return to your car within about 20 more minutes.

GOOMBURRA STATE FOREST: MISTAKE MOUNTAINS

North of Cunninghams Gap lies a remote and seldom visited stretch of the Main Range. Part of it belongs under the jurisdiction of Goomburra State Forest, while the remainder has been preserved as the Mt. Mistake section of Main Range National Park. It is here that the 100 km (62 mile) crescent of the Scenic Rim officially begins. As yet, the region has few hiking trails, and all of those begin in Goomburra State Forest, the focal

point of the following descriptions. This northern extension of the Main
Range offers unusual views from ridgetop lookouts, lovely streams and
waterfalls, and uncrowded hiking. Goomburra and the Mistake Range
should appeal to outdoor enthusiasts who love tranquil, unspoiled, scenic parks.

Road access. From Brisbane drive southwest on Route 15, the Cunning-
ham Highway, to a point around 29 km (18 miles) past Cunninghams
Gap and just beyond Gladfield. Turn right at the sign for the village of
Goomburra and follow all signs to it. After about 6 km (3.75 miles) you
reach an intersection at which two roads head off to the right in a sort of
Y. You make the "hard" right turn, following a sign to Inverramsay and
Goomburra State Forest, and then drive a further 25 km (15.5 miles),
with the last 6 km (3.75 miles) on gravel. You will pass many small camps
with romantic names. Ignore them and continue into the state forest,
where the next move depends on your hiking and camping plans.

The first three trails listed below begin in close proximity to each
other. To reach them, bear left off the main Goomburra State Forest road
just before you reach Poplar Flat Campground. The secondary road you
have entered, passable only in dry weather, crosses a creek and immediately climbs the range. In really rainy conditions, forest rangers will close
a gate across it. After about 4.25 km (2.75 miles) look for a spacious clearing to the left of the road. This is the parking area for the Araucaria Falls
Track. Another 1.25 km (0.75 miles) brings you to the Sylvesters Lookout

Strangler fig

trailhead. After 1.5 rough km more (1 mile), the road terminates at a large clearing for the Mt. Castle Lookout. This clearing would also serve visitors planning to walk the Winder Track, in case that trail reopens anytime soon.

The trailhead for the fourth featured walk, the Cascade Trail/Ridge Trail Loop, is located at the end of the road in Manna Gum Campground.

Camping. The forest's two campgrounds, Poplar Flat and Manna Gum, are located alongside the main park road. Pick whichever you like and pay your camping fee. Both campgrounds have cows roaming around.

Season. Any, but avoid a visit during rainy weather on account of possible road closures.

1. Sylvesters Lookout

> **Distance: 1.5 km (1 mile) round trip**
> **Time: 15 minutes**
> **Difficulty: easy**
> **Attractions: rainforest, great downrange views**

Though advertised as a 750 meter (0.5 mile) stroll, the Sylvesters Lookout track is actually even shorter than that. The trail leads through pristine, spectacular rainforest out to a viewing platform suspended over the cliff edge. En route you enter the Mt. Mistake National Park. Unfortunately, the QNPWS has temporarily closed the platform. Still, you can easily see past it across the plains and hills to the east and down the range toward Cunninghams Gap. You return the same way.

2. Mt. Castle Lookout

Distance: 1.25 km (0.75 miles) round trip
Time: 20 minutes
Difficulty: easy
Attractions: a unique and stirring vantage point

This track leads through an enchanting rainforest studded with impressive hoop pines. These tall and very straight trees have rough, knobby bark, faint banding, and a coniferous appearance, even though they are not true pines. At the overlook you would expect to contemplate the eastern plains; instead, you find yourself face to face with the formidable massif of Mt. Castle, a sheer walled mesa that appears nearly inaccessible. It is an impressive sight, reminiscent of the Lost World plateau in Lamington. Return via the same trail.

3. Araucaria Trail

Distance: 3 km (1.75 miles) round trip
Time: 1 hour and 15 minutes
Difficulty: moderately easy
Attractions: an attractive waterfall in a lush gorge

The Araucaria Trail sign promises that the walk will require two hours, but it should not take nearly that long. It is an easy hike except for a steep and slippery trans-creek section of trail at the very end.

Begin by crossing a small creek on rocks and continuing into the rainforest. The trail soon widens and offers easy passage amid fine forest scenery resounding with the sharp calls of the eastern whipbird. After about 15 minutes, the trail starts downhill and soon bends right past a huge hoop pine (*Araucaria cunninghamii*, the trail's namesake tree). It drops down to the north branch of Dalrymple Creek at the top of Araucaria Falls, whence you can gaze downstream over a rainforest topped by more lofty hoop pines. Cross the creek and descend on switchbacks to the foot of the falls. A bit of rockhopping will give you an unobstructed view of this exquisite cascade. Return as you came.

4. Cascade Trail/Ridge Trail Loop

Distance: 8 km (5 miles) round trip
Time: 2.5 hours
Difficulty: moderately easy
Attractions: rainforest, several nice falls, views from the ridge

The loop depicted here combines sections of two trails that could also be walked separately as shorter circuits. They work well as a longer loop, however, since their best features complement one another.

Begin on the Cascade Trail, because directional signs assume you will be walking it upstream. Locate the sign for the Cascade Trail at the far end of Manna Gum Campground, down by Dalrymple Creek. You cross the creek almost immediately, the first of 19 crossings, all of which can be done by rockhopping. At first the trail wends its way through eucalypt forest past pale Sydney blue gum trees. After about a half hour, the trail divides, with the short right fork dropping down to the base of a low but attractive cascade. Returning to the main trail, you pass a marker proclaiming the boundary of the World Heritage Rainforest Reserve. And, sure enough, the rainforest does begin around here, as epiphytes, lianas, walkingstick palms, piccabeen palms, and other characteristic species start to appear.

Continuing through the rainforest, you will glimpse two more small falls below the trail, now traversing along the slope of a ravine. After a tiring climb, the trail finally reaches a much larger cascade that drops about 20 meters (65 feet) in two stages. To enjoy the best view of the lower falls, detour down a short spur to the right. Back on the main walking track, you cross a rusty cable, then follow the trail as it veers right to the upper falls. This is the only place where one might lose the trail. To locate its continuation, scramble up the rocks to a little pool below the upper falls and look to the left. Notice the trail departing up-hill through dense vegetation. Follow it as it winds around the head of Dalrymple Creek and then widens into a disused 4-WD track.

About 15 minutes past the last falls, a sign will point the way to the Ridge Trail, which requires a left turn and then a tiring climb up another abandoned road. If you don't feel like making the climb, you can pro-ceed straight ahead instead of turning left at this junction, and the Cas-cade Trail will take you back to the campground. You would cut 2 km (1.25 miles) off the walk by remaining on the Cascade Trail. Assuming you opt for the Ridge Trail, you struggle uphill until it gains the ridgetop and heads west. From this point you enjoy inspiring views across the Goomburra Valley toward the Mistake Range, as are now several hundred meters higher than Dalrymple Creek where you had previously walked. Meandering through eucalypt forest, the trail begins its descent, at first gradually, but then precipitously. The last 20 minutes of walking require care on the steep, gravelly, eroded trail. Cow pies strewn about also detract from its aesthetic appeal. Near the end, the trail becomes vague, and you may find yourself emerging on the road below Manna Gum Campground. If so, just turn right and walk back up to your car.

Mt. Barney National Park

Among Australian bushwalkers and rock climbers, Mt. Barney has a rare mystique. Because of its rugged terrain, big walls, and paucity of trails, this park has tended to attract the hardy and highly experienced outdoorsperson—at least until recently. But gradually the park has opened up to slightly less rugged hikers as trails have been improved. Most notably, fit and energetic walkers with no special rockclimbing or orienteering skills can now ascend Mt. Barney itself. The park service has marked and upgraded an old hiker-made trail from Yellow Pinch Campground to Mt. Barney saddle. This South Ridge Trail, contemptuously dubbed "Peasants Ridge" by the rockclimbing confraternity, will prove tiring but is not really dangerous to any reasonably fit hiker. Of course, climbers have pioneered many other routes up Mt. Barney, but all of them involve at least some rockclimbing. Below is a summary of the main features of the peasants' route. As a card-carrying peasant, I found it tough enough!

Mt. Barney National Park includes a number of other high and rather remote peaks. Unlike Mt. Barney, which is composed of granophyre (a rock type similar to granite), the neighboring peaks are mostly made of rhyolite like the famous Main Range mountains. If you find yourself drawn to this scenic and wild part of tropical Australia, you may want to make forays into these more remote sections of the park. Since such hikes would mostly be off-trail, you would need a topo map, compass,

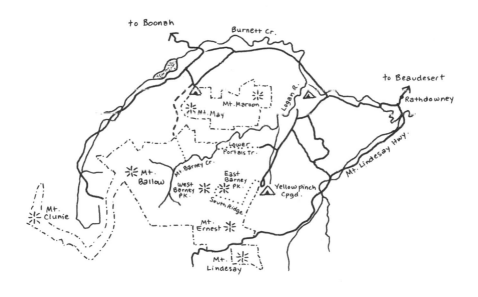

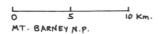

MT. BARNEY N.P.

and one of the guidebooks specializing in cross-country routes. As of today, the park has only two official walking tracks, both reviewed here.

Road access. From the Brisbane area, drive south on the Mt. Lindesay Highway toward Beaudesert. From north of the city or the airport, you can now easily reach the Mt. Lindesay Highway by taking the Gateway Motorway around the city to its junction with the Logan Motorway, on which you just drive west one exit to the Mt. Lindesay. Continuing south, drive 1 km (0.62 mile) past Rathdowney and take a right on the Boonah–Rathdowney road. Travel 8 km (5 miles) west until you see signs for Lower Portals/Barney View. Turn left here onto the Upper Logan Road. Continue on past the Barney View turnoff, following signs to Lower Portals and Yellow Pinch.

If you want to hike to Lower Portals, drive about 8 km (5 miles) south from the Boonah–Rathdowney road, looking for Lower Portals Road, a right turn. Follow the latter to where it ends at a car park about 2 km (1.25 miles) farther. If you intend to climb Mt. Barney, just keep driving south, following all signs to Yellow Pinch. The trail begins at the Yellow Pinch Campground.

Camping. You can camp at Beaudesert Shire's Yellow Pinch Campground, which has no tap water available and rather indifferent amenities. Otherwise you might try Mt. Barney Lodge, reached by a left turn just before Yellow Pinch, which offers cabins and camping.

Besides these drive-in campgrounds, Mt. Barney National Park contains 14 backcountry campsites, some of which can accommodate up to 30 visitors. In the context of the trails described here, some of these campsites deserve further comment. First, Lower Portals (site #5) has several camping spots beside Barney Creek at the end of the Lower Portals Trail. Also, those ascending Mt. Barney can camp at either of two places on the saddle between East and West Peaks (sites #6 and #7). In addition there are 3 sites (#8, #9, and #10) along Cronan Creek on the old road leading from Yellow Pinch Campground to the start of South Ridge Trail.

Hikers could trim several kilometers off the ascent by camping at Cronan Creek the previous night, leaving their overnight gear on site, and then ascending the next day carrying only a daypack. The park imposes quotas on all these backcountry sites, so you should reserve a spot either by calling or writing. Write to The Ranger, QNPWS, M/S 342, Boonah, Qld. 4310, or phone (07) 5463-5041. Calling ahead is preferable, since you can then ascertain whether or not the site you want is full and, if it is, adjust your plans on the spot.

Season. Avoid hiking in Mt. Barney N.P. during the hottest days of summer, since both trails are exposed to direct sun in many places, and during the few really chilly winter days. Otherwise, any season is fine.

Buttress roots

1. Lower Portals

> **Distance: 7.5 km (4.75 miles) round trip**
> **Time: 2 hours**
> **Difficulty: moderately easy**
> **Attractions: a swift creek with deep pools amid boulders**

Although the Lower Portals Hike has little to recommend it en route, it leads to a perfectly delightful campsite. Begin at the Lower Portals carpark and follow the obvious trail across an uninspiring open eucalypt landscape. After 3.5 km (2.25 miles) you reach Barney Creek. Cross it on rocks, and then head left along its edge to the designated sites at trail's end. The Lower Portals would be a fine place to spend a lazy summer afternoon swimming and relaxing in the creek's deep, cool pools, or daydreaming under a shade tree. More ambitious hikers could scramble up a hill to the right for views of the creek's upper reaches or rockhop and route-find far upstream. Return by the same trail.

2. Mt. Barney Ascent

> **Distance: 15.25 km (9.5 miles) round trip**
> **Time: 7.5 to 9 hours, including summit time**
> **Difficulty: difficult**
> **Attractions: wildflowers, best views in southeast Queensland,**
> **kudos for climbing the region's second highest peak**

Ascending Mt. Barney involves an elevation gain, from Yellow Pinch Campground to East Peak, of more than 1000 meters (3300 feet). At least among mountains with trails to the summit, that would put it just behind Bartle Frere in northern Queensland as the biggest climb in tropical Australia. Make no mistake: climbing Mt. Barney will tax all but the most hardened hikers. But ordinarily fit people can do this climb and will not regret it, because the views along the way and especially from the summit are unrivaled.

One can ascend the mountain in either of two ways: as a day hike from Yellow Pinch Campground (the trailhead) or as an overnight with a camp on the saddle between East and West Peaks. The time suggested here for the entire hike assumes that it's being done as a dayhike. Dragging a heavy backpack up to the saddle would add perhaps 2 or 3 hours to total trail time. The steepness of the route would make backpacking a punishing ordeal. Still, a camp at the saddle would enable hikers to enjoy the most beautiful light on Mt. Barney and surrounding peaks around sunset and sunrise.

Bring water along, especially for the climb, since you will find it only near the summit in a little stream. Try to get an early start, whether to avoid climbing in the heat during the warmer months of the year or to beat gathering darkness from May to October.

You start the climb by walking to the end of Yellow Pinch Campground, passing a gate, and roadwalking about 4 km (2.5 miles) to a sign for South (Peasants) Ridge/East Peak. The roadwalk should take most people an hour or less. At the sign, go right onto an old, terribly rutted 4-WD road and follow it for about 30 minutes until it peters out at a landslide area above a palm-filled ravine. Beyond here, the trail narrows and climbs relentlessly up a wooded slope. Soon you will notice orange arrows directing you along the trail whenever the correct route appears in doubt.

For another hour you struggle ever upward, sometimes over rough terrain. At two places you must scramble up steep rock slabs using hand- and footholds. Although some people might find those sections daunting, they are really not that hard. All the while you pass through luxuriant grass tree, wildflower, and banksia growth. Incidentally, the sharp-pointed grass tree "leaves" could injure your eyes, so wear some protection such as sunglasses. Rarely will you enjoy grand vistas yet, but every now and then you will glimpse Mounts Ernest and Lindesay just across the valley and in the distance the McPherson Range.

Eventually the trail traverses left along a low, moist cliff. It takes you gradually higher until you emerge above Barney Saddle. You must then descend about 50 meters (175 feet) to a large clearing amid surprisingly dense forest on the saddle itself. The abundant walking stick palms remind you that, even at this altitude, you have not left tropical Australia behind.

From the clearing on up to East Peak, route-finding becomes a serious problem. To locate the trail's continuation, follow these directions. First, walk across the clearing on the saddle and find an obvious trail heading down the other side. Walk down it about 30 meters and look for a fairly well-defined trail heading off to the right. Take this trail and fight through brush to a small creek. Cross it near a log. On the other side you will encounter another, smaller clearing where a bare patch marks the spot of a hut that once stood here. From the hut site look right and you should notice a trail ascending parallel to the creek. Follow it as it swings back to the creek. At a small pool amid some flat rocks, look left. You should discern a faint trail amid the vegetation that heads away from the creek and toward a ridge.

Past this point, you will struggle. The trail has no more arrows to mark its course, so you have to figure out the route on your own. That becomes increasingly difficult as the route crosses open rock, divides into several branches and false spurs, and grows much fainter. You will inevitably lose it repeatedly on your way up. Therefore, before tackling this final push, survey the most likely route to the summit and, when in doubt, move toward it. If you have lost the trail, you will eventually intersect it again, because there just aren't that many places it could go. When off the trail, try to walk on rock slabs rather than wading through underbrush, since the latter grows so thickly that you can't always see where you are stepping.

After much travail you will attain a kind of false summit. From that point the trail becomes more distinct, and you should stay on it most of the way to the top. From the saddle to East Peak should take a bit less than an hour, provided you don't lose the trail too often.

Summit vistas seem to extend forever. South of you looms Mt. Lindesay's wedding cake profile. Beyond it you can gaze far down into New South Wales. To the west rise rainforest-clad Mt. Ballow and, more distantly, the Main Range. The latter counts one peak, Mt. Superbus, that is even higher than Mt. Barney. Far to the east look for the McPherson Range and, just behind it, the angular summit of Mt. Warning. Toward the north you can readily identify Mts. Maroon and May, as well as the far-off profile of the D'Aguilar Range north of Brisbane and over 80 km (50 miles) away. I have seen no better views anywhere in tropical Australia.

The return walk to the saddle should prove less arduous, since you will be able to locate the trail more easily from above than from below. All in all, it will probably take about an hour less to descend from East Peak to the carpark than it took to ascend there. When you reach the tricky rock scrambles described earlier, you may find it easiest to turn around and face the rock, downclimbing by the same foot- and handholds you used to get up.

Chapter 4

THE GRANITE BELT

Queensland and New South Wales share a high, cool plateau stretching several hundred kilometers from around Warwick, Qld., south to the Gibraltar Ranges, well inland from the Scenic Rim. In some places, granite domes, balanced rocks, and dramatic cliffs loom above surrounding meadows and forests, enticing hikers to explore an intriguing, unique landscape. Australians call this region the "Granite Belt," after its predominant rock type, and have set aside several superb national parks to preserve its wildest, most scenic reaches.

More than most regions in this book, the high altitude Granite Belt experiences severe seasonal variations of climate. During the winter months, temperatures can drop below freezing, and snow on the domes is not an uncommon sight. Spring brings profuse displays of wildflowers, but chilly nights. So, if you choose to visit these parks in the cool

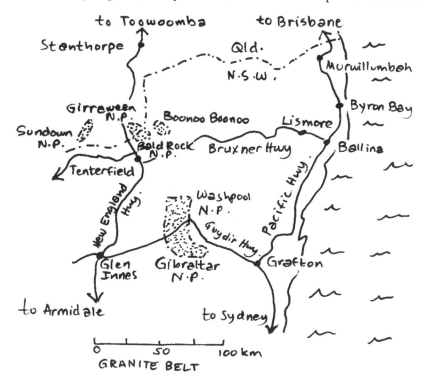

GRANITE BELT

season, expect conditions similar to those you might encounter in the Adirondacks or Rockies in October, and bring appropriate clothing and equipment. The Granite Belt also receives substantial rainfall, though nowhere near as much as the nearby Scenic Rim. If showers pass through when you are there, do not try to climb the steeper domes. Their slopes pose a challenge even in dry weather; when wet, they would make footing treacherous and could cause long, life-threatening falls.

Despite such difficulties, Granite Belt parks will enthrall most hikers. Scrambling up and down the domes can be good fun, especially for kids. Photographers will have a field day in parks like Girraween, Gibraltar Ranges, and Boonoo Boonoo, capturing on film balanced rocks, surreal slopes, and high waterfalls. Finally, these parks offer excellent opportunities to encounter wildlife, especially kangaroos, wallabies, and unusual birds. Their forests also differ from those farther east, with picturesque eucalypt species, some temperate rainforest, and amazing displays of Christmas bells and other flowers in early summer.

Road access poses few problems. All the parks described here can be reached on spur roads off the New England Highway which runs from just north of Sydney on up past Toowoomba, Queensland.

GIRRAWEEN NATIONAL PARK

Girraween National Park, lying mostly above 900 meters (3000 feet), may remind Americans vaguely of Yosemite's domes or the rocky, bald tops of the Adirondack Mountains. Geology partly accounts for the park's rugged and scenic landforms. Most of the region is rather dry and quite cold by Australian standards. Frosts are common in winter, and snow falls occasionally. You will encounter no rainforest here; rather, open eucalypt woodlands cover most of Girraween, at least in its lower, more temperate zones. On the higher ridges and peaks above 1100 meters (3600 feet), bare granite predominates, in some cases, acres of it, interspersed by stunted trees and wildflowers. Atop these balds, and indeed even in some of the eucalypt forests, reposes the oddest assortment of balanced rocks, Stonehenge-like monoliths, "arches," and grottoes to be found this side of southern Utah. The best hikes in the park lead trekkers up to, or close by, the summits of the highest granite peaks.

Road access. From Brisbane or Toowoomba, drive to Warwick, then follow the New England Highway south past Stanthorpe. The main park entrance road branches off about 25 km (15.5 miles) south of this small town. From the south, follow the New England highway about 30 km (18.5 miles) north from Tenterfield, N.S.W., to the park road.

Camping. Girraween has two campgrounds, Bald Rock Creek and Castle Rock. Sometimes one of these will be closed if the other can handle visitors by itself. The campgrounds have the usual QNPWS amenities, including a supply of firewood. Self-registration is the rule, though it is wise to call or write ahead for reservations, especially if you hope to visit the park on a weekend.

Season. October through April would be best, though one could certainly visit during warm spells in winter as well.

1. Mt. Norman/Castle Rock

> **Distance: 10.5 km (6.5 miles) round trip**
> **Time: 5 hours**
> **Difficulty: moderately difficult if climbing the summit**
> **Attractions: highest granite dome in the park, acres of bare rock, the "Eye of the Needle"**

To reach Mt. Norman, you begin at the Castle Rock Camping Area, which is the second campground accessed from the park road, a few hundred meters past the turnoff to Bald Rock Creek Camping Area. Proceed to the far end of the loop drive through the campground to the "walking tracks" signboard. The trail to Mt. Norman also gives access to Castle Rock and to the Sphinx/Turtle Rock area of the park, described below.

   The trail is graded and fairly easy at the start. You gradually gain elevation as you pass by various eye-catching arrangements of boul-

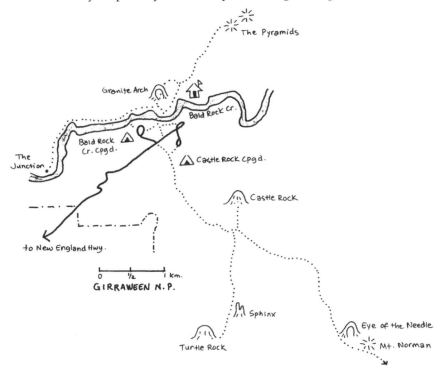

ders. After about 2 km (1.25 miles) you arrive at an important junction. The trail to your left leads to Castle Rock (0.5 km / 0.3 mile distant) and Mt. Norman (3.5 km / 2.25 miles farther), while the trail to your right heads toward the Sphinx (1.5 km / 1 mile) and Turtle Rock (1.75 km / 1.1 miles). Go left at this junction.

Very shortly thereafter you can branch off left on a short spur to Castle Rock. The spur trail winds slowly upward amid titanic boulders until it encounters bare granite. Follow white blazes up onto the rock, through a joint-fissure in the dome, and out onto a sloping terrace. The blazes lead you far around a line of low cliffs to a point where you can scramble up to the very top of the dome. The route may prove a bit scary, as you are walking "sidehill" along steep rock slopes. But the traverse looks worse than it really is. If you stay close to the low cliff line on your right, the angle is less extreme, and you can grip the cliff wall for support. Views from the summit are breathtaking, and just below the summit they are almost as good.

Retrace your steps back to the main trail to Mt. Norman and turn left. After winding through tall eucalypt woods and crossing a creek, the trail heads toward another expanse of granite. The rock formations will pique your interest, as will the tiny rivulets of water that flow from small springs and gouge channels in the granite. Soon you reach a false summit, which you bypass on the left. Continue on around, following white blazes up another large expanse of bare rock to enter high-elevation forest. Before long, you attain the base of Mt. Norman's summit, a veritable garden of enormous granite monoliths. Two monoliths have fallen together to form a pseudo-arch called Eye of the Needle, a spectacular and photogenic feature.

Beyond the Eye, you pass through a sort of tunnel amid the boulders. Pay close attention to your route here so you do not

Hikers ascend Mt. Norman

get lost on the way back. Shortly, you attain a decisive point in your journey. Continuing on south brings you to a superb overlook. It is possible to follow a trail from here down into the valley to a picnic area, 2 km (1.25 miles) distant. This picnic area is also accessible by 4-WD road.

To climb Mt. Norman, however, you do not continue toward the picnic area. Instead, you leave the trail where it plummets into the valley and go left from the overlook for a few meters. Facing the rocks above you, you notice a rocky gully, which is the route to the summit. This primitive, unmarked route requires you to inch your way upward, along a ledge, to a small tree. From the tree, you ascend to another ledge and scramble up a narrow chimney. The route is difficult, as parts of it are very exposed, and a fall here could be dangerous. Still, many people successfully attempt it every day. Even if you pass up the trip to the summit, you will not be disappointed by the views and the local scenery. Return the way you came.

2. The Sphinx/Turtle Rock

> **Distance: 7.5 km (4.75 miles) round trip**
> **Time: 2.5 or 3 hours**
> **Difficulty: moderately easy**
> **Attractions: the park's most famous and most photographed**
> **feature, plus freelance exploration around Turtle Rock**

These fascinating formations merit a visit, whether as a side trip from Mt. Norman or a separate hike. To reach them, follow the Mt. Norman trail from the campground as described above. When you reach the first trail junction, turn right. From here, the Sphinx is 1.5 km (1 mile) and Turtle Rock is 1.75 km.

The trail climbs gradually to these balds until, almost before you realize it, you are standing before the Sphinx. The signature of Girraween, it is an enormous granite tower, capped by a head-like balanced rock. The Brobdingnagian boulders all around it should also interest hikers, as should the Zen-like feel of the stunted trees growing against backdrops of sheer, smooth granite.

From the Sphinx, Turtle Rock is only about 5 minutes away. Follow a faint path as far as you can, then walk right up to, and along, the lowest cliffs of the dome. You soon notice a fairly obvious gully that leads upward, and, from its top, a tilting ramp of rock takes you to a spot just below the summit. From that vantage point, you enjoy superb views of the Sphinx and much else.

There is also a similar ravine, a bit farther on, that heads toward the interior of the dome. If you climb it, you come to a lovely eucalypt grove and a strange, shadowy, joint-type fissure. Wedged above you in the narrow fissure are four huge boulders. It's a magical place.

Backtrack to your car.

3. The Pyramid

> Distance: 3 km (1.75 miles) round trip
> Time: 1.5 hours
> Difficulty: moderately difficult
> Attractions: amazing views of Second Pyramid, balanced rocks

Just past Castle Rock Camping Area, there is a turnoff on the left for a picnic ground. The trailhead is located here. The trail crosses Bald Rock Creek on bridges. Passing through a meadow, it intersects two trails almost immediately, one to The Junction and the other to Granite Arch, 150 meters distant. In the spring, hikers are treated to extravagant wildflower displays in this vicinity.

Past the second junction, the trail climbs on stairs to the base of the Pyramid. It proceeds onto the bare granite slopes, marked by white "footprints" all the way to the top. Since this is the steepest of Girraween's commonly climbed domes, special caution is required, especially on the descent. Beware of snakes as well, which sometimes can be spotted sunning themselves on the rocks. The climb is tiring, but well worth the effort. As you climb higher, the fluted, rounded form of the Second Pyramid heaves into view. Near the top, it makes an awesome backdrop for an enormous, precariously balanced boulder. The summit itself is surreal. From the highest point you can see the whole park spread out below in a sort of bowl, bounded and studded by more granite balds—a geologic revelation.

After descending the Pyramid the way you came, detour to see Granite Arch on the trail referred to above. It is not actually a true arch, but rather consists of slabs of granite that have fallen together. The trail passes directly under it.

BALD ROCK NATIONAL PARK

Bald Rock in New South Wales shares a border with Girraween National Park in Queensland, so the features in both are similar: open eucalypt forests, topped by granite domes. Because some roads and trails in the parks connect, cross-border hikes are possible. Although Girraween is better known and more heavily visited, the great domes of Bald Rock may be even more impressive than those of their neighbor. Bald Rock has a slightly different, more rustic ambience, too, given its smaller size, more basic camping facilities, and more difficult access.

Road access. From either the north or south, take the New England Highway to the general vicinity of the park. From the north, as you enter the town of Stanthorpe, watch for signs to Amosfield and/or the Mt. Lindesay Highway. Turn left here. At Amosfield, 16 km (10 miles) distant, go south (right) and drive 21 km (13 miles) on a mostly unpaved but fairly good road. Turn right at the park entrance road and travel 6 km (3.75 miles) to the campground and trailheads.

From the south, drive through Tenterfield, N.S.W., watching for signs to the Mt. Lindesay Highway and Woodenbong. After 29 km (18 miles) turn left onto the national park access road.

Camping. The park's small campground has individual sites with grills and, in a few places, picnic tables. Firewood and water are also provided. However, the Park Service recommends that you boil the water before drinking it.

Season. Same as for Girraween.

1. Bald Rock Summit

> Distance: 2.25 to 5 km (1.5 to 3 miles) round trip, depending on the route chosen
> Time: 1 to 1.5 hours
> Difficulty: moderately easy
> Attractions: the rock itself, granite formations in surrounding forest, views

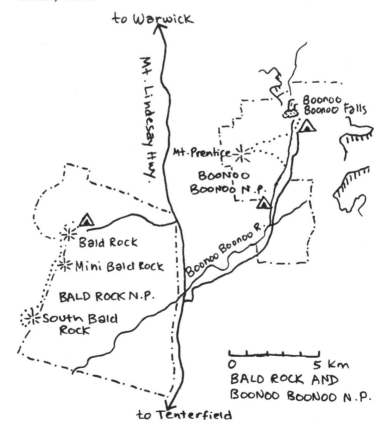

Bald Rock is said to be the largest granite dome in Australia. It measures 750 meters long by 500 meters wide (2475 feet by 1650 feet) and looms some 200 meters (650 feet) above the surrounding forest, which itself occupies a high plateau. The summit is listed at 1341 meters (4400 feet) in elevation, which would put it in a class with Mt. Barney and Mt. Superbus, the highest peaks across the border in southeast Queensland. Statistics aside, Bald Rock has an aesthetic appeal matched by no other dome in the region. Its surface is fluted in places, like Second Pyramid in Girraween, and is graced by "tapestried," vertical striping caused by mineral stains.

From the picnic area adjacent to the campground at road's end, you may ascend Bald Rock by either of two routes: the steep, direct way (a little over 1 km) or the more roundabout and gradual climb, called the Bungoona Walk (2.5 km / 1.5 miles). Both trails are well worth your time and can be combined to form a loop. For safety reasons, it is better to ascend via the steep route and return on the gentler route.

At the picnic area, locate the kiosk display. Go straight ahead, following signs for the summit. Quickly the trail heads out onto bare granite, marked by white paint splotches. Head right up the steep, bare slope to a wooded ridge. The trail veers right and winds around to a viewpoint, just before the summit, where the tapestry wall of Bald Rock falls away below you. The summit itself offers exceptional views in good weather. From the summit, the white splotches continue through heath to the northwest side of Bald Rock, looping back to the viewpoint mentioned earlier. Retrace your steps until reaching the signed junction 400 meters from the summit. Take the right fork at the sign to return via the Bungoona Walk.

This route is slightly longer than the more direct descent, but worthwhile, as it leads past and sometimes through strange, arch like boulder arrangements, exquisite orchid gardens perched atop bare rock, and eucalypt forest thickly carpeted with ferns.

Incidentally, New South Wales park rangers encourage careful exploration of parts of Bald Rock that are not on the official routes, so feel free to roam a bit.

2. South Bald Rock/Border Link Trail

> **Distance: 14 km (8.75 miles) round trip**
> **Time: 4 to 6 hours**
> **Difficulty: moderate**
> **Attractions: rock aesthetics, solitude, views**

If you want to try a more adventurous hike with the promise of solitude, consider walking out to South Bald Rock. Though less lofty than its neighbor, South Bald Rock has a different and captivating aesthetic. Although you can complete this trip in only a few hours, you might enjoy making it an all-day outing so you have plenty of time to explore the summit and to climb other balds.

The hike begins at the rest area and campground, very near to the trails that ascend Bald Rock. Locate the sign for the Border Link Trail. The trail soon merges with an old (though still used) 4-WD track. This old road detours north around Bald Rock, giving views of gargantuan granite monoliths below the slope.

Before long you reach a junction that bids you to go left toward South Bald Rock, 6 km (3.75 miles) distant. Here the trail meets the border fence between Queensland and New South Wales and parallels it for most of the trip out. You shortly come to an unsigned Y-intersection. Go right and downhill, following the fence.

The old road soon runs through the fence and veers sharply left. Ignore an old grassy track, continuing straight ahead. You pass mini Bald Rock on the right and another bald on the left. Eventually, a road comes in from the left at a locked gate. At this point check your watch; walking at a steady pace, you have about 35 minutes left to South Bald Rock. Plan to monitor your progress carefully.

Next, notice a balanced rock on the right just before the road heads out onto bare granite. To the left, you spot the rise of a granite ridge. Coming off the bare stretch, your road heads left and downhill, following the granite ridge closely. In order to climb the ridge, walk a bit farther until its sides grow less steep and look for a break in the barbed wire fence. Go on through the fence at the break and walk alongside the ridge until you see a place to scramble up.

Beyond the ridge, on the right, lie a meadow and then a house-sized boulder. Just past the latter, notice a rather large rock on the left with a prominent yellow spot. These are important landmarks in helping you find and ascend South Bald Rock. About 50 meters past the yellow-spotted boulder, look for a faint trace of a track veering left at the point where the road jogs right. Through the trees you can discern South Bald Rock.

Either from here or from another spot about 50 meters farther down the trail, where ferns grow densely, you can head off cross-country toward the bald. The route is easy once you get past the underbrush and onto the granite. Bushwhack toward an area where a long ravine or ramp angles up the rock. The terrain almost forces you into it, as you get squeezed between the rock itself and a neighboring granite ridge. Follow the ravine all the way up, noting landmarks for the return walk. Near the top, look for a collection of boulders and an old campsite. Here you head directly up the final slopes of South Bald Rock. Notice that it really is bald, save for a single tree growing from a fissure part way up. Its almost perfectly smooth, muscular surface, plus its huge tors and vertical slabs, give it a spare, otherworldly atmosphere. The summit is very easy to climb, even when wet. Views from the top are excellent.

Above: *Wongi Sandblow, Fraser Island*
Overleaf: *Piccabeen palms in fog, Eungella National Park*
Below: *Reflections on Noosa River, Great Sandy National Park*

Natural Bridge, Springbrook National Park

*Female king parrot,
Lamington National Park*

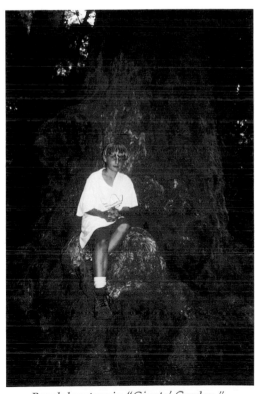

*Brush box tree in "Giants' Garden,"
Lamington National Park*

Snorkeling over the Great Barrier Reef

Cape Tribulation coastline

Bald Rock summit, Bald Rock National Park

*Rainbow Falls, Blackdown Tableland
National Park*

*Scribbly gum,
Noosa National Park*

Mt. Mitchell, Main Range National Park

Hinchinbrook Island from the mainland

Above: *McAllisters Gorge, Sundown National Park*
Overleaf: *Rainforest, Eungella National Park*
Below: *Violet Gorge, Carnarvon National Park*

One can also climb South Bald Rock by following the road clear around to the back side. However, that alternative involves a much longer ascent.

When you are finished with your explorations, retrace your steps back to your car.

BOONOO BOONOO NATIONAL PARK

This small park of only 2422 hectares (6000 acres), situated very near to Bald Rock, exists mainly to protect magnificent Boonoo Boonoo (pronounced "bunna boonoo") Falls. Yet the park has other, more subtle attractions as well: a cool climate, plentiful wildlife, well-preserved stands of eucalyptus, banksia, and cypress pine, and some lovely pools both above and below the waterfall. Ideally, one would visit it in conjunction with a trip to Bald Rock.

Road access. Same as for Bald Rock National Park, except that the entrance road lies about 5 km (3 miles) south of there along the Mt. Lindesay Highway. A corrugated dirt road 14 km (8.75 miles) long leads into the park.

Camping. The park has two campgrounds that offer primitive camping. Cypress Rest Area is about 8 km (5 miles) down the access road, on the left, while Boonoo Boonoo Falls Rest Area is at road's end.

Season. Warmer months would be best, but since trails in this park are less exposed to frigid winds than those in its neighbors, winter walks would not be too bad either.

1. Boonoo Boonoo Falls

> **Distance: 2 km (1.25 miles) round trip**
> **Time: 1 hour**
> **Difficulty: easy to platform; moderately difficult to bottom of falls**
> **Attractions: pools, falls**

The trailhead, marked by a signboard, is located at Boonoo Boonoo Rest Area. After 100 meters the well-engineered gravel path splits. The left fork, a 100 meter spur, goes to Top Pool, a swimming hole above the falls. The other fork passes some small cascades created as the creek traverses a granite slope. About 200 meters past the junction, it reaches a viewing platform from which the upper tier of Boonoo Boonoo Falls can be appreciated. To see the waterfall in its entirety, you must proceed down the trail past the platform. The trail deteriorates in quality as it switchbacks to a viewpoint from which the lower tier of the waterfall is visible. This viewpoint is about 10 minutes from the platform. Past the viewpoint, it is another 10 minutes to the base of the falls. This portion of the trail is very steep and requires some hand-over-hand maneuvering. At the bottom, both tiers of the waterfall finally come into view. Retrace your steps back to the parking area.

SUNDOWN NATIONAL PARK

It is customary to describe Queensland's Sundown National Park in conjunction with Girraween and Bald Rock because of their proximity. However, it does not belong, strictly speaking, to the Granite Belt, and it bears little resemblance to the area's other parks. Geographically, Sundown lies in the "traprock" zone, a region in which ancient sea sediments and scraped surface rock were pushed inland and subjected to severe pressures and deformations some 300 million years ago. Sundown differs in climate and flora as well, being located in a rather dry, hot, hilly part of the state that is quite unlike the cool, granite plateaus farther east. Summer hiking, in fact, is not advisable here, for temperatures can exceed 40° C (104° F).

Australian bushwalkers often reserve special praise for this park, conjuring its "outback" atmosphere and lauding the unique beauty of

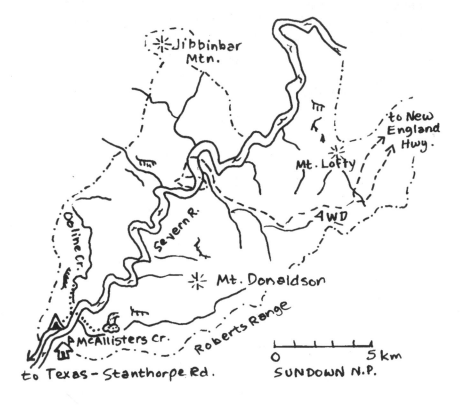

its redrock canyons. These claims may seem inflated to anyone who has hiked the chasms of Australia's Red Center or the American Southwest. However, the park's defiles do have their moments; McAllisters Gorge is especially interesting. If you lower your expectations and visit Sundown prepared for pleasant rock-hopping through mildly scenic, uncrowded gorges, you will not be disappointed. People eager for multiday, trailless trekking will particularly enjoy this park, since many such trips can be undertaken, with the aid of a compass and topo map, along the Severn River and its tributaries. Conditions for hiking vary tremendously depending upon how much water is in the streambeds. The times and difficulty ratings given below apply to hiking at low water levels. At higher water levels, the gorges are more scenic, since their waterfalls are running, but they are also more challenging to explore. Check with rangers before finalizing your plans.

Road access. From the south, take the New England Highway through Tenterfield, N.S.W. A few kilometers north of town, turn left onto the Bruxner Highway toward Bonshaw. Drive for about 55 km (34 miles) until you come to a sign for Glenlyon Dam. Turn right here, and continue on to a T-intersection. Turn right again, in the direction of Stanthorpe. From here it is perhaps 10 km (6 miles) to the turnoff for Sundown National Park. The park road, which is dirt and in mediocre condition, is about 4 km (2.5 miles) long. Broadwater Campground is at the road's end.

From the north, drive toward Stanthorpe, Queensland. Follow the bypass of the town on the New England Highway, and turn onto the road toward Texas. After about 35 km (21.75 miles), go left at a junction. Proceed another 30 km to a second junction, where you head toward Glenlyon Dam. You reach the park access road after 15 km (9.25 miles).

Camping. Broadwater Camping Area provides individual sites with grills and firewood, but (as usual) no tables. Bring your own water or draw it from a tank at the ranger's residence, a couple of kilometers back up the park road. Self-register upon arrival.

Season. To avoid extreme heat, it's best to visit from May until November. Also, summer brings thunderstorms which could cause flash floods in the gorges.

1. Ooline Gorge

> **Distance: 5 km (3 miles) round trip**
> **Time: 1.5 hours**
> **Difficulty: moderately easy**
> **Attractions: pouroffs, pools**

This gorge, just a short walk up the Severn River from the campground, affords enjoyable though unspectacular walking in a leafy defile. The unsigned route begins near a display kiosk in the campground at road's end. The rough but safe track follows a fence as it parallels the upstream course of the river. Within about 15 minutes of walking, you descend to the usually dry bed of Ooline Creek. Go left here to enter the gorge or detour first to the right, if you wish, to swim in the "Permanent Pool" at the confluence of Ooline Creek and the Severn River.

There is no trail up Ooline Gorge. You must rockhop the entire way, sometimes through grass and vegetation, sometimes skirting small pools. It is relatively easy until you reach a rock pool and pour-

Kangaroo, Girraween National Park

off. Probably one could bypass the pouroff on the right, though that would be tricky. Otherwise, stop here and return the way you came.

2. McAllisters Creek

> Distance: 6.5 km (4 miles) round trip to Split Rock Falls; 8 km (5 miles) round trip to Double Falls
>
> Time: 2 hours to base of Split Rock Falls; 3 or 4 hours to Double Falls
>
> Difficulty: moderately easy to Split Rock Falls; moderately difficult to Double Falls
>
> Attractions: pools, pouroffs, cliffs

Advertised as a redrock gorge, McAllisters Creek fits that description only in its upper reaches. Still, this hike can be recommended for the beauty of its rock pools and pouroffs (waterfalls in wet times) even in the "dark rock" sections.

Commence the walk from the kiosk displays at road's end, crossing the Severn River and cutting across to the stony bed of McAllisters Creek, just slightly downstream from your starting point. At first, the walking is tedious as you seek firm footing on rocks that constantly shift and roll. But after about 15 minutes the gorge's walls close in and you more often hike on smooth rock, the scoured-out bed of the creek. The rock pools and basins become more picturesque and the gorge walls become higher as you progress upstream. Above one pool which must be skirted on the right, red, fractured rock crops out for the first time.

After about an hour of walking, you arrive at a narrow but deep pool behind which rises a steep, smooth pouroff. You can easily climb it by skirting the pool's edge at the far right and ascending a fracture that presents numerous convenient foot- and handholds. At the top, you behold still another pool and pouroff, which for most people is unclimbable. This pouroff has a chockstone above it. Although Split Rock Falls is immediately behind the pouroff, your view of it from below is blocked. Still, this small section of McAllisters Creek proves outstandingly beautiful.

One can bypass Split Rock Falls by going back downstream past the lower pouroff, then looking for a rocky chute on the left. Ascend it carefully, as a misstep could cause a rockslide. Near the top, you traverse left and make your way across the steep, brushy slopes above the gorge. Soon, you will notice a way to descend back into the creekbed, which you encounter just at the top of Split Rock Falls. From there, the going is easy and scenic, though brief, since Double Falls, reached in about twenty minutes, poses for most hikers a barrier to further upstream exploration. Retrace your steps to your car.

WASHPOOL NATIONAL PARK

High in the Gibraltar Ranges, on the Gwydir Highway linking Glen Innes and Grafton, New South Wales, lie two national parks that together form a World Heritage Area. The northern park, Washpool, protects two extensive tracts of temperate rainforest—one of which, the Willowie Scrub, is N.S.W.'s largest—as well as deep river gorges and plenty of drier, eucalypt forest. Mostly wilderness, Washpool remains an almost undiscovered gem. It includes two pleasant campgrounds that attract few visitors and enough trails to occupy most hikers for a day or two. As a bonus, the park is home to lyrebirds, satin bowerbirds, and the small wallabies known as pademelons.

Road access. From southeast Queensland, drive south on the New England Highway past Girraween National Park and Tenterfield, N.S.W., to the town of Glen Innes. There, turn east on the Gwydir Highway and travel about 70 km (43.25 miles) to the park entrance road, a left turn. Alternatively, drive south on Route 1 from Brisbane to Grafton, N.S.W., and turn west on the Gwydir Highway, traveling about 90 km (55.75 miles) to the park entrance.

Camping. Washpool provides two campgrounds. The Coombadjha Rest Area is a grassy meadow across Coombadjha Creek from a parking lot.

Back up the road a few hundred meters lies the Bellbird Rest Area, offering individually designated sites and a shelter (with fireplace) in case of inclement weather.

Season. October through May would be best, but winter warm spells would allow for pleasant hiking as well.

1. Washpool Walk

> **Distance: 10 km (6.25 miles) round trip**
> **Time: 3 to 4 hours**
> **Difficulty: moderately easy**
> **Attractions: temperate rainforest, waterfalls**

This is the premier hike in the park. Drive to the Coombadjha Rest Area at road's end to locate the trailhead, which is just to the right of the parking lot. The trail follows Coombadjha Creek for several kilometers, though mostly far above it, passing through temperate rainforest. The number of tree species is fewer than in the tropics, and buttress roots, epiphytes, and lianas are much less common here than farther north. The hike is quite high, varying from about 800 to 950 meters in elevation (2600 to 3000 feet), and therefore tends to be cool. Because of both its altitude and its more southerly location, this trail offers a different experience from those in the Border Ranges or Mt. Warning.

After about 1.5 hours and a gradual ascent, you reach a detour to Summit Falls, whose three cascades reward hikers with fine scenery and pleasant pools. A few more minutes of walking bring you into a drier,

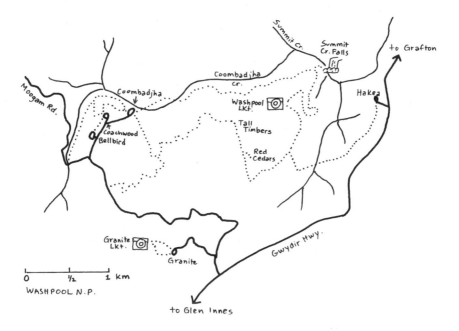

more open forest with a detour to Washpool Lookout, a rock promontory that affords views over giant eucalypts to the Washpool Valley and surrounding ridges. This is a great place to relax and enjoy the park.

A bit farther on, you notice a third spur trail down to a few giant red cedars spared by loggers in earlier decades. These specimens—not true cedars, but actually deciduous trees—have survived more than 1000 years and should impress anyone with their majesty and beauty. A tip of the hat to the enlightened loggers who fought to preserve this stand of valuable cedars and have them included in the national park.

Back on the main trail, a short distance past the cedars spur, you come upon a backcountry campsite with fire grills and a restroom. Beyond this spot, known as Tall Timbers, the trail becomes an old logging road for about 2 km (1.25 miles). Along here you may see some interesting avian life, possibly even a lyrebird. Before long, the Washpool Walk leaves the logging road and heads back down to the Coombadjha Rest Area to complete the loop. The logging road itself, now called the Acacia Walk, meanders for another 2 km or so and ends at the main park road, which would leave you about a 20 minute walk along this road to your vehicle.

2. Coombadjha Walk/Coachwood Walk/Blue Gum Walk

Distance: 1 km (0.62 mile) round trip
Time: 25 minutes
Difficulty: easy
Attractions: a chance to learn about Washpool's forests

This short stroll comes highly recommended, especially if you can do it before the Washpool Walk. The best place to begin is the Coachwood Picnic Area, where free brochures supply interpretation of various numbered and lettered features along the trail. The brochure introduces the temperate rainforest environment and helps you identify the area's most common trees and ferns, especially the coachwood, Sydney bluegum, and corkwood. The Coachwood Walk soon joins the longer Coombadjha Walk at the creek, near delightful Coachwood Pool. From here, the marked trail continues on to the right and eventually leads to Coombadjha Rest Area about 400 meters farther down the trail. En route, it takes you along the creek past exceptionally clear pools, riffles, and fern gardens. Alternatively, from Coachwood Pool, you can go left and follow Coombadjha Creek down to a branch of the park road, then roadwalk back to the campground.

GIBRALTAR RANGES NATIONAL PARK

Though very close to Washpool, Gibraltar Ranges National Park has a quite different landscape. Here the gray granite of the New England

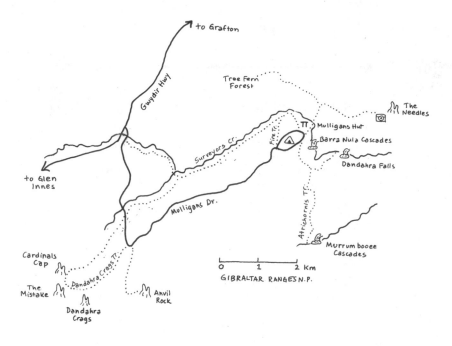

Batholith crops out in domes that rise above the forests and wetlands, much as in Girraween and Bald Rock National Parks. Several of the best trails wind past, or over, these granite domes, so hiking in the Gibraltar Ranges offers wider panoramas than the forest trails of Washpool. Together, the two parks protect nearly 45,000 hectares (112,000 acres) of wild country.

Road access. Follow directions for Washpool National Park, except that the Gibraltar Ranges park access road is about 2 km further west.

Camping. The park has a very large campground (rest area) at Mulligans Hut near Little Dandahra Creek. It offers all the amenities one might expect, including even hot showers. There is no need to reserve sites in advance.

Season. Same as for Washpool.

1. Dandahra Falls

> **Distance: 5 km (3 miles) round trip**
> **Time: 2 hours**
> **Difficulty: moderate**
> **Attractions: a very high waterfall in a wild valley**

To pick up the trail, walk down to Mulligans Hut Picnic Area near the campground. The old hut is a wood cabin with a masonry fireplace. The trail heads across a creek toward several different destinations and soon divides. The Barra Nula Cascades spur heads left, but your trail continues straight as the Atrichornis Track. At first, the way (following an old 4-WD road) passes through familiar open eucalypt forest—the summer haunt of yellow-tailed black cockatoos. Before long, however, it plunges into rainforest. At the division of the Dandahra Falls and Atrichornis tracks you will go left toward the falls. Almost immediately you arrive at a Y intersection. The right fork begins the Junction Spur Trail, so you should stay left, going downhill. Walk through a forest in which mottled, tooth-leafed coachwood predominates, though a spur will take you to an enormous remnant white beech.

Soon the trail reaches a granite balanced rock that affords views into the deep, remote Dandahra Valley below. Hikers now commence a steep descent, down hundreds of steps, that ends on the rocky banks of the creek. Here you must walk and rockhop downstream about 200 meters to reach the top of the falls. Be sure to stay to the right during the rockhop, as the trail resumes near the falls on the right bank. The overhang to the right of the falls gives hikers a dizzying glimpse of the awesome 240 meter (900 foot) drop of Dandahra Falls into a gloomy chasm. Don't attempt to leap across the creek just above the falls, as you could be swept over. It is possible to rockhop upstream to a small waterfall with an excellent swimming hole below it. The return trip to your car requires a double back, so brace yourself for a stiff climb.

2. Barra Nula Cascades

> **Distance: 1 km (0.62 mile) round trip**
> **Time: 30 minutes**
> **Difficulty: moderate**
> **Attractions: rockhopping, swimming, falls**

This short, pleasant hike begins at Mulligans Hut, along the creek. Turn right, proceeding downstream, and pick up the Atrichornis Trail that goes toward Murrumbooee Cascades and Dandahra Falls. After 300 meters your trail branches off to the left and intersects the creek. Here the trail ends and you have to boulder-hop the rest of the way. Cross the creek here and head downstream, rounding a bend. About 200 meters from the creek-crossing you arrive at Barra Nula Cascades, a small double waterfall. There are swimming holes here, too. Retrace your route back to the car.

3. The Needles

> **Distance: 6 km (3.75 miles) round trip**
> **Time: 2 hours**
> **Difficulty: moderately easy**
> **Attractions: rock formations, views, some nice rainforest**

The trail begins at Mulligans Hut. It crosses the creek immediately, then proceeds 1 km (0.62 mile) to a junction with an old 4-WD road. The left fork here goes to Tree Fern Forest, but you bear right, entering a rainforest area. The trail negotiates many ups and downs before its final descent to Needles Lookdown, an overlook of the Mann River Valley. From the offi-

Grass trees, Gibraltar National Park

cial overlook you can easily backtrack and scramble up to the top of a rocky bald to inspect the needles more closely. Return the way you came.

4. *The Anvil*

> **Distance: 4 km (2.5 miles) round trip**
> **Time: 1 hour**
> **Difficulty: moderately easy**
> **Attractions: rock formations, views, wildflowers in season**

The trailhead for this pleasant hike is located off the park road 5.6 km / 3.5 miles south of the Gwydir Highway. Park across the road from the trailhead. The trail crosses several different habitats—woodland, meadow, and swamp (there is a metal walkway over the boggy sections)—and winds past huge granite boulders, balanced rocks, wildflower gardens, and grass trees. The terrain is characterized by gentle ups and downs. From an identifying sign at km 1.5 (mile 1) you receive your first look at the Anvil; step back into the meadow here a few meters for an unobstructed view. The trail leads around to the back of the formation and then stops. It is too steep to climb all the way to the Anvil's base, though you can get part way up fairly easily. Double back to your car.

5. *Dandahra Crags Loop*

> **Distance: 10 km (6.25 miles) round trip, including roadwalk**
> **Time: 3 hours**
> **Difficulty: moderately easy, except for the moderate climb of the**
> **Crags**
> **Attractions: wildflowers in season, granite formations**

You can either complete the circuit described below, which involves a 2 km (1.25 mile) roadwalk at its conclusion, or opt for a shorter, in-and-out hike from the Dandahra Crags trailhead (5 km / 3 miles round trip, not including spur trails to granite outcrops). Hikers who eschew the long loop will not miss much, since the trail's points of interest are concentrated in the Dandahra Crags area.

The loop starts at a signed trailhead, roughly 3 km (1.75 miles) past the visitor center on the park road. Unfortunately, there is no official parking area here, so just pull off the road wherever it seems safe and convenient. You will be hiking one segment of a longer trail that actually crosses the road at this point, so be sure that you orient yourself properly by going southwest when you start out.

The first 3 km (1.75 miles) or so follow an old 4-WD road through a rather boggy meadow resplendent with red and yellow Christmas bells during the southern summer. Before long, the trail passes a mitre-shaped rock formation known as the Cardinals Cap as well as another granite bald, the Mistake. There appears to be no easy way to ascend either, or even to obtain an unobstructed view, since the area around them is brushy.

Walking a few minutes more brings you to a side trail that heads over to Dandahra Crags. This huge double outcrop, at 1100 meters (3600 feet) elevation, offers fantastic views, especially to the south. Hazy blue ridges stretch off into the distance, while in the foreground, massive granite boulders and shady grottoes please the eye. The side trail leads right to and partly up the granite slabs, eventually petering out. You need to invent your own route to the top, though cairns left by other hikers help to show the best way. Climbing up the rough granite should not prove too difficult for most people, even on relatively steep slopes. Pay attention to your ascent route, because you must find the spur trail again when you leave the rock.

Returning to the main trail, you pass two more interesting outcrops with the fanciful names of Djaragans Warriors and Janoolas Children. The former offers intricate passageways and cool recesses through the granite. Grass trees growing amid the boulders create tempting photographic possibilities. Another half hour past Djaragans Warriors takes you to the park road. If you are roadwalking back to your car, you will need to turn left here.

Chapter 5

SAND, SEA, AND ISLANDS

South of the Great Barrier Reef, the Australian coast lies exposed to the full force of Pacific breakers. Over millennia, wave action, sediments washed down from nearby highlands, and ocean currents have created a unique environment of sand dunes, ridges, islands, and beaches. In some places, the great sandhills have been overgrown by dense vegetation, even rainforest; elsewhere, dune sand still moves along the track of the prevailing winds, smothering forests and heath. Once coveted only for its timber and for construction-grade sand, this sand and sea province attracted the attention of the environmental community starting in the 1970s. As conservationists realized the value of remote coastal ecosystems, they demanded that extractive industries cease. After some hard-fought battles, preservation has been assured for such gems as Fraser Island, the Cooloola Coast, and Noosa and Burrum Coast National Parks.

Although most visitors come to surf, swim, and sunbathe, the coastal province offers ample hiking opportunities as well, not to mention canoeing and beachcombing. In fact, some parks have walking trails long enough for extended backpack trips, a rarity in tropical Australia. Moreover, the environments that hikers will experience prove more diverse than one might expect. Bundjalung National Park in northern New South Wales boasts one of the region's longest and loveliest beaches. Fraser Island and Cooloola both have beautiful freshwater lakes and extensive, old growth rainforest. Noosa National Park preserves secluded coves, tidepools, and picturesque "scribbly gum" trees. The Noosa River, together with the chain of lakes on its lower stretches, forms an everglades environment that has been completely protected. Campsites have been developed along the river to allow canoeists to paddle in, stay overnight, and hike to various attractions in the park. Only a few places in the United States, such as Everglades National Park and Okeefenokee Swamp, offer anything comparable.

Here, too, at the meeting of land and ocean, you can anticipate some memorable encounters with wildlife. Unhybridized dingoes (wild dogs) inhabit Fraser Island and will approach campers quite closely (sometimes too much so). Dolphins regularly come into Tin Can Bay near Great Sandy National Park and swim with visitors. Off Fraser Island, humpback whales congregate in late winter; indeed, they now support a whole tourist industry of whale-watching boats. And, of course, birdwatchers will sight a wide range of marine, estuarine, and land birds in the coastal province.

All of the parks described below lie within easy driving range of Route 1, the main east coast artery. However, Fraser Island has connections to the mainland only by ferry and requires a 4-WD vehicle, while parts of the Cooloola region are similarly hard to access without 4-WD.

to Rockhampton

Bundaberg

Burrum Coast N.P.

Great Sandy N.P.

Fraser Island

Maryborough

Great Sandy N.P. (Cooloola)

Noosa N.P.

Mt. Coolum N.P.

Gympie

Bruce Hwy

Brisbane

Toowoomba

Pacific Hwy

QLD.

N.S.W.

Lismore

Ballina

Bundjalung N.P.

0   100 Km
SAND, SEA, ISLANDS

to Sydney

BUNDJALUNG NATIONAL PARK

The coast of New South Wales has some of the world's finest beaches. But even in this exalted company, the beach at Bundjalung National Park stands out. It stretches all the way from Iluka in the south to Evans Head in the north and has been protected as near-wilderness for most of its length. Cars have access to it only in a couple of places. Behind the beach, Bundjalung encloses 17,700 hectares (44,000 acres) of coastal forests, swamps, and lagoons. The park also has creeks and rivers suitable for canoeing.

Road access. The easiest way to reach the park is by turning off the Pacific Highway (Route 1) on the road to Iluka, about 50 km (30 miles) south of Ballina. Drive down this road about 15 km (9.25 miles) and look for signs to Woody Head Campground on your left, just past the Shark Bay turnoff.

Camping. Woody Head is a large campground with all the amenities, including hot showers and even a few picnic tables. On certain weekends and holidays, the popular campground can fill up in a hurry, so it is best to book a reserva tion; phone (066) 46-6134, mornings. The park also maintains three primitive campgrounds (called "rest areas") clustered at the end of Gap Road in the north.

Season. Any.

In the area. The resort town of Byron Bay draws raves for its beaches, picturesque lighthouse, and extensive trail system. The

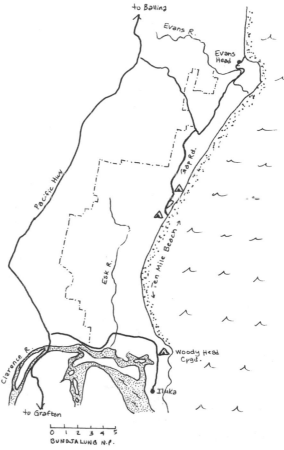

BUNDJALUNG N.P.

countercultural influence here is strong, as it is in much of northeastern New South Wales.

1. Bundjalung Beach

Distance: variable
Time: variable
Difficulty: easy
Attractions: sand, sun, swimming

From the campground, walk to the beach. Turn left and stroll north for as long as you like. There is no trail, but the walking is utterly unproblematical. Fishing and shelling prospects are good, and the crowds thin out as you get farther from the campground. Best of all, the ocean breakers are less powerful here than at many other coastal beaches, so you can usually go swimming without much trepidation. It truly doesn't get any better than this!

NOOSA NATIONAL PARK

Tucked in between the trendy, fast-growing resort towns of Noosa Heads and Sunshine Beach, Noosa National Park is the most heavily visited park in Australia. It will not satisfy wilderness seekers, but it offers so much else that almost every visitor will find something to appreciate here. Covering only 454 hectares (1120 acres), the small park nevertheless displays an astonishing variety of landscapes: pandanus-fringed

Bundjalung National Park

coastal bluffs with tidepools and beaches below; Australian "heath" on windy ridges; tall, open, eucalypt forest; and even palm groves and patches of rainforest.

Moreover, the park's excellent trails form an intricate network allowing for many scenic loop hikes and variations on routes. If you should choose to walk all the way through the park, catching a bus back to your car is easy. Wildlife may not rival, say, the Bunyas, but you have a fair chance of seeing goannas and koalas, and the prospects for birdwatching are excellent. Finally, the coastal views from several of the trails have few equals in southeast Queensland.

I have worked out a series of loop trips by splicing together sections of various trails. However, these loops are in no sense "official," so you should not expect them to be identified as such on park signs. Because there are so many trail junctions, and also because information given on the signs is not always as complete or as unambiguous as it should be, it is easy to become rather disoriented here; thus, you must take extra care to monitor your progress as you hike.

Road access. From Brisbane, take the Bruce Highway (Route 1) north, following signs to the Sunshine Coast. Exit at Route 70, the Sunshine Motorway, and follow it north toward Noosa Heads. Exit either at the roundabout leading to Peregian Beach and the David Low Way (Route 6), which terminates in Noosa Heads, or drive farther to a T intersection at the Noosa–Eumundi Road, turning right toward Noosa Heads.

From the north, take the Bruce Highway (Route 1) to the Cooroy exit. From Cooroy, follow signs to Noosa Heads via Tewantin. To get to the main park entrance, drive to Hastings Street, the main thoroughfare of Noosa's shopping district. At the roundabout, just in front of the tourist information center, go right and drive one block. Turn left here and continue straight ahead for about 1 km (0.62 mile) until the road ends at a parking lot. The park headquarters, or visitor center, is located here. Directions for finding other park entrances are provided below.

Camping. The national park has no facilities. However, Noosa Shire runs a public camping area at Munna Point on the Noosa River, just minutes from the center of town. This campground has few tent sites, but they are right on the water. There are also several caravan parks in the area, including one, the Sunrise Holiday Village in Sunrise Beach, that is only steps from the ocean.

Season. Any.

In the area. When you visit the park, by all means check out the many attractions of Noosa Heads and environs. Numerous restaurants, shops, and nightclubs make this a premier travel destination, bearing certain resemblances to Carmel, California, or Key West, Florida, but with a casual charm all its own. A trip up the Noosa River, either by tour boat or canoe, is a must for wilderness lovers who come to this region; see description below, under Great Sandy National Park, Cooloola Section. Also consider a shopping trip to the large, upscale flea-market in nearby Eumundi, which operates on Saturday mornings year-round.

1. Palm Grove Loop

> **Distance: 1 km (0.62 mile) round trip**
> **Time: 30 minutes**
> **Difficulty: easy**
> **Attractions: rainforest flora and fauna**

This short, interpretive trail begins and ends at the picnic area behind park headquarters. With signs to identify trees and plants, it provides a good introduction to the park's ecology. Most of the time, it winds through rainforest, where lianas and piccabeen palms are especially prolific. At about the halfway mark, you enter a drier, transition zone but soon loop

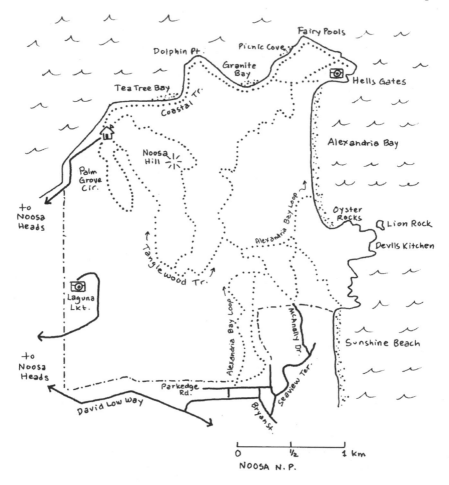

NOOSA N. P.

back into coastal rainforest. The Palm Grove Loop gives you a feeling of having experienced a remote and beautiful wilderness, despite its proximity to Noosa's beaches and restaurants.

2. Noosa Hill

> **Distance: 3.75 km (2.5 miles) round trip**
> **Time: 1 hour**
> **Difficulty: moderately easy**
> **Attractions: scribbly gum trees, scenic views**

The trail commences behind park headquarters, just to the left of the rest rooms. Find the sign for the Tanglewood Trail, and follow that trail into the rainforest. You remain on the Tanglewood Trail for 1 km (0.62 mile), when you intersect the trail to Noosa Hill, a left turn. Ascend the hill, passing many whitish-gray or light yellow scribbly gum trees. These trees grow very large on the southwest side of Noosa Hill and display an amazing range of forms. You will recognize them instantly from the wiggly lines incised by insects burrowing under their smooth bark.

Near the hilltop, you take a short spur trail up to the viewing area. From here you enjoy (slightly obstructed) vistas over the Pacific, the Cooloola Coast, and south to Lake Weyba on the Noosa River.

Returning to the main trail, you now have 1.25 km (0.75 mile) back to park headquarters. There will be some terrific views out to sea as you descend. The trail's end brings you out on a service road above the main parking lot.

3. Coastal Track/Tanglewood Loop

> **Distance: 7 km (4.5 miles) round trip**
> **Time: 1.5 hours, plus detours to beaches**
> **Difficulty: moderately easy**
> **Attractions: coastal views, diverse ecosystems, koalas**

The start of this beautiful, popular hike is at the far end of the parking lot for the main section of the park, near the visitor center and information kiosk. Carry water, especially in summer, when the first few kilometers of the trail can get uncomfortably hot.

The blacktopped walkway is marked with a sign that directs you toward Hells Gate and other, closer destinations. Around the parking lot and in the first kilometer of the trail, look sharp for koalas. These adorable creatures tend to be quiescent during the daytime, and you can often spot them resting in the forking branches of eucalyptus trees, off which they feed.

The trail affords magnificent views across Laguna Bay toward the Cooloola Coast. On a clear day you can see for 50 or 60 km. The tall, angular peak in the background is Mt. Cooroora, north of Noosa. You will walk by rocky headlands, tidal pools brimming with marine life, and several cove beaches such as Tea Tree Bay, about 700 meters (0.4 mile) from the trailhead, and Granite Bay, at km 1.5 (mile 1). Even when rough surf precludes swimming on more exposed beaches, you can usually swim in these protected coves. Sometimes, dolphins and even whales can be spotted in this vicinity. The one blemish on this otherwise spectacular walk is the array of dead pandanus trees, decimated by an insect infestation that the park service is attempting to combat.

Beyond Granite Bay, ignore the connecting trail to the Tanglewood Track, which you will reach later on via a longer, more scenic route. Continue straight ahead to Hells Gates, at km 2.75/mile 1.75. The "gates" is a narrow defile in the cliff, below the promontory on which you stand, that catches the brunt of huge Pacific breakers.

Rounding the point, you now pick up the Tanglewood Track toward Park Headquarters, 4.25 km (2.6 miles) distant. Within 500 meters (0.3 mile) you pass a turnoff on the left to Alexandria Bay, a long cove-type beach, and another on the right to the Coastal Track. At both of these junctions, continue straight ahead and remain on the Tanglewood Track. Soon you will move beyond the scrubby coastal zone into shadier eucalypt forest and even a mini-rainforest around a small ravine. Past here, notice a photogenic stand of grass trees.

When you have come about 6.25 km (4 miles) you begin to encounter many more turnoffs to various destinations. Stay on the Tanglewood Track, enjoying the park's famous scribbly gums. In the last kilometer of the trail, you enter a pocket of coastal rainforest. There are some impressive fig trees, brush boxes, and hoop pines along the way. Look for noisy pittas and yellow-breasted Australian robins in the understory. The trail emerges at a picnic area above the parking lot; often you can see goannas and brush turkeys scavenging for food here.

4. McAnally Drive to Alexandria Bay Loop

Distance: 5 km (3 miles) round trip
Time: 1.5 hours
Difficulty: moderately easy
Attractions: varied scenery, beautiful beaches

The trailhead is in the suburb of Sunshine Beach. Take the Sunshine Beach exit off the David Low Way (Route 6). You are now on Pacific Avenue. Follow Pacific Avenue to a roundabout and go left here onto Ferguson Street. Continue on Ferguson Street until it deadends at Bryan Street. Turn left here and then take the first right onto Seaview Terrace. Follow this street, which curves toward the beach and then goes uphill. You will pass Surfside Court; take the next left, onto McAnally Drive. Park along the left side of this steep road, but not in the circle at the end (a towaway zone) or in front of "No Standing" signs. The trail begins at the far end of the circle.

At the very beginning, the trail forks. Ignore the left-hand track (on which you will return later on) and go straight ahead toward Alexandria Bay, 1 km distant. The trail descends as you pass through a low banksia/grass tree environment with occasional views out over the blue Pacific. The trail dips down to cross a marsh on a boardwalk and then ascends to a junction. A spur trail to the right leads to the north end of Sunshine Beach, only 700 meters (0.4 mile) distant. It is a worthwhile detour, but your trail goes straight ahead here and soon intersects a wider track. Turn right onto this track, which descends to Alexandria Bay through an open woodland of eucalypti, casuarinas, and cedars. On your left, obscured by vegetation, is a small stream. Because of the fresh water here, this is a prime birdwatching area, and you may glimpse some of Australia's colorful wrens flitting about in the scrub.

About 15 minutes from your trailhead, you arrive at Alexandria Bay's gorgeous, undeveloped beach. The beach attracts walkers, surfers, and, at the south end, a few nudists. Turn left at the beach and walk up to the pandanus-clad headland at the far north end. Here you will spot a sign for the Tanglewood Track and Coastal Track. Leave the beach here and ascend on the trail for 120 meters to a junction. The Tanglewood Track extends in both directions here. Turn left and remain on the Tanglewood for several kilometers, ignoring signs for the Coastal Track.

The trail meanders uphill, passing out of the banksia zone into taller, melaleuca forest. About 45 or 50 minutes out from your trailhead, you reach another junction. Do not turn left toward Alexandria Bay, but continue straight ahead, remaining on the Tanglewood Track. The trail now enters a small patch of semi-rainforest with many looping, trailing vines. It then emerges into more open country covered by brilliant green foxtail sedge. Notice a few whitish scribbly gums on the right, their barks decorated by wavy insect tracks.

The next junction, about an hour out, offers the choice of staying on the Tanglewood Track or veering off left toward Alexandria Bay and McAnally Drive (both 1.25 km away). Go in the direction of McAnally Drive here and also at the two junctions that follow. The last 300 meters of the trip are highly scenic, as you look out over the Pacific and southward all the way to Mt. Coolum, the squat peak toward which the beach curves. At a final unmarked fork, go left and you emerge back on McAnally Drive at your car.

5. Parkedge Road to Alexandria Bay Loop

Distance: 4.5 km (2.75 miles) round trip plus beach and headland walking
Time: 1.25 hours plus digressions
Difficulty: moderately easy
Attractions: beach, forest, views

For trailhead access, turn northeast onto Solway Drive in the suburb of Sunshine Beach from David Low Way (Route 6). Take the second left, onto Bryan Street, which brings you to Parkedge Road. Turn left onto Parkedge Road and park near the entrance gate.

Take the trail into the forest. Within 50 meters you reach an intersection. Alexandria Bay can be reached by either trail, but you should go straight ahead here for a clockwise loop. Continue on, turning right to follow Alexandria Bay signs at the next junction, about 500 meters (0.3 mile) distant. Around here you enter a "heath" landscape in which banksia, grass trees, and other low-growing flora predominate. You will enjoy wide vistas over rolling hills to the Pacific.

The trail descends slowly to a 4-way intersection. Go left here toward Alexandria Bay, 1.25 km (0.75 mile) away. The trail descends through a small swamp in which ferns and gnarled paperbark trees abound. At the next junction, a 3-way, you head right, toward Alexandria Bay (the left fork goes to the Tanglewood Track and Hells Gate). From here, the trail descends, passing an unmarked jeep road on the left and a lovely paperbark stand. You soon come to yet another junction. Your trail goes left here, descending steadily to Alexandria Bay, though you may wish first to detour right and walk 700 meters to see the north end of Sunshine Beach.

When you arrive at Alexandria Bay, you turn left and walk all the way up the beach to the far end. Before you do that, however, you can detour to explore the headland on the right side of the beach, which has inspiring views up the coast and, farther on, overlooks rocky Devils Kitchen, a small, surf-pounded bay. However, there is no official trail here, and some scrambling is necessary.

At the far north end of the beach, you pick up a trail that soon branches. Take the left branch, marked "Tanglewood Track/Park Headquarters." Past there, follow all signs to Parkedge Road. Eventually you reach a 4-way intersection at which two of the trails lead back to Parkedge Road. Go straight ahead here to complete the loop back to your car.

TEWANTIN STATE FOREST

Just outside Tewantin, a village near Noosa Heads, lie scattered patches of forest that have much to please the visitor. Hikes are short but enjoyable and highly scenic.

Road access. From Noosa Heads, follow signs to Tewantin. Continue out of Tewantin in the direction of Cooroy on Route 6. Pass a golf course and a service station. About 500 meters later, after a road junction, look for a small road heading left that is signed "Tewantin State Forest: Wooroi Day Use Area." This leads to the trailhead for hike #1.

For hike #2, continue down Route 6 toward Cooroy. About a kilometer beyond the Wooroi Day Use turnoff, look for signs on the right for Mt. Tinbeerwah. Turn here and proceed uphill to a parking lot. The road is not completely paved, and one section may have a nasty washout, so drive carefully.

Camping. See listing for Noosa National Park.

Season. Any.

1. Palm Grove Walking Track

Distance: 1.5 km (1 mile) round trip
Time: 30 minutes
Difficulty: easy
Attractions: birdlife, palm groves

At the parking lot, follow the signs onto the path, ignoring a side track to the left that is blocked off by a log. Continue past a small bridge, taking the left fork, which will bring you around in a loop to the same spot. Notice the different varieties of palms: cabbage tree at first, then piccabeens in "Picabeen Valley," the wettest, shadiest section of the trail. Listen for the sharp call of the whipbird along here. The track boasts some very imposing eucalypt specimens as well, one of which has a hollow large enough to accommodate several kids.

Koalas

2. Mt. Tinbeerwah Summit Lookout

Distance: 1 km (0.62 mile) round trip
Time: 30 minutes
Difficulty: moderately easy
Attractions: best views in the area

From the parking lot, follow the constructed, cement path (which is wheelchair-accessible for about half its length) uphill. The last section passes over bare rock and has some steps. At the top, you are greeted by a stunning 360° panorama. The view takes in the Noosa River, all of the area's lakes, and Laguna Bay to the east. To the west rises the Blackall Range, and to the south you can see the Glass House Mountains, about 60 km (almost 40 miles) away. Other, lesser peaks lie spread out in the near foreground. This is an ideal track for sunrise or sunset. Retrace your steps back to your car.

MT. COOLUM NATIONAL PARK

Mt. Coolum, Australia's largest rock monolith aside from Ayers Rock, rises amid the suburbia, beaches, and golf courses of the Sunshine Coast. Despite its surroundings this ancient volcanic plug affords vistas up and down the coast and offers a fine walk that will get your blood circulating.

Road access. From Coolum, drive south on Route 6 (David Low Way) through Pt. Arkwright and Yaroomba to the hamlet of Mt. Coolum. Just past a resort golf course, turn right onto Centenary Hts. Road. Soon you come to a Y intersection. Go right here. Immediately after you execute this turn, there will be a short dirt road on the left that leads to a parking lot and the start of the Mt. Coolum Walking Track.

Camping. None in the park, so you should visit it from a Noosa base camp.

Season. Any.

1. Mt. Coolum Walking Track

Distance: 3 km (2 miles) round trip
Time: 1 hour
Difficulty: moderately easy
Attractions: views

The walk commences just north of some nearly vertical cliffs that face the Pacific. The trail first takes you through sparse, often hot eucalypt woodland, including some stands of scribbly gum. Before long it bends southward, climbing relentlessly, to bring you out above the cliffline.

Once you have surmounted this obstacle the trail levels out somewhat, and it's an easy stroll to the summit. The views, which reach to the Glass House Mountains, reward the exertion of the climb. But communications equipment on the top of Mt. Coolum detracts from its ambience. Still, if you are in the area, the park deserves a visit. Return as you came.

GREAT SANDY NATIONAL PARK: COOLOOLA SECTION

Just north of chic, bustling Noosa Heads begins a long, almost empty coastline that stretches north nearly to Fraser Island. Once slated for development, this wild shore, the Cooloola Coast, has since become a national park that rivals even its famous northern neighbor. Fraser and Cooloola (which means "cypress pine" in one of the Aboriginal languages) have much in common, not least because they were once joined together by a land bridge. Both have sand blows, lakes, marshes, rainforests, wide beaches, and vast expanses of eucalypti forest, as well as sharing Great Sandy National Park. But the Cooloola section has some unique features. First, it preserves a great part of the basin of the Noosa River, a placid stream that flows through a series of large, shallow, brackish lakes, draining finally into Laguna Bay right off Noosa spit. The river and lakes together form what Australians call the Noosa Everglades, a favorite haunt of fishermen and canoeists. Much of the Everglades lies within the national park and affords unique opportunities for paddling, camping, and exploring (see below).

Second, Cooloola, like Fraser Island, has one of the few trails in tropical Australia long enough for a multi-day trek. The Cooloola Wilderness Trail covers 48 km (29.75 miles) and offers four established backcountry campsites, three with fresh water.

Finally, Cooloola offers easier access than Fraser Island, since many of the roads that enter it are either paved or gravel/dirt thoroughfares suitable for 2-WD vehicles. Thus, one need not rely on expensive ferry trips and jeep rentals or taxi hires to get around. Visit this special place soon, before industrial tourism transforms it.

Road access. For northern Cooloola hikes, drive to Gympie on the Bruce Highway (Route 1). Turn onto the well-marked road to Rainbow Beach/Tin Can Bay. After 46 km (28.5 miles) the road splits, with the left fork heading toward Tin Can Bay and the right fork going to Rainbow Beach. Turn right here, toward Rainbow Beach, which is about 30 km (18.5 miles) distant. The Cooloola Wilderness Trail begins 8 km (5 miles) past the previously mentioned fork on this road; hikes to Lake Poona and Freshwater Lake commence at Bymien Picnic Area, a few kilometers east of the road; the Carlo Sandblow trip starts in the town itself. See below for details.

Several canoe and hiking trips take off from Elanda Point or Boreen Point on Lake Cootharaba. To reach these settlements from Noosa, drive to Tewantin, following the Cooroy–Tewantin Road through the town's main shopping district. About two blocks past it, there is a small sign for Boreen Point. Turn right here and then take the first left, just past a

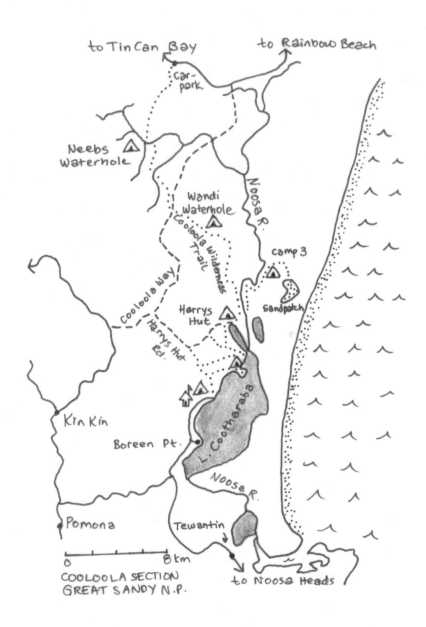

COOLOOLA SECTION
GREAT SANDY N.P.

schoolyard. Follow the Boreen Point Road (Route 6) for about 20 km (12.5 miles), which will involve a right at a T intersection between Tewantin and Boreen Point. Then you will come to another intersection, at which you go left toward Elanda Point on a gravel road, or else directly into Boreen Point, depending on your plans.

One can also reach certain trailheads from the Harrys Hut Road. These complicated directions are provided below, under "camping."

Camping. The Cooloola section of Great Sandy National Park has only one campsite that can be reached in an ordinary car, the Noosa River Camping Area (aka "Harrys Hut"), which is reached from Noosa as follows. Take Route 6 west to Cooroy and thence to Pomona. Just past that hamlet, the road forks and you head left on the Kin Kin Road. At Kin Kin continue on Route 6 to and then past Wahpunga. About 11 km (6.75 miles) beyond Kin Kin, you will see a sign for the Cooloola Way, a decent gravel road. Follow it for 4 km (2.5 miles) to the Harrys Hut road and turn right. The Noosa River Camping Area lies at the end of this road and offers excellent facilities. This road can be a little rough and perhaps impassable after heavy rain. But the Harrys Hut area does give access to some choice sections of the Cooloola Wilderness Trail, in case you do not

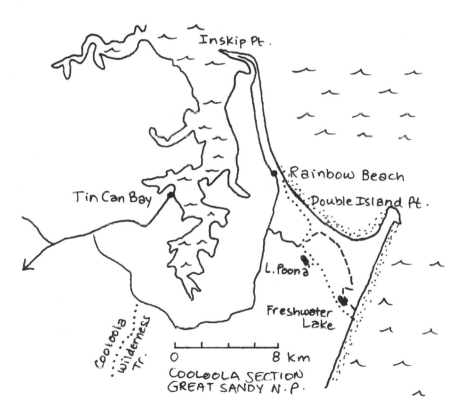

Inskip Pt.

Rainbow Beach

Double Island Pt.

Tin Can Bay

L. Poona

Freshwater Lake

Cooloola Wilderness Tr.

0   8 km

COOLOOLA SECTION
GREAT SANDY N.P.

wish to hike its entire length. If you have a boat you can also camp at any of 10 campsites right along the Noosa River. See hike #7 for details.

If not camping in the Noosa River area, visitors will need to seek out a commercial campground. In the south, Elanda Point offers adequate facilities beside the lake, and plenty of kangaroos on the grassy grounds. Expect crowds here, especially on holiday weekends. There is also a caravan park and a small shire campground in Boreen Point. In the north, you have to stay at a commercial caravan park in Rainbow Beach, unless you have 4-WD vehicle for the journey out to one of the area's two campsites.

About 30 minutes' drive from the national park's north end is the charming village of Tin Can Bay. At the town's marina and dock you will often find playful dolphins who will swim with you and allow you to pet them, especially if you have fish to offer. Fish can be purchased at a shop adjacent to the dock. The dolphins tend to come into the shallow water here on the morning high tide. It's thrilling to swim with these wild but friendly creatures.

Season. May through October for the lowest-lying sections. In the warmer months heat, mosquitoes, and muddy trails make walking around the Noosa River and Kin Kin Creek less pleasant. However, the Carlo Sandblow and the Freshwater/Poona area in northern Cooloola would still be fine even in summer.

In the area. From the town of Tewantin, near Noosa, a car ferry crosses the Noosa River and gives access to the Cooloola beach. With 4-WD, you can drive up the beach at low tide, all the way to Double Island Point. Attractions along the way include colored sands, towering bluffs, and the *Cherry Venture*, a rusting, wrecked freighter half buried by beach sand. You can camp almost anywhere on the beach once you pass the Noosa Shire boundary (marked).

1. Lake Poona

> **Distance: 4.5 km (2.75 miles) round trip**
> **Time: 1.5 hours**
> **Difficulty: moderately easy**
> **Attractions: a picturesque lake fine for swimming**

Drive down the road to Rainbow Point for about 26 km (16 miles) past the turnoff for Tin Can Bay. Turn right onto Freshwater Road and proceed for 3 km (1.75 miles) to Bymien Picnic Area. Beyond this point, the road is impassable to 2-WD vehicles.

From Bymien Picnic Area, a pleasant spot with tables and toilets, walk down the main trail through the rainforest for 600 meters (650 yards), intersecting the track to Freshwater Lake. Turn right here and hike uphill over somewhat rocky terrain for another 600 meters. As the track tops out, there will be a signed trail to Lake Poona on the right. The lake is 1 km (0.62 miles) away. Your trail crosses a low ridge before descending steadily to the tea-colored lake. Though logged in the past, the forest near the lake still contains impressive lilly pilly, blackbutt, kauri pine, hoop pine, strangler fig, and rosewood trees. The lake itself is oval, forest-fringed, and a bit reedy. It has a couple of tiny but popular beaches from which you can launch a lazy float in the tannin-darkened waters. Gnarled, intricately patterned melaleuca trees grace the shoreline and even extend into the lake. These swamp-loving, whitish trees, also called paperbarks, have an almost bonsai-like quality.

Return the way you came. On the way back, you can do the 260 meter Dundathu Circuit, which branches off the trail close to the picnic area. The trail passes through rainforest with healthy specimens of kauri and hoop pines, quandongs, piccabeen palms, and strangler figs. Christmas orchids also bloom here in season.

2. Freshwater Lake

Distance: 15 km (9.25 miles) round trip; additional 3 km (1.75 miles) round trip to ocean
Time: 4.5 or 5 hours
Difficulty: moderately easy
Attractions: spectacular rainforest, a good trail, the lake

For information on how to reach the trailhead at Bymien Creek Picnic Area, consult the description for Lake Poona (hike #1). The routes to Freshwater Lake and Lake Poona initially coincide. From the carpark, stroll 600 meters on a narrow, winding trail through the rainforest. When you intersect an old logging road, turn right, and ascend the rocky track to a low pass. The Lake Poona Trail takes off here, but you continue straight ahead, descending gently parallel to the Freshwater Creek drainage.

About 1.5 km (1 mile) before you reach the lake, you meet a jeep road that serves as a firebreak. Ignore this road and continue walking straight ahead as the trail descends to the lake. The vegetation changes now; you are out of the true rainforest and into a more open area of eucalypt vegetation. Freshwater Lake is rather reedy, but people swim in its lower end. A path traces the lake's circumference. Beyond the lake, the main trail goes on to a campground at the ocean, 1.5 km (1 mile) distant, usually used by 4-WD parties. Backtrack to your car.

3. Carlo Sandblow

Distance: 1.25 km (0.75 mile) round trip
Time: 30 minutes
Difficulty: moderately easy
Attractions: Sahara in the tropics, beautiful views

As you enter the town of Rainbow Beach, take the first road to the right, which is Double Island Drive. Almost immediately, go left onto Turana Street and follow it a few blocks to a T intersection. Turn right at the T onto Green Valley Drive, and then turn left at the next intersection, going uphill. An immediate right puts you on Cooloola Drive, which you follow uphill through a residential neighborhood until it becomes a cul-de-sac, Rainbow Heights Circle. There are two water towers here. An obscure driveway on the left leads down to a parking area and trailhead. Be sure to wear sunglasses to protect your eyes from glare and blowing sand.

The trail gently ascends and then winds along a ridge with views of both the Pacific and Tin Can Bay. Notice the fine scribbly gums en route. At the end of the trail, there is a hang-gliding platform from which you can walk out onto the sand, in any direction you like. The ceaseless wind will soon efface your tracks. The sandblow is surprisingly large and almost completely barren of vegetation, save at its edges, where a few stunted trees have survived. Walking south, you will enjoy superlative views of the Cooloola Coast clear down to Double Island Point.

Northward, you can discern Tin Can Bay, Inskip Point, and—on a clear day—Fraser Island.

4. Kin Kin Creek/Kinaba Point

Distance: 11 km (6.75 miles) round trip
Time: 3 or 4 hours
Difficulty: easy
Attractions: superb rainforest, palm groves, lake views

Be sure to bring along insect repellent on this hike. Avoid the trail in the wet season, when it is likely to be muddy.

The hike begins at Elanda Point campground on the shore of Lake Cootharaba, the largest of the lakes formed by the Noosa River. You begin by paying a fee to the caravan park owner for parking your car in his lot. Then walk around to the right of the office and follow signs into a lakeside rainforest. You soon come to two T intersections in close proximity to each other. Go left at the first and right (onto a jeep road) at the second, following signs to Kinaba Point. Bird life is abundant in the meadows and shrubs that line the road. The first section of the hike goes through pastureland, but you soon plunge into dark, deep, wet rainforest with overhanging palm fronds shading the track. As you near the point, notice the lush growth and huge rainforest trees alongside the trail near tea-colored Kin Kin Creek.

At the end of the trail is the Kinaba Information Center, which has a boat dock, exhibits, toilet, boardwalks, and a glassed-in sitting room. The information center is located at the north end of Lake Cootharaba, near Kinaba Island and the start of the Noosa Everglades. Since tour boats visit here, you probably will not have the area to yourself. Return the way you came. It would be easy to combine this hike with another out to Kin Kin Creek to make a day of it; see below.

5. Fig Tree Walk

Distance: 9.5 km (6 miles) round trip
Time: 2.5 hours
Difficulty: easy
Attractions: no crowds, nice mixed forest, lake views, and
    swimming

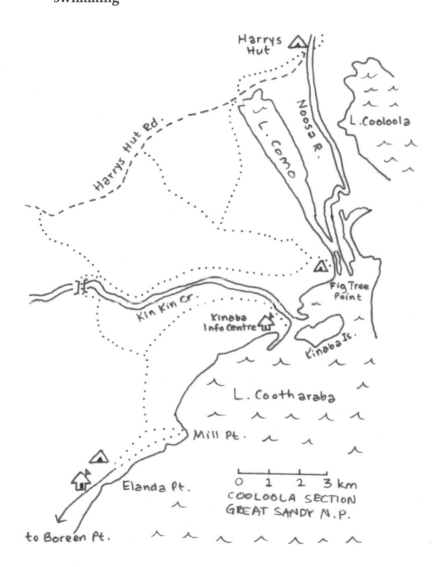

The trailhead is accessed from the Harrys Hut road, off Cooloola Way, about 2 km (1.25 miles) past the signed boundary for Cooloola National Park. For directions to the Harrys Hut road, see the section on camping in Cooloola, above.

The trail follows an abandoned 4-WD road through melaleuca forest for most of its length. It is well-maintained and fairly level, with gentle ups and downs. After about 20 minutes of walking, you intersect the Cooloola Wilderness Trail (see description, below). Go straight here and continue to another junction, where you turn left and proceed to Fig Tree Point, only 700 meters (0.4 mile) distant. Fig Tree Point, surrounded by rainforest, is a beautiful spot on Fig Tree Lake, a bay of Lake Cootharaba. A picnic area, campground, toilets, and dock are here. From the point, the left-hand channel of the Noosa River leads to Lake Como, and you are likely to see boats entering and exiting the Everglades. Retrace your steps to return to the parking lot.

6. Cooloola Wilderness Trail

Distance: 48 km (29.75 miles) one way
Time: 2 or 3 days
Difficulty: difficult in 2 days; moderate in 3
Attractions: solitude, beautiful campsites, scribbly gums,
    rainforest

The trailhead is located just to the right of the Rainbow Beach road, 6 km (3.75 miles) beyond the turnoff to Tin Can Bay. As you pull off the highway, look for the trail signboard, 150 meters ahead to your left. Park your car here. Logistically, the hike is difficult unless you can do a car shuttle or arrange for a pick-up at Elanda Point, where the trail ends.

Scarcely known to overseas visitors, the Cooloola Wilderness Trail offers one of the longest backcountry hikes in tropical Australia, at least on a regularly maintained walking track. The trail is well-constructed and easy to follow throughout, though a few stream crossings might dismay some people. For maximum enjoyment, allow 3 days for the trip, rather than exhausting yourself by rushing it.

The trailhead display at Mullen carpark has self-registration envelopes for backcountry camp sites. Calculate what you owe and drop the form along with your payment in the slot. The sign here advertises distances to various destinations along the way and gives the total number of kilometers as 44.6. Note, however, that the sign underestimates the trail's length by almost 3.5 km (2.25 miles), as explained below.

The first 16.5 km (10.25 mile) section of the trail is pleasant enough, but somewhat monotonous, with few real highlights. Wear long pants to protect your legs against sharp scrub bushes. You stroll through open, breezy, sunny forest and heath dominated by banksias. Occasionally, you gain views to the east and south, and you even get a glimpse of the distant Cooloola Sandpatch from a ridgetop.

Neebs Waterholes, at km 8.75/mile 5.5, mark a transition. The waterholes are actually a sluggish stretch of the upper Noosa River and have a serene, intimate beauty. Your first reliable source of potable water is located here, as is a small campsite. To continue down the trail, you must cross the small river as best you can, perhaps by shinnying across fallen logs. Take care, as the crossing can be slippery.

Beyond Neebs, the forest grows somewhat taller, and grasses and grass trees replace scrub. About 1.5 km (1 mile) past the river crossing, you walk on an old 4-WD road for a while, which speeds you along. Soon, though, you hit a section of trail that may be drowned under a foot or more of water during wet periods of the year. If that is the case, you must wade for about 60 meters to reach dry land. Look for blue ribbons on trees to guide you across the drowned trail.

You come to Cooloola Way, a rough road through the park, at km 16.5 (mile 10.25). A sign here informs you that Wandi Waterholes lie only about 4.75 km (3 miles) ahead. The clearing near Wandi Waterholes makes a great campsite for the first night of the trip. The area is surrounded by an extensive scribbly gum forest that marches down to the edge of this lakelike tributary of the Noosa River. The surface of the waterholes often remains calm enough to create a perfect mirror of the picturesque white gums. Although some maps of the area show a camping area just beyond a stream, the park service has recently cut a new spur trail to a clearing above Wandi and well away from the water in an effort to preserve its purity. Fires are forbidden here. To continue south, you must first walk back on the spur to the main trail. Almost immediately, you must cross Wandi Creek; you may want to wear sandals while doing so.

Past Wandi, the trail increasingly coincides with abandoned 4-WD roads, so you breeze along. In less than 2 hours, you encounter the now broad Noosa River on the left. Just before reaching the river you walk through an open heathland that offers terrific views of the Cooloola Sand patch on the ridge to your east. The route then follows the banks to the Noosa River Camping Area, commonly called Harrys Hut, at km 30.75 (mile 19). Once again, there is a sign that gives inaccurate information about the distance to the trail's end at Elanda Point, which is actually not 13.9 km but rather 17.25 km (10.75 miles) ahead. If you plan to set up camp later on at Fig Tree Point (described below), it is advisable to fill all your canteens here, since the Noosa River at Fig Tree Point is already brackish.

The trail now becomes the Harrys Hut road. You must roadwalk for about 20 minutes before the trail veers off the road to the right, just past the actual hut of a local man named Harry Spring. Since the trail soon comes back to the road, you can simply continue on the road here, if you prefer, until you notice a sign showing the trail plunging into the rainforest

Kookaburra

on the left. Bear in mind that although the map makes it seem as though the trail crosses the road, the trail in fact joins the road and coincides with it for about 500 meters (550 yards) before departing again to the left.

Now begins an exceptionally beautiful section of trail overtopped by cabbage palms, flooded gums, and other rainforest trees. You also cross a sort of causeway made of logs through a melaleuca swamp. Beware of losing your footing here; the logs can be slippery when wet and mud-covered.

Past the swamp and more rainforest, the trail reaches another 4-WD track. Turn left here, heading in the direction of Fig Tree Point. After about 30 minutes, you will see a sign that gives the distance to Fig Tree Point as 700 meters (0.4 mile), and to Elanda Point as 10.5 km (6.5 miles)—an accurate figure, for a change.

The main trail turns right at the sign, but you should plan to detour first to Fig Tree Point, an attractive campground and a good destination for the second night of your trip. The point is at the north end of Fig Tree Lake, near channels that enter the Noosa River Everglades and Lake Como.

The final leg of the hike from Fig Tree Point to Elanda Point takes between 2.5 and 3 hours to complete. At least some of this 10.5 km (6.5 mile) stretch will include lush rainforest and glimpses of placid Kin Kin Creek, on your left. After about 1.5 hours of walking, you reach a bridge over the creek (contrary to the map, which says there is no bridge). Beyond the bridge, the trail has little to offer except farm roads, cow pies, and sore feet. However, you can expect to see packs of kangaroos as you plod across the meadows near Elanda Point, where the trail ends.

7. Noosa River/Cooloola Sandpatch Paddle and Hike

**Distance: 29 km (18 miles) by canoe, plus 12 km (7.5 miles)
hiking, round trip**

Time: 6–7 hours paddling; 2.5 hours walking

**Difficulty: difficult if done in one day; moderately difficult as
an overnight trip**

**Attractions: Noosa River Everglades, one of Queensland's
biggest sandpatches, views**

Road Access. Drive to Boreen Point as described in the park introduction. When you reach that village, drive until you see the Top Shop on your right. Turn right, go down a hill, and you will find a caravan park and water taxi service, the Everglades Waterfront Holidays, at the bottom on the left. To set up a drop off and pick up, phone (07) 5485-3147 or 5485-3164.

Camping. Ideally, you would camp at one of the Noosa River sites such as camp 3. To do so you must make an advance reservation and pay a fee. Contact the Kinaba Information Centre, via Elanda, MS 1537, Tewantin, QLD.

This trip combines two modes of wilderness travel into a single outdoor adventure through two very different but equally beautiful settings. To be sure, one could hike to the Cooloola Sandpatch without any canoeing, but it would be difficult logistically. Likewise, one could easily canoe all through the Noosa River basin without hiking a step. But the trip suggested here represents a classic Australian way to see both river and sandpatch. The trip is best done as an overnighter. To do it all in one day is exhausting (particularly if you opt not to hire the water taxi).

You can begin the canoe trip either at Elanda Point or Boreen Point, both on Lake Cootharaba. I strongly recommend the Boreen Point option even though it costs more. From there you can avail yourself of the local water taxi service which will take you all the way up to the Kinaba Information Center at the head of Lake Cootharaba, provide you with a canoe, and pick you up at whatever time you specify, all for a reasonable price. The taxi service avoids a paddle across Lake Cootharaba, an often windy, choppy body of water that swamps canoes regularly and forces many paddlers to "walk" their canoes across miles of shallows. The service will also sell you an inexpensive map that explains how to negotiate the maze of channels that lead to the Noosa River.

For the canoe trip, "official" guidelines suggest a time of 2 hours and 40 minutes to paddle from Kinaba Center to Camp 3, a distance of 14.5 km (9 miles). However, that figure may prove optimistic as applied to less experienced paddlers, or canoeists battling strong winds.

You start by entering an inconspicuous channel near Kinaba and then route-finding for about 25 minutes up to Fig Tree Point dock, which is also accessible by foot (see hike # 5). From here you push off into more complex channels (often marked by signs), and soon reach the Noosa River. Canoeing between Fig Tree and the next rest stop, the Noosa River Camping Area (universally known as Harrys Hut), 5 km (3 miles) away, should take about 1.5 hours for average paddlers. This is the zone in which brackish water becomes fresh and potable (though darkened to a tea-color by tannin). The river in this stretch often has a tranquil, mirror-like surface that perfectly reflects the gnarled, leaning melaleucas, cabbage palms, and gums that overhang it. Morning mist or a reddish-gold sunset only add to the timeless magic of this lovely, unspoiled river.

It is possible to hike to Cooloola Sandpatch from Harrys Hut on a trail that passes through Camps 1, 2, and 3. However, this plan requires that you swim or otherwise cross the Noosa River in both directions, and it involves a much longer trek.

After a rest at Harrys Hut, about half way to your destination, continue on upriver for another 7.5 km (4.75 miles), or about 1.5 hours of paddling time. For purposes of this description I'll assume you will stop at Camp 3 on the right bank of the river. If you have a permit, you can camp there; otherwise, you will stop and moor your craft while walking to Cooloola Sandpatch. Note that there is no water along the trail to the Sandpatch.

To begin the hiking segment of this journey, walk from the Camp 3 dock through the small campground and locate a sign directing you to the sandpatch. Follow the trail into a sandy banksia and casuarina flat. At first, you walk on a service road, but after 500 meters the trail departs the road, forking off to the right. Initially quite level, it rises gradually and then more steeply on switchbacks toward the long high ridge (nearly 200 meters / 650 feet high in places) that walls off the Noosa River drainage from the Pacific. The vegetation also changes subtly, as some scribbly gums and acres of low-growing grass trees make their appearance. After 45 minutes or so, the trail gains the top of a secondary ridge and levels out, swinging to the left. Soon you glimpse the still distant sandpatch, as well as Lakes Cooloola and Como, through the trees. Another half hour or more brings you right to the margin of the Sahara-like sandpatch. Further exploration simply involves freelancing fun on the dunes. Views take in (from various points) the deep blue Pacific, Lake Cootharaba, much of the lower Noosa basin, and remote peaks to the north and west. Return to Camp 3 by the same trail.

The trip back to Kinaba poses few problems except finding the proper channels. Signs that were obvious going upriver are often partly hidden going downriver. To avoid confusion, try to recall the appearance of channel junctions by glancing back at them as you paddle upriver and remembering which way you steered at each key point.

Dingo

FRASER ISLAND

Fraser Island, reachable only by ferry boat, has impressive credentials: it is the world's largest sand island, with an area of 184,000 hectares (455,000 acres), and Australia's fourth largest island overall; it boasts the world's largest "perched lake" (Lake Boomanjin) as well as dunes that rise to 240 meters (775 feet); its offshore waters are a humpback whale playground; and the whole island has been World Heritage listed. But somehow even these superlatives fail to convey the unique charm of the place.

The northern half of the island (the least accessible part) has been entrusted to Great Sandy National Park. The southern half has become a recreation area with a few tiny towns and resorts as well as most of the hiking trails. The west coast, on Hervey and Platypus Bays, is lined with mangroves and narrow beaches; the east coast, on the Pacific Ocean, has a magnificent, wide beach that extends unbroken for 101 kilometers (62.5 miles). Cruising up and down the beach at low tide in a 4-WD vehicle, visiting such attractions as the Colored Sands, Rainbow Gorge, and the Champagne Pools, is a favorite Fraser Island pastime. Renting a 4-WD, either on the mainland or at the island's Eurong village, adds considerable expense, but also opens up many more possibilities for exploration.

Fortunately, however, there is much here to please non-motorized tourists as well. Easily accessible walking tracks form a broad arc linking many of Fraser Island's renowned lakes with its eastern beaches. They wind north and south from the island's main campground, Central Station, and introduce trekkers to two types of lakes: "window lakes" (those at water level) and "perched lakes" (those nestled in dunes above the water table). Although the island contains some active dunes or sand blows, it mostly consists of ancient sand ridges that have stabilized and been densely vegetated. Hikers will experience a surprising range of forest ecosystems, from coastal scrub to towering rainforests. Loggers cut satinay, New England blackbutt, and other valuable trees until 1992, when the island's forests achieved total protection from further logging. Except for gear-grinding 4-WD vehicles, Fraser has a remote, timeless ambience. Out on the trails—except where they intersect roads—you will be able to savor this serene beauty.

All visitors are advised to purchase a Sunmap Tourist Map of Fraser Island before starting their trip and to bring water or else a filtration system of some sort, since lake water is suspect.

Road access. Follow the Bruce Highway (Route 1) to the Maryborough/ Hervey Bay exit. Follow Hervey Bay signs out of Maryborough, until in about 15 km (9.25 miles) you see a sign for River Heads. Turn right here. Keep going in the direction of River Heads until, a few kilometers from the end of the road, you reach a store on the left that sells camping permits and ferry tickets. Arrange these details, then either park by the store (to reduce the potential for car clouting) or in the lot at the ferry launch. If you are on foot, you do not need to reserve ferry tickets ahead of time, but reservations are essential for passage if you are bringing an automobile; phone (07) 4124-1900.

Once you have arrived on the island, you can walk or drive to Central Station, 8 km (5 miles) from the ferry landing or hire a taxi to take you there. For taxi service you must phone in advance; the number is (07) 4127-8188. The driver will also do pick-ups and drop-offs elsewhere on the island. Be aware, however, that taxi hire is rather expensive.

Camping. Central Station is a lovely, spacious, park-like place along Wanggoolba Creek. Extravagant epiphytes and bold dingoes, cockatoos, and kookaburras make your stay in this old logging camp memorable. The campground provides grills, hot showers, firewood, picnic tables, shelters, water, and a telephone. People can also camp at Lake McKenzie, Lake Boomanjin, and Dilli Village (a private resort), as well as anywhere along the beach. There is no official camping at Eurong.

Season. Any, but can be buggy in summer.

1. Wanggoolba Creek/Pile Valley

> **Distance: 4 km (2.5 miles) round trip**
> **Time: 1 or 1.5 hours**
> **Difficulty: moderately easy**
> **Attractions: clear rainforest creek, enormous satinay trees**

This scenic walk begins near the information display at Central Station. Head upstream on the boardwalk along Wanggoolba Creek, one of the great beauty spots of Fraser Island. The creek, with its white sand bottom, is exceptionally clear and photogenic. Piccabeen palms dominate the rainforest here, but specimens of giant angiopteris fern, growing right out of the water, steal the show. Birds are abundant. After slightly over 1 km, you cross the creek on a bridge. The trail first heads north and then turns east as it ascends a drier ridge toward Pile Valley, home to a stand of statuesque satinay trees, over 60 meters (200 feet) high. The trail ends at a parking area on a 4-WD road. Retrace your steps back to Central Station.

2. Central Station to Lake McKenzie

Distance: 10 km (6.25 miles) round trip
Time: 4.5 hours
Difficulty: moderately easy
**Attractions: beautiful lakes with small beaches, eucalypt forest,
    rainforest scenery**

This popular hike starts near the Central Station information display. Follow the Wanggoolba Creek Trail through deep rainforest for a short distance and then cross the stream on a sturdy log bridge. The trail ascends and descends a ridge, amid drier eucalypt forest. It passes a small marsh before dropping down to clear, beautiful Basin Lake, which is accessible via a short spur.

From here, you encounter more forested ridges on your way to Lake McKenzie. The lovely beaches here can be crowded at times because of easy road access for 4-WD vehicles. After a refreshing swim, return the way you came.

3. Central Station to Dilli Village

> **Distance: 20 km (12.5 miles) one way**
> **Time: 6–8 hours of walking, ideally done in two days**
> **Difficulty: moderately difficult as a day hike; otherwise moderate**
> **Attractions: lakes, sandblow, forests**

This is one of the premier treks on Fraser Island. It is possible to complete the hike in one day and camp near the beach at Dilli Village, then taxi back to the ferry (or to Central Station, if you left a vehicle there). A better alternative is to camp en route at Lake Boomanjin and then proceed to Dilli Village the next morning, planning to meet a taxi there.

The trail starts across the road from the campground. It climbs steeply, sometimes on stairs, up a ridge through forest and macrozamia. After

Lake McKenzie, Fraser Island

about 2 km (1.25 miles) of pleasant walking, you descend to a 4-WD road near Lake Jennings. If you want to swim in the lake or even see it, you need to take the following detour: turn right onto the road, walking for about 200 meters, and then go left at a junction. Another 10 minutes brings you to a small beach beside the lake. Retrace your steps to the main trail.

The trail crosses the 4-WD road mentioned above, then climbs a long ridge above and to the left of Lake Jennings. Eventually it meanders down to Lake Birrabeen, 6 km (3.75 miles) from Central Station. You can swim in this exceptionally clear lake from a reedy beach by the trail, observing the tour bus hordes on the larger beach across the lake. Because the lake is shallow, it remains warm even into the autumn months.

Next the trail passes a small picnic area and wanders by a reed-choked lagoon before reaching the beautiful, dazzlingly white beach at Lake Benaroon. Behind the beach are fascinatingly distorted melaleucas. From this point, the trail temporarily deteriorates. It struggles through thick vegetation far around the lakeshore until finally heading south into the ridge country again. On the ridges, overhanging branches and dead-fall across the trail may impede your progress. However, fine tree specimens along the way provide constant interest: huge blackbutts, smooth-barked apples (reddish in color), and white scribbly gums grace this long, little-used stretch of trail.

After a few hours of walking, you finally reach picturesque Lake Boomanjin. The trail turns right here, skirting the lake's north shore, and crosses a flat covered by glaring white sand. This open section can be very hot, and it is important to bring an ample water supply with you. Soon you arrive at Lake Boomanjin Campground, a shady oasis popular with 4-WD enthusiasts. It lies 13.5 km (8.5 miles) from Central Station.

The final 6.5 km (4 mile) section of the hike, from Lake Boomanjin to Dilli Village, takes only about 2 hours to complete, since the trail improves and climbs less steeply. The highlight of this area is surely the Wongi Sandblow. After about 2.5 km (1.5 miles) you see a ridge rise up to the left of the trail out of fairly level terrain. Atop it lies the sandblow, a large area of shifting dunes. The official trail skirts the sandblow, but there soon appears a very steep, hiker-made route up which you can scramble to gain access to this fascinating feature. Climb this slide, leaving packs behind if you wish, and you emerge into a mini-Sahara of golden sand. Views are exhilarating; you can see all the way from the edge of Lake Boomanjin to the Pacific Ocean. Kids love to roll around and run down the steep dune faces.

Back on the main trail, you follow ridge tops and eventually descend toward Dilli Village, a rustic resort cum campground about 150 meters from the beach. It has the usual amenities plus a swimming hole. Don't miss the sunrise from the vast windswept beach behind the village.

BURRUM COAST NATIONAL PARK: WOODGATE SECTION

The Burrum River flows into Hervey Bay not far south of Bundaberg. The QNPWS has recently consolidated three smaller parks into the new Burrum Coast National Park, thus preserving some vital wildlife habitat. Since Fraser Island across the bay has been carefully protected as well, this stretch of Australian littoral seems likely to escape the frenetic development occurring farther south. Of the park's three sections, only Woodgate is easily accessible to hikers.

Burrum cannot match more glamorous parks for scenery, given its flat terrain and somewhat monotonous forests. Nevertheless, it has quiet beauty, abundant birdlife, and calm water for swimming. Don't make a special trip here, but if you are in the Hervey Bay area for whale-watching (see below), consider a detour to this tranquil part of the coast.

Road access. From Childers on the Bruce Highway, drive east for 2 km (1.25 miles), take the turnoff to Goodwood, and then travel 45 km (28 miles) to the town of Woodgate. The road, though narrow, is paved all the way.

From Bundaberg, follow signs to Goodwood and from there to Woodgate. Once in town, directions depend on which hike you choose to do. See below for information.

Camping. The park has a pleasant, low-key campground on the beach, though one that is sometimes plagued by insects. However, you need a 4-WD vehicle to drive there over a soft, sandy road. Backpackers would have no trouble walking down this road (which would take under an hour) and setting up camp. Otherwise, you can always stay at the caravan park in town, where you must content yourself with a tiny patch of grass among trailers and RVs.

Season. Any but summer, although early spring may mean controlled burns and charred landscape.

In the area. If you visit the Hervey Bay region from August to October, you might consider taking a humpback whale-watching tour. Various companies operate tours, which normally are an all-day affair, with lunch provided. In season, whale sightings are virtually guaranteed. Although tour operators are not supposed to get within 100 meters of them, the whales are curious creatures that often approach boats much more closely than that. The best views occur when the whales "breach," soaring completely out of the water. Dolphins are common in the bay, and dugongs (sea cows) are sometimes spotted as well. A bonus of these tours is that you are treated to beautiful views of the northern part of Fraser Island, with its tall cliffs, white and reddish sand, and long, empty beaches. Be sure to pick a day when the seas are calm and the weather is favorable.

1. Melaleuca Trail

Distance: 10.75 km (6.75 miles) round trip
Time: 3 hours
Difficulty: moderately easy
Attractions: forest, bird-blind near a pond

To reach the trailhead, drive on through the town of Woodgate until you reach 12th Avenue. Turn right here. Signs will direct you to Walkers Point Road. From there, continue until you see signs for the hiking trails on the left side of the road, not far past the turnoff for the campground.

Much of this trail's vegetation was scarred by controlled burns in 1996. However, given the fast rate of regrowth in sunny Queensland, it should soon be presentable again. The easy-to-follow trail sometimes cuts narrowly through forest and at other times follows old 4-WD roads. Along the way it visits various plant communities, including melaleuca, cabbage palm, and wetland. It passes very near to the beach for about 1 km (0.62 mile), allowing you to take a swim if you so choose. It also goes by both a bird-blind—a popular spot—and the park's laid-back, beach front campground, which has cold showers but no picnic tables. Eventually, the trail loops back around to your starting point.

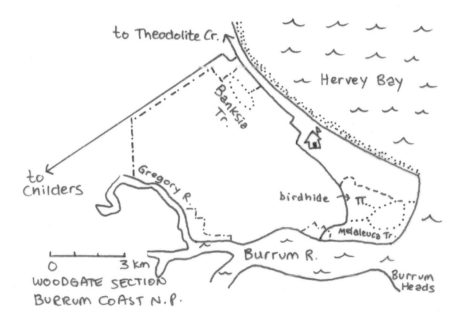

2. Banksia Loop

Distance: 5.75 km (3.5 miles) round trip
Time: 1.5 hours
Difficulty: easy
Attractions: melaleuca swamp, palm grove

To reach the trailhead, drive to the main road of Woodgate village, which goes along the beach, and turn onto 6th Avenue. In about 50 meters look for a trailhead signboard. Pull in and park here. Since the area may be buggy, it is wise to take insect repellent along.

The wide, level trail wanders through various swamp and forest habitats, and it is a good venue for bird-watching. It begins as a paved path that soon turns into a boardwalk as it passes through a lovely melaleuca swamp. At the end of the boardwalk, after you have gone about 400 meters (0.25 mile), the trail forks, intersecting the Banksia Loop proper. Turn right onto the loop and enter a forested area. The trail soon winds past a lovely palm grove. Later on, banksia is the predominant form of vegetation. At two points, the trail temporarily follows jeep roads through scrubby country before closing the loop. Return to your car via the boardwalk.

Chapter 6

ESCARPMENT AND RANGE

The vast majority of visitors to tropical Australia stick to well-established routes along the coast or fly instead to the Northern Territory. The parks of interior Queensland have yet to be fully discovered by international trekkers. Yet some of the most dramatic scenery, plentiful wildlife, and best trails lie inland and should not be missed.

The terrain of the interior varies greatly. Rugged ranges dissect much of southern Queensland, sometimes supporting rainforest in moist uplands or sheltered ravines. The more isolated ranges often boast rare and beautiful plant species. Farther north and west, the land grows drier;

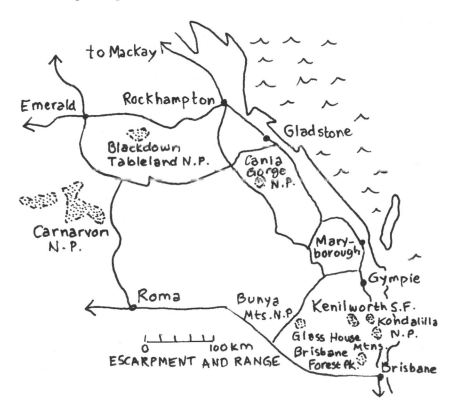

colorful canyons and escarpments impart to parks like Carnarvon Gorge a look that is reminiscent of the American Southwest.

Wherever you go in the vast hinterland, you will feel a sense of Australia as it used to be. Long stretches of empty highway connect small settlements that serve far-flung agricultural and pastoral operations. Social life revolves around cafes, pubs, and bowling clubs. The people of "regional" Australia display a genuine warmth toward visitors, and brief queries will often evolve into interesting conversations. You may garner valuable advice about a nearby trail, swimming hole, or dirt road. And you will likely gain some insight into the struggles of rural Australians to survive drought, floods, fires, and falling commodity prices.

Roads to the hinterland parks described here do not quite measure up to those nearer the coast. In some cases you will have to drive miles on gravel or dirt road. Even the paved roads frequently consist of only one lane and require extra care while driving.

BUNYA MOUNTAINS NATIONAL PARK

Though less renowned than some of Queensland's other parks, the Bunya Mountains offer visitors varied and scenic hiking, loads of wildlife, and— of course—specimens of the area's namesake tree, the pagoda-shaped bunya pine. The ancestral peak from which today's Bunya Mountains were formed arose between 23 and 24 million years ago. Like Mt. Warning farther south, it was a shield volcano, a broad, gently sloping cone created by successive flows of basaltic lava. The contemporary range, with its cliffs and waterfalls, has eroded a great deal but still reaches elevations of 1135 meters (3725 feet), towering above the surrounding plains.

The woodlands atop the Bunyas run the gamut from moist rainforest to dry rainforest, and dry eucalypt forest to dry, closed scrub. In the rainforest, especially above 850 meters (3000 feet), you will behold the rare, stately bunya pines. Given proper conditions, they form a rather open, dome-like crown with most of their sharp-pointed leaflets out at the end of the branches. Today they grow only here and, in a few isolated locations, around the Blackall Range and Atherton Tableland. Thus, Bunya Mountains National Park resembles Redwood National Park in California in protecting an ancient, unique, and majestic tree species that has few refuges left. Besides its architectonic beauty, the tree has another remarkable trait: every 3 years it produces pineapple-sized "pinecones" containing hundreds of delicious bunya nuts. As late as the 20th century, Aboriginal bands would hasten to harvest nuts from this sacred tree, wherever it bore fruit. Today you can collect some yourself or purchase them from nearby stores. Just be careful that a cone doesn't fall on you as you hike the trails!

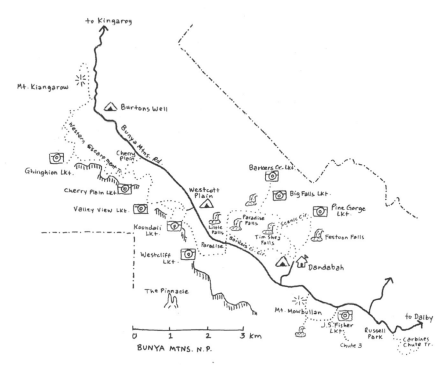

BUNYA MTNS. N.P.

Apart from the rainforest, with its bunyas, strangler figs, "stinging" (gympie) trees, and red cedars, the park offers opportunities to walk the edge of its western escarpment through quite different ecosystems. Out there, space, light, open woodlands, and long vistas entice visitors. But wherever you walk or camp in this park, you will see wildlife in abundance. Few parks in Australia can match the Bunya Mountains for diversity and numbers of birds and animals. Marsupials are especially plentiful.

Road access. From the east (e.g., Brisbane or the Sunshine Coast), follow highways to Yarraman. Head south 20 km (12.5 miles) and then back northwest to Maidenwell. In that hamlet, signs point the way to the park, another 28 km (17.5 miles) away over a decent road with some gravel surface.

From the south (e.g., Toowoomba or the New England region), take the road to Jondaryan, then drive to the park via Maclagan. This is the steepest, most tortuous route, and it also has some gravel.

From the north, a paved but serpentine road leads to the park from Kingaroy, a fair-sized town.

Camping. The park has three campgrounds. Dandabah, the most popular, has hot showers and must often be booked months in advance. There are restaurants and inns nearby. Burtons Well Campground is perhaps the best, with seclusion, views, and rainshelter. Westcott offers a wide, grassy clearing and scattered picnic tables. The last two campgrounds work on the self-registration system. To reserve sites at Dandabah, phone (07) 4668-3127.

Season. Any, but bear in mind that the park can be cold at night, year round. Chilly fogs may delay morning warm-ups, and in the winter, snow might even dust the heights. Plan accordingly, bringing along warm clothes and sleeping bags.

In the area. Tarong National Park, though adjacent to the Bunya Mountains, is drier and lower. It features interesting granite formations, magnificent grass trees, and Coombah Falls, a seasonal waterfall. If you are passing through Maidenwell in transit to the Bunyas, the waterfall is worth a visit. In Maidenwell, look for signs to Coombah Falls, only 2 km (1.25 miles) from the center of town on a road that is partly paved. Drive to the parking area and overlook at the road's end. The short trail descends on about 50 steps to the waterfall and, below it, a large pool bounded on one side by cliffs. Even when no water is flowing over the falls, this is a lovely spot.

1. Western Escarpment Trail

> **Distance: 16 km (10 miles) one way, including Mt. Kiangarow ascent**
> **Time: 5 or 6 hours**
> **Difficulty: moderately easy**
> **Attractions: views, solitude, wildlife, variety of ecosystems**

The "Western Escarpment Trail" assembles 5 separate walking tracks into a single longer jaunt. Obviously, you could follow the park brochure and do any of them individually, though you would miss the pleasures of a day (nearly) alone in the bush. Bear in mind that since this is a one-way trip, you will either need to be picked up or walk the road back to your vehicle.

Begin at the unsigned, but "iconed," trailhead opposite the upper end of Burtons Well Campground. After 200 meters, look for a sign directing you to Mt. Kiangarow, a little over 1 km (0.62 mile) distant. Don't neglect to walk this part of the trail; it presents superb views both east and west and leads to the park's highest point (1135 meters/3725 feet). Wear long pants here, since stinging nettles trailside may cause discomfort.

Backtracking to the main trail, head southwest along the escarpment toward Cherry Plains Picnic Area, about 6 km (3.75 miles) away. At first, you pass through fairly dense forest dominated by massive, thin-leaved stringybark trees and occasional Queensland bluegums with mottled, brownish bark. At Ghinghion Lookout, watch for falcons, grey goshawks (a rare species), and other members of the hawk family. Beyond the lookout, the trail follows the edge of the cliff, so you enjoy continuous views out toward the endless plain of the Darling Downs, one of the state's top farming regions. By all means, take the 700 meter/0.4 mile (each way) spur track to Bottle Tree Bluff. This is an open, grassy environment studded with oddly shaped grass trees and home to parrots, wallabies, and other creatures. At the Bottle Tree Bluff trail junction you will have another 1.5 km (1 mile) to Cherry Plains Picnic Area.

Past the Bottle Tree Bluff spur, the trail alternates between patches of rainforest and the more open escarpment environment. Assuming you continue the hike rather than ending it at Cherry Plains, follow signs to Westcott Picnic Area. Just past the unmarked Valley View Lookout, you will see signs directing you back toward Cherry Plains or onward toward Westcott. Right below this point is a third sign indicating the Koondai Circuit. Take this track. It will lead eventually to Westcott Picnic Area, but via the escarpment with its superior views.

When you reach the big clearing at Westcott Picnic Area look to your right for another trailhead, this one with no directional signs but several icons. Follow this trail, which takes you on to West Cliff Lookout and Paradise Parking Area, where your hike ends. The lookout, about a 20 minute walk past Westcott, offers more sweeping views across Darling Downs and lots of eucalypti with peeling bark. Beyond the lookout, the trail winds back into the rainforest, traversing one of the Bunyas' famous grassy "balds" known as Little Pocket. It ends at the main park road, opposite Paradise Parking Area.

2. Barkers Creek Circuit

Distance: 10 km (6.25 miles) round trip
Time: 3 or 3.5 hours
Difficulty: moderately easy
Attractions: profuse bird life, falls, beautiful rainforest

This rainforest trail starts at the Paradise Parking Area, along the main park road. After 300 meters (1000 feet) the actual loop begins. Go left here at this junction. The trail descends slightly to the first major point of interest, Paradise Falls, located only 350 meters (0.2 mile) past the junction. It is an idyllic spot where water trickles down a cliff face that is covered with vegetation. Little Falls, at km 1.25 (mile 0.75), is similar.

About 10 minutes past Little Falls, you emerge briefly out of the rainforest to lateral across one of the Bunya "balds," enjoying distant views to the east from this grassy meadow. Soon you arrive at a spur, 700 meters (0.4 mile) one way, to Big Falls, quite an impressive sight after a rain, but otherwise perhaps hardly flowing at all.

Back on the main trail, continue clockwise around the loop to another clearing, this one sporting grass trees. A junction with the Scenic

Circuit is just past here; go right to continue around the loop, after detouring briefly (if you wish) down the Scenic Circuit to see Tim Read Falls.

The Barkers Creek Trail now enters a zone with a large concentration of fig trees. In fact, the trail passes directly through one of them, shortly before the first of a pair of junctions leading to Dandabah Campground and Picnic Area. Turn right at both of these junctions. From here it is about 3 km (1.75 miles) back to the carpark, on a gently undulating path.

3. Scenic Circuit

Distance: 4 km (2.5 miles) round trip
Time: 1.5 hours
Difficulty: easy
Attractions: well-preserved rainforest with falls and bunya
pines

Bunya pine

The Scenic Circuit appeals to park visitors of all ages and experience levels; hence, it becomes very crowded at times. Still, the towering bunyas and strangler figs, charming Festoon Falls, and the cathedral-like atmosphere should compensate for the throngs of people.

Begin at the Dandabah Picnic Area, just down the road from the campground. Notice several huge bunya pines near the start of the trail. Some of them bear horizontal scars that may have been made by Aborigines seeking footholds to climb for the nuts. After 0.75 km, you descend to the base of Festoon Falls, reached by a short spur trail. The small cascade trickles through dense vegetation over rich, black basalt. There are huge stinging trees (gympies) across the creek.

Shortly, you arrive at a spur to Pine Gorge Lookout, a disappointment because it affords views of a nuclear power plant in the valley below. A bit farther, look for an enormous, scarred, double-trunked bunya pine. Past here you approach a creek and spot Tim Shea Falls, another small cascade that issues into a dark, slightly gloomy pool.

As you near the end of the circuit, be alert for a large hoop pine, easily distinguished from the bunya by its upward pointing branches and more closed, almost ropelike structure. A short distance from here, the trail actually passes through an immense, open-trunked strangler fig; you will miss it if you take one of the hiker-made shortcuts on this part of the route. About 100 meters farther on, you intersect the Barkers Creek Trail. Go left here to complete the circuit back to the Picnic Area and your car.

4. Cunjevoi Falls/Chute No. 3

Distance: 6 km (3.75 miles) round trip, including road walk
Time: 1.5 to 2 hours
Difficulty: moderately easy
Attractions: solitude, bunya pines

The local shire council maintains this near-loop trail in Russell Park, just outside the Bunya Mountains National Park boundary. Their standards do not match those of the QNPWS, however, and as a result the track is sometimes overgrown and hard to follow. Wear long pants, since nettles and other thorny shrubs would otherwise cause much misery. Also, beware of snakes where the vegetation is thick.

Begin at Fischers Lookout (1073 meters/3520 feet elevation) and walk downhill across the meadow. You will soon reach the forest and, with luck, find far more bunya cones than in the national park. Be careful not to lose the trail as you pass a gympie (stinging) tree with a hole in it. Immediately past that tree, go left, ignoring a false path to the right.

You will then come to a sign pointing the way toward both Cunjevoi Falls (170 meters/560 feet high), at the terminus of a spur trail, and the main road picnic area (trail's end), 2 km (1.25 miles) distant. Cunjevoi Falls, like others in the area, is dry at certain seasons of the year. However, the down-canyon views are always impressive, so you might want to stroll out to see it anyway.

Back on the main trail, you ascend a slope to Little Mount Mowbullan through very thick grass. Although I did not encounter any snakes on this stretch of trail, I worried about them, because I could not see where I was stepping. Here the trail is difficult to follow, especially on top of the "mountain" itself. Persevere and you will follow it over the top and down into the forest again. Before long, note a sign pointing back up toward Little Mount Mowbullan near a dry creekbed. Forge straight ahead past this sign and under some vines, and you'll hit a one-time 4-WD road, now a forest trail. Continue uphill to another sign indicating that Chute No. 3 is 700 meters (0.4 mile) away on a spur trail. Walk on out to the top of the old logging chute, now mostly disappeared. You will enjoy fine, open country and views down-canyon from here. Return to the main trail and proceed for 800 meters (0.5 mile) alongside a fence to close the loop at the main road picnic area.

5. Carbines Chute

Distance: 2 km (1.25 miles) round trip
Time: 30 minutes
Difficulty: easy
Attractions: rainforest, wildlife

This short, graded, nature trail in Russell Park, just outside the national park boundary, is wheelchair accessible.

It starts opposite Munros Camp, 1 km (0.62 mile) down the road to Darby. Wallabies frequent Munros Camp and cross the road just above it, so exercise caution when driving.

The trail descends gently through beautiful, healthy rainforest to a fenced overlook with (rather unexceptional) views to the west. Signs along the track identify the many species of trees that you see, including gympies, tree ferns, hollywood, incense wood, axehandle wood, and piccabeen palm. Vines run riot here, as on so many trails in the Bunyas. Carbines Chute, visible at the trail's end, was once used by loggers to slide felled trees down the mountain slopes. The hiker-made track past the overlook is steep and dangerous. Return to the parking area the way you came.

BRISBANE FOREST PARK

The D'Aguilar Range rises near Brisbane and extends for over 30 km (18.5 miles) toward the northwest. Though far from a pristine wilderness, the range has been granted protection from intensive development. It contains a few private inholdings, but most of the range has now been placed under state forest or national park stewardship as a greenbelt preserve. Collectively, these refuges (including Maiala, Jollys Lookout, Manorina, and Boombana National Parks) go by the name of the Brisbane Forest Park. Although it does not belong in a class with Lamington or the Border Ranges, it has extensive forests remarkably close to the city and some worthwhile hiking trails. Visitors staying in Brisbane who want to leaven the pleasures of urban life with a few quiet walks would find the Forest Park attractive.

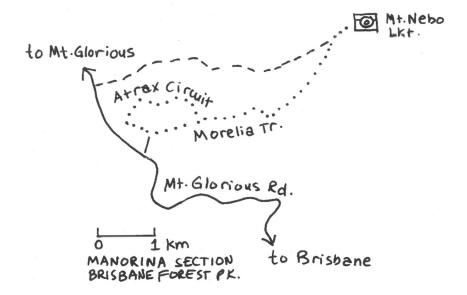

Road access. Route 31 (Waterworks Road), usually signed for "The Gap," will take motorists from near downtown Brisbane to the park boundary. From there just follow the same road (now the Mt. Nebo Road) until you reach the desired trailhead. For the first two hikes park at the Manorina National Park campground, on the right just a couple of kilometers past Mt. Nebo village and clearly marked. The third hike begins at the Maiala National Park picnic ground, on the right not far beyond the village of Mt. Glorious, but not so clearly signed.

Camping. Manorina Bush Camp, only a few minutes' drive north of Mt. Nebo village, has level, well-constructed tent sites in a leafy, peaceful setting, complete with peacocks. Water, restrooms, and grills are provided. To camp there, you first need to obtain a permit from the Brisbane Forest Park Information Center on the left side of Waterworks Road, just as it leaves Brisbane and enters the park to become Mt. Nebo Road.

1. Morelia Walk

> **Distance: 6 km (3.75 miles) round trip**
> **Time: 1.5 hours**
> **Difficulty: easy**
> **Attractions: varied forest scenery, nice views at lookout**

Begin this pleasant stroll at the Manorina Campground mentioned above. Signs will point you to the beginning of the trail, which meanders gradually up a ridge behind the campground. You will pass by some stately eucalypti and occasionally through remnant rainforest in shaded ravines. One strangler fig supports a pepper vine as thick as a treetrunk. After about 45 minutes the trail intersects an old 4-WD road at which you turn right. In another 50 meters you will reach the summit of Mt. Nebo, where a flat, open, rock platform affords views across the Samford Valley clear out to the Pacific Ocean and even to offshore islands. Return as you came.

2. Atrax Self-guided Walk

Distance: 750 meters (0.5 mile) round trip
Time: 15 minutes
Difficulty: easy
Attractions: learning about creatures of the forest

This short loop branches off the Morelia Trail near its beginning and winds back around behind the campground. It features signs describing the animals in Manorina National Park, most of which are nocturnal. These signs explain facets of the animals' appearance, habits, tracks, and potential predators. One could probably use this trail to "spotlight" a few of these remarkable creatures, but beware of one broken down bridge on any such night walk.

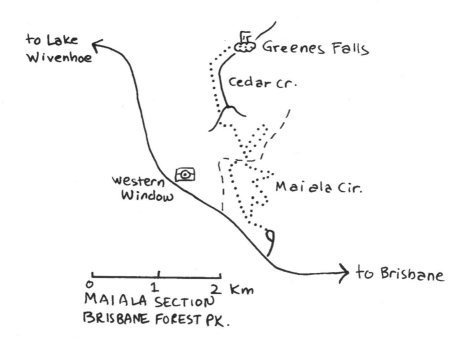

3. Maiala Circuit/Greenes Falls

Distance: 5 km (3 miles) round trip to Greenes Falls
Time: 1 hour for the portion now open (see below)
Difficulty: easy
Attractions: creeks and rainforest

The walk to Greenes Falls used to be a favorite of Brisbanites, but the last one kilometer has recently been closed for repairs, so (as of this writing) visitors can only go as far as a dirt access road from which the last leg to the falls departs. Still, you can do this walk as a loop of approximately 3 km and enjoy the high, cool rainforest. The trail passes along several creeks that sustain magnificent forest giants untouched by loggers. It takes off from the parking lot of Maiala National Park, just west of the village of Mt. Glorious on the previously described Mt. Nebo Rd.

KONDALILLA AND MAPLETON FALLS
NATIONAL PARKS

The Blackall Range behind Queensland's Sunshine Coast once harbored extensive rainforest. By now most of it has been felled for its valuable timber trees and to create pastureland or homesites. Still, in this fashionable and rapidly developing district, two national parks have been established to preserve remnants of the Blackalls as they used to be. Mapleton Falls, the smaller of the two, protects a patch of rainforest, open eucalypt forest, and escarpment, as well as its namesake waterfall. Kondalilla is large enough that you could spend hours or even a whole day there enjoying its swimming holes and deep, rainforest-clad gorge. Picabeen palms reach stately proportions here, and platypuses may be spotted in the streams around twilight. Kondalilla Falls itself tumbles 80 meters (260 feet) into Skene Creek.

Road access. For Mapleton Falls: from the Bruce Highway (Route 1) drive into Nambour and from there follow signs up to the village of Mapleton. In the village, turn right onto the Obi Obi Road (signed for Mapleton Falls) and drive about 4 km (2.5 miles) until you spot another sign for the park. Turn right there and continue to the parking lot, about 1 km (0.62 mile) farther. You can also reach Mapleton on the tourist drive that runs atop the Blackall Range from near Landsborough to Nambour.

For Kondalilla: from the Bruce Highway you can reach the just-mentioned tourist drive from north or south. In either case you will find the entrance to Kondalilla National Park between the villages of Montville and Mapleton, near the hamlet of Flaxton about 3 km (1.75 miles) north of Montville.

Camping. Neither park allows camping, so you must rely on commercial accommodations or else drive a bit further to campgrounds in Kenilworth State Forest described in a later section.

1. Mapleton Falls Loop

> **Distance: 1.25 km (0.75 mile) round trip**
> **Time: 30 minutes**
> **Difficulty: easy**
> **Attractions: views, birding, the falls (if viewing platform is ever repaired)**

This very short hike would normally begin with a sidetrip to the Mapleton Falls overlook platform adjacent to the parking lot. However, it is closed for the time being, so one cannot actually see the falls well from anywhere on a trail. Still, the short loop trail makes for a pleasant walk. You saunter down from the parking lot to a grassy picnic area and from there across a creek and into the forest. At a junction you can go either way, but this description assumes that you take the right fork. At first rainforest species predominate, but drier eucalypti replace them as the trail winds uphill and passes some agricultural land. On the margin of forest and field you may encounter an amazing variety of bird species if you walk slowly and listen for diverse calls and songs. The trail soon traverses around to a short spur that leads to Peregrine Overlook. This lofty perch offers fine vistas across a rugged and still rather wild landscape of ranges and valleys. In a few minutes the trail completes its circuit, and you return to the picnic area and your car.

2. Kondalilla Falls Circuit

> **Distance 4.5 km (2.75 miles) round trip**
> **Time: 2 hours**
> **Difficulty: moderate**
> **Attractions: a high waterfall, outstanding rainforest in the gorge below the falls, a deep pool**

From the parking lot, walk down through the picnic ground amid exceptional specimens of epiphytes and follow signs for the Kondalilla Falls Circuit, which actually includes almost all of the Picnic Creek Circuit as well. At first the trail descends almost imperceptibly through wet eucalypt forest alongside Picnic Creek. Hikers will pass by some miniature cascades and small pools en route to the escarpment over which Kondalilla Falls (the word means "rushing waters" in an Aboriginal tongue) drops 80 meters (260 feet). Soon the trail descend more steeply, often on steps, to a junction with Skene Creek (a tributary of Obi Obi Creek) where a huge pool attracts plenty of swimmers in summer. Around the pool you will find peerless views into the Skene Creek val-

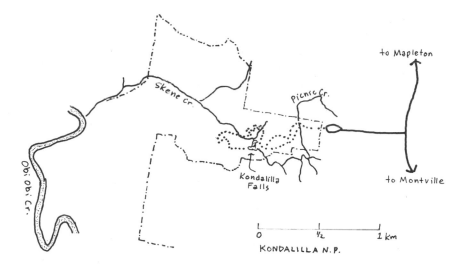

KONDALILLA N.P.

ley. Sometimes, playtpuses are spotted here. Just below the pool the falls plunge into a verdant rainforest gorge, but can't be appreciated from the top.

Your trail now commences a steep descent into this gorge through lush rainforest. Notable in the flora here are young bunya pines and a stately grove of piccabeen palms on the south-facing slope. The trail brings hikers around to an overlook of the falls, but to see them best one must rockhop a little way up the creek from the point where the trail approaches the falls most closely.

Past the falls the trail begins its steep climb back up to the top of the escarpment, offering some enchanting rainforest walking on the way. Follow the signs back toward the parking lot. The trail will take you there via a slightly different route than you came until it reaches Picnic Creek again.

GLASS HOUSE MOUNTAINS NATIONAL PARK

A "hot spot" in the earth's crust once underlay Australia's eastern rim. As the continent drifted slowly northward, the hot spot kept thrusting up new volcanoes until about twenty million years ago, including (among others) the Tweed Volcano which created the eastern Scenic Rim. Yet, the most striking, instantly recognizable mementoes of ancient volcanic fury are the Glass House Mountains.

This curious company of towers and rounded hills looms above the Bruce Highway starting about 50 km (30 miles) north of Brisbane. The "mountains" are actually volcanic plugs, the solidified lava cores of much-eroded ancient volcanoes. Many are grandly scenic, while a few, as described below, can be easily climbed, affording amazing vistas over the steeper ones and on to Brisbane and the coast. Bear in mind that the national park does not protect the entire area around these peaks; rather, each section of park covers only the peak itself and its immediate surroundings. Between the mountains stretch pineapple fields, state forest lands, and rural lots.

Road access. Described below for each individual hike.

Camping. Beerburrum State Forest has developed a camping area just off the Bruce Highway about 11 km (6.75 miles) south of the Sunshine Motorway turnoff. To reach it from the south, drive north on the Bruce Highway (Route 1) past the Glass House Mountains, watching carefully for a sign indicating the crossing of Coochin Creek. Then prepare to turn off, as Roys Road, the access point for the camping area, lies only 2 km (1.25 miles) up the highway. The Roys Road turnoff is not a standard

freeway exit; it is simply a crossover point on the median strip preceded by a short turn lane off the right (passing) lane. Roys Road is located about 67 km (41.5 miles) north of Brisbane.

From the north, as you approach the Glass House Mountains look for Bells Creek Road heading off to the left, then prepare to turn, since Roys Road is only about 2 km (1.25 miles) past Bells Creek Road. This is an easier turn, because you do not have to cross a busy freeway from the fast lane. Once on Roys Road, drive 5 km (3 miles) farther, where

Mt. Coonowrin, one of the Glass House Mountains   a sign advertises the campground. You could also choose a commercial campground nearer to the Glass House Mountains.

Season. Any, although winter winds on the summits could prove chilly.

In the area. If you would like to see or photograph the Glass House Mountains from unusual vantage points, you might enjoy either of two sidetrips. First, you can drive up toward the village of Maleny from a Bruce Highway turnoff near Landsborough. Shortly before you reach the village, look for a signed left turn to Mary Cairncross Park. This lofty perch looks over the entire Glass House group from above and has especially striking views around sunset.

Second, you can take the Bruce Highway to the Bribie Island exit and drive east about 20 km (12.5 miles) across the bridge to this sand island on the coast. Then turn left and wend your way along the shore. You will enjoy unusual views from several small waterside parks across the Pumicestone Passage to the Glass House Mountains. Bribie Island also offers unlimited and straightforward beachwalking opportunities on the ocean side.

1. Mt. Ngungun

Distance: 3 km (1.75 miles) round trip
Time: 1 or 1.5 hours
Difficulty: moderate
Attractions: unsurpassed views of Mts. Beerwah and Coonowrin

Road access. Locate the Glass House Mountains Tourist Drive on a road map. One can reach it either from the south via Beerburrum or from the north via Landsborough. From the little town of Glass House Mountains, just off this road, follow signs southwest onto Coonowrin Road. Just past Glasshouse Mountains Preschool, turn right onto Fullertons Road. After about 1 km (0.62 mile) more, look for a parking area on the right for Mt. Ngungun. The trail begins there.

Though Ngungun (253 meters/830 feet high) presents no danger to hikers, the trail to its summit may prove challenging for some because of its steepness and sections of hand-over-hand climbing. This can be a hot hike in summer, so bringing water is advisable. Wear boots, since the rough terrain puts considerable stress on ankles.

The trail proceeds on a level for the first 100 meters then ascends on "stairs" for a short distance. Beyond them it climbs relentlessly up to and past Ngungun Cave. More climbing up very steep grades brings hikers to a flat area with good views of Mt. Tibrogargan (364 meters/ 1195 feet high). Past this vantage point, the trail heads upward again over one slightly tricky patch of bare rock to a ridgetop, then laterals to the left to a point where one enjoys fantastic views west to Mts. Beerwah

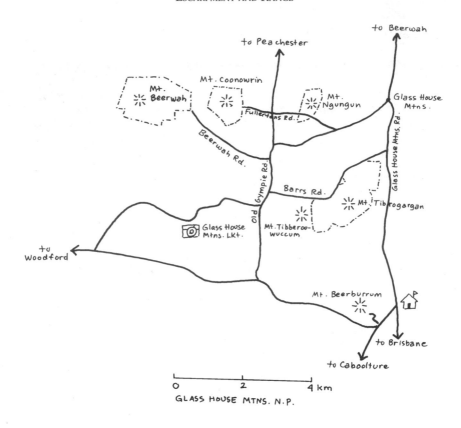

GLASS HOUSE MTNS. N.P.

(556 meters / 1825 feet) and Coonowrin (377 meters / 1235 feet). The two peaks almost "line up" from the Ngungun vantage point. Coonowrin or "Crookneck" is the very steep peak with an angular profile. Return as you came.

2. Mt. Coonowrin Base

Distance: 2 km (1.25 miles) round trip
Time: 45 minutes
Difficulty: moderate
Attractions: a close-up look at this bizarre peak

Road access. Take the Glass House Mountains Road from either its northern or southern junction with the Bruce Highway (Route 1) and follow it to a spur that leads into the village of Glass House Mountains. From the village follow the Coonowrin Road west until you hit the Old Gympie Road. Turn right (north) and then left at the marked turnoff for Coonowrin. The ascent to Coonowrin's (aka Crookneck's) summit is suitable only for experienced rock climbers, but one can scramble up to the base of its "tower" without danger. Wearing boots would be wise.

From the small parking area, a rough path heads uphill, at first quite gradually, but growing ever steeper as it climbs. You will soon reach a rock outcrop a bit below the true base of Coonowrin. Struggle up this outcrop and you will quickly make it to the beginning of Coonwrin's precipitous rock face. You can contour around the base to the left for 100 meters or so and perhaps find a good vantage point to see nearby Mt. Beerwah. Return as you came.

3. Mt. Beerburrum

Distance: 1.5 km (1 mile) round trip
Time: 30–45 minutes
Difficulty: moderately easy
Attractions: views to south and southeast

Road access. Just south of the town of Beerburrum on the Glasshouse Mountains Road look for a signed right-hand turn to Mt. Beerburrum National Park. Drive down this secondary road to a picnic area and park there.

Though quite short, the Beerburrum Trail climbs steeply up a paved fire road all the way to the summit (280 meters/920 feet). From there, one can ascend a ladder to the firetower on the summit for unobstructed vistas in every direction. On a clear day, the view takes in Brisbane's central city skyscrapers, the Gateway Bridge, the distant profile of the McPherson Range, the much closer Blackall and D'Aguilar Ranges, and offshore islands like Bribie, Moreton, and possibly North Stradbroke, not to mention all the other Glass House Mountains. In short, this is one of the finest panoramas in the coastal hinterlands. Return by the same road you ascended.

4. Wild Horse Mountain Lookout

Distance: 1.5 km (1 mile) round trip
Time: 30 minutes
Difficulty: moderate
Attractions: views of Glass House Mountains and vicinity

Road access. Take the exit for Wild Horse Mountain Lookout off the Bruce Highway (Route 1) at Johnston Road. Drive on an unpaved road for about a kilometer, following signs to the parking area. Gas stations on either side of the highway here offer free, regularly scheduled shuttle service to the lookout.

The trail climbs the "mountain" (really a hill) by means of a very steep paved road. Your views, limited at first to the surrounding state forest and cultivated fields, improve dramatically as you ascend, though you can never completely escape traffic noise from the Bruce Highway. The

123 meter (400 foot) high mountain was named after the wild horses that used to roam free here. At the top there is a shelter with interpretive signs and exhibits. In addition to the Glass House Mountains, you can see the Pacific coast near Bribie Island. Backtrack to your car.

KENILWORTH STATE FOREST: CONONDALE RANGE

About an hour's drive west of Noosa Heads rises the Conondale Range, now partly protected as a national park. As yet the park has no official walking trails; however, the Kenilworth State Forest lands adjacent to the national park have been developed for camping and hiking and have similar terrain. The Conondale region would not strike most hikers as spectacular, but it does offer pleasant walking and campsites that are extremely popular with local people, yet almost unknown to tourists. The hikes described here include attractive rainforest, creeks and falls, as well as a summit lookout.

Road access. From north or south travel the Bruce Highway (Route 1) to a point just north of Eumundi, then turn west at the Kenilworth sign. From Noosa one would reach the same point by driving to Eumundi, bearing right at the Kenilworth sign in that village, then crossing the Bruce Highway. Next, drive about 50 km (30 miles) west through the village of Kenilworth in the direction of Maleny. About 5 km (3 miles) past Kenilworth, look for the trailhead and parking area for the Fig Tree Walk, if you plan to do that one. The parking lot lies just past the Little Yabba Creek bridge.

For the other hikes, continue on down the road past the bridge for a few hundred meters, then turn right onto the Booloumba Creek Road (aka the Kenilworth Forestry Road). Specific hike directions given below will take their bearings from points along this gravel loop drive.

One can also reach the Conondale Range from Mapleton Falls or Kondalilla National Parks by driving down from the Blackall Range on the steep Obi Obi Road, which is reached by the directions given above for Mapleton Falls.

Finally, the road to and through Kenilworth goes all the way to Maleny, so it would provide convenient access from that end for those coming from the Glass House Mountains.

Camping. Kenilworth State Forest has four spacious campgrounds, located just off the Booloumba Creek Road about 6 km (3.75 miles) after the turnoff from the Kenilworth–Maleny Road. Choose whichever strikes your fancy.

In the area. Expansive views of the Glass House Mountains and the Pacific Ocean can be enjoyed from the tablelands near the state forest. The village of Mapleton, in particular, boasts fashionable restaurants and gift shops. The relative coolness of the area is an added attraction during the summer months.

1. Fig Tree Walk

Distance: 1.25 km (0.75 mile) round trip
Time: 20 minutes
Difficulty: easy
Attractions: enormous strangler figs

Start this easy stroll at the parking area along the Maleny–Kenilworth road as noted above. Walk across Little Yabba Creek Bridge to the trailhead, then head into beautiful rainforest on a gravel and boardwalk track that stays level all the way. The trail circles around one huge, ancient strangler fig, then winds past other rainforest giants, including the notorious stinging tree (gympie). Interpretive signs aid your understanding and enjoyment of this remnant rainforest at the confluence of the Mary River and Little Yabba Creek.

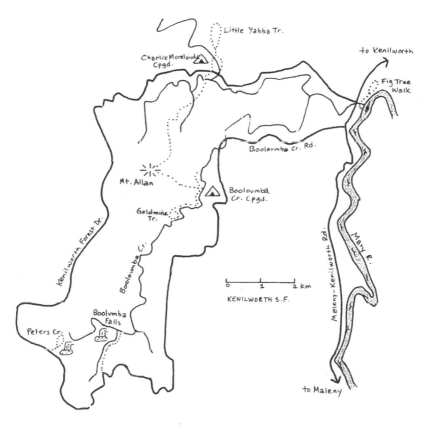

2. Gold Mine Walk

Distance: 5.25 km (2.5 miles) round trip
Time: 1.75 hours
Difficulty: easy
Attractions: rainforest and a historic mine

The Gold Mine Walk starts at camping area #2 (clearly marked as you drive through the state forest campground), although it has connector trails to campsites #1 and #3 as well. It ascends within 5 minutes to a junction with the Mt. Allan Trail (see below), but Gold Mine hikers stay left at this intersection. The trail soon drops into an especially attractive section of rainforest dominated by palms. Though heavily logged at one time, Kenilworth State Forest has not lost all its majestic trees. As the rainforest closes in, the trail meets Booloumba Creek and follows it for most of its "outbound" journey. Along the creek hikers occasionally enjoy views upstream and to nearby ridges. Near the end of the trail a short loop to the old gold mine departs. Stairs eventually lead up to the mine, which has been blocked off for safety reasons. It offers little to the eye but much to the imagination as one reflects on the immense difficulties that must have confronted the miners. The mine also provides lodging to 2 species of bat. Past the mine one completes the loop by a short stroll of 300 meters (0.2 mile). From that point on, hikers simply follow the same trail they used to walk up Booloumba Creek. Be sure to listen for bellbirds and wampoo pigeons in the forest.

3. Mt. Allan Track

Distance: 4 km (2.5 miles) round trip
Time: 2 or 2.5 hours
Difficulty: moderate
Attractions: forest scenery and views on top

Mt. Allan affords the finest views in the Conondales. A fire tower on top allows hikers to climb up above the trees and take in a 360° panorama that extends all the way to the old volcanic hills near Eumundi and Pomona, about 40 km (25 miles) distant.

To start this hike, locate either camping area #1 or #2 in the Kenilworth State Forest campground. The track up Mt. Allan branches off the Gold Mine Walk after about 0.5 km (0.3 mile), near Booloumba Creek and forges relentlessly uphill for another 1.5 km (1 mile), with only a brief respite along a ridge about an hour into the walk. At times hikers will be climbing or descending on a grade steep enough that footing can be treacherous. Exercise special care in wet weather. Because the trail passes mostly through open eucalypt forest, long vistas across nearby ridges occasionally present themselves.

Once you attain the summit and spend some time there, you can choose to descend a different way, along a 4.5 km (2.75 mile) trail to Charlie Moreland State Forest. But that option would entail return transportation problems at the end. Also, one could easily combine the Gold Mine and Mt. Allan tracks in one longer walk.

CANIA GORGE NATIONAL PARK

Above Moon Creek (Cania Gorge) in southeastern Queensland runs a buff colored escarpment incised by steep-walled Russell Gully. Cania Gorge National Park preserves the gully, another ravine on the far side of Moon Creek, and much of the escarpment top. Hikers will discover surprisingly many trails in the area, both within the park boundaries and on adjacent land. But the real gem of Cania Gorge National Park is Russell Gully. Its colorful, eroded sandstone walls tower above a verdant rainforest dominated by palms and tree ferns. Dripping springs and clear creeks, in combination with the shade of the forest, create an oasis-like atmosphere reminiscent of some of Carnarvon National Park's side canyons (see next section). As a bonus, campers at the nearby tourist park will get to enjoy plenty of wildlife: kangaroos, rufous betongs, and platypuses, plus abundant, varied birdlife. Cania Gorge, though not well-known, has much to offer visitors and makes a convenient stopover on the way to or from the Carnarvon/Blackdown Tableland region.

Road access. From Brisbane take the Bruce Highway (Route 1) north to a junction with the Wide Bay Highway just north of Gympie. Follow the Wide Bay to Kilkivan and continue to Goomeri, where you turn right (north) onto the Burnett Highway and drive about 250 km (155 miles) north to Monto. From there, follow the Moonford Cania Dam Road, a one-lane byway, another 13 km (8 miles) to the main picnic area and trailheads. You can also reach Cania Gorge from the north via Biloela and the Burnett Highway.

Camping. Since camping is not allowed in the national park, you might consider Cania Gorge Tourist Park. The owners provide a broad, un-crowded lawn for tents, hot showers, and sheltered cooking facilities. As noted, the attractions of this campground are the wild creatures that seem to show up regularly for handouts, especially the miniature walla-bies called betongs.

1. Dripping Rock/The Overhang

>Distance: 1.5 km (1 mile) round trip, plus sidetrips
>Time: 1.5 hours
>Difficulty: easy
>Attractions: colorful gorge walls, rainforest pockets

This short walk begins at the picnic area and leads to several beautiful spots around Russell Gully. You cross the creek and continue through open forest until reaching a sign directing you either up or down the gully. You can turn right and visit Dragon and Bloodwood Caves (they are actually more like alcoves), moderately interesting walks that take about a half hour round trip. Then, returning to the sign mentioned before, you can continue on upstream, deeper into Russell Gully. You reach a seep spring at Dripping Rock about 1 km (0.62 mile) from the picnic area. From there you have another 500 meters (0.3 mile) of spectacular walking, often on boardwalks along the cliff walls, to the Overhang, an alcove in a shady, palm and tree fern-lined section of the Gully. Notice the Aboriginal artwork—handprints and a snake—to your left on boulders. The aesthetic effect of the intense emerald green vegetation against the red-hued sandstone is unforgettable. Return as you came.

2. Ferntree Pool

Distance: 5 km (3 miles) round trip
Time: 1.5 hours
Difficulty: moderately easy
Attractions: eucalypt forest, a picturesque small pool

Less interesting than the previous hike but still enjoyable, the Ferntree Pool walk takes you through much drier country. You need to drive about 1 km (0.62 mile) south, in the direction of Monto, from the picnic area to find the trailhead. From there, the track follows Doctors Gully through a very open and sometimes hot eucalypt forest until reaching the pool. You see many species of ferns en route, especially as you near the pool, which is surrounded by them. The pool itself is usually quite still and reflects the ferns and small rock shelf behind it. In all this is a pleasant walk, well worth undertaking.

3. Platypus Walk

Distance: 600 meters (650 yards) round trip
Time: 30 minutes
Difficulty: easy
Attractions: possible platypus sightings, birdlife

This pleasant walk along Three Moon Creek starts across the road from the office at Cania Gorge Tourist Park. It descends on steps to the creek and follows the left bank closely, allowing access to spots where one might hope to see a platypus. Early morning and early evening present the most favorable opportunities for platypus viewing.

CARNARVON NATIONAL PARK

If you imagine the slot canyons of the American Southwest endowed with permanent streams, waterfalls, palms, and primeval ferns, you will form some idea of this park's special appeal. Carnarvon National Park actually includes four separate, very large sections, of which only the Carnarvon Gorge section is as yet easily accessible for ordinary cars. But if you have some extra time and money, by all means visit the other sections by 4-WD as well, for they reputedly have some real scenic gems. Below I will describe only hikes in and around the gorge.

About 200 million years ago, what is now central Queensland formed a shallow basin into which flowed sediment-laden streams from the surrounding country. These sediments eventually were transformed into sandstone, then capped by harder basalt from later volcanic eruptions. In time, uplifting and erosion created the Consuelo Tableland and the deep canyons that drain it, including Carnarvon Gorge and its tributary "slot" canyons. By American standards, Carnarvon's walls do not rise exceptionally high, but their whitish tint makes a beautiful backdrop for the deeper green of the large gum trees and casuarinas on the valley floor.

Yet the gorge itself pales in comparison with its side canyons, some of which narrow down so much that they receive sunlight for only a half hour per day. Then too, some of the tributary gorges have miniature waterfalls that photographers crowd around to shoot during those rare illuminated moments. As if the side canyons weren't enough, Carnarvon Gorge also preserves some first-class Aboriginal rock art sites, among the finest in eastern Australia. In short, this is not a park you want to miss, even though reaching it from the coast takes some time.

Road access. From Brisbane follow Route 2 (a freeway) toward Ipswich, then cut off onto the Warrego Highway, Route 54, toward Toowoomba. Follow the Warrego all the way to Roma (about a five-hour drive), then turn right (north) on the Carnarvon Developmental Road. Follow this often narrow, one lane road for about 200 km (125 miles) and turn left on the signposted park access road. After 45 km (28 miles), about half of it paved, you reach the main campground.

From points north, follow the Carnarvon Developmental road south from Emerald via Springsure and Rolleston to the park turnoff. The last 75 km (46.5 miles) of that road had not yet been paved as of this writing.

Camping. The Carnarvon Gorge campground has about 80 sites but can still fill up completely during school holidays and some weekends. By all means, reserve a spot in advance if you plan to visit at these popular times. The campground has only cold showers, but a few sites do have tables. Also, you must bring your own firewood, as the park provides none and forbids gathering any. If you book ahead, you might request one of the sites that has a picnic table.

You can also camp at a lovely backcountry site about 10 km (6.2 miles) upcanyon known as "Big Bend." A platypus inhabits the rock pool nearby, emerging at dawn and dusk. Spending at least one night at Big Bend would give you adequate time to walk up the gorge and explore its many side canyons. Otherwise, you would face an almost 20 km (12.5 mile) hike, not counting trips to the rock art sites and tributaries: too much to attempt in a single day without rushing.

In a pinch you can buy gasoline and a few supplies from the Oasis Lodge, 3 km (1.75 miles) from the campground. Remember that water from Carnarvon Creek must be purified; otherwise, fill up canteens at the campground and carry along all you will need.

1. Mickey Creek/Warrumba Gorge

Distance: about 4 km (2.5 miles) round trip
Time: 1.5 hours
Difficulty: moderately easy, with some scrambling
Attractions: deep, narrow, verdant gorges

The two branches of this Carnarvon Creek tributary make an excellent short hike. From the campground drive about 1.5 km (1 mile) back up the park road to reach the signposted trailhead on your right. Mickey Creek is a pleasant canyon with a flowing stream, but its neighbor, Warrumbah, will impress most visitors even more. It is a very narrow slot, similar to some in Arizona or Utah, but lined with palms and tree ferns. Like other Carnarvon side canyons, Warrumbah receives little direct sunlight, so if you want to see it illuminated, plan to be there around

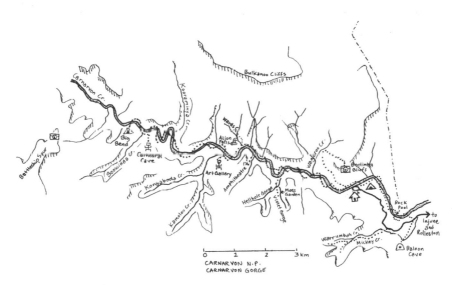

noon. In some places Warrumbah narrows so much that you can touch both walls with outstretched arms. The hike route leads out along Mickey Creek for perhaps 1 km (0.62 mile), at which point the canyon forks and you simply walk up each branch in turn. Mickey is the left fork and Warrumbah the right. Return the way you came.

2. Baloon Cave

Distance: 1 km (0.62 mile) round trip
Time: 20 minutes
Difficulty: easy
Attractions: rock art and informative trailside plaques

Baloon Cave shelters some fine Aboriginal rock art, though these drawings cannot match the panels in Carnarvon Gorge itself. To see it you drive back about 2 km (1.25 miles) from the campground to a signed trailhead to the right of the road. Walk through a landscape of primitive-looking macrozamia plants, pausing to

Carnarvon Gorge

read the interesting comments on Aboriginal culture and the uses the original inhabitants made of local flora. At the panel you will find mainly stenciled handprints. Return as you came.

3. Rock Pool

Distance: 600 meters (650 yards) round trip from carpark, or 4 km (2.5 miles) round trip from main campground
Time: 10 minutes from carpark, or 1 hour from campground
Difficulty : easy
Attractions: a great swimming hole

The rock pool is exactly what its name suggests: a large natural pool below an immense boulder, deep enough for swimming and having its own little sand beach. If you just want to swim, walk down from the signed carpark on the left side of the road about 1 km back up the road from the campground. The trail descends slightly to a picnic area, crossing the creek on rocks and veering to the right to intersect the pool. Alternatively, you can stroll down to the pool from the campground and enjoy the bird and animal life in this quiet stretch of Carnarvon Gorge.

4. Nature Trail

Distance: 1.25 km (0.75 miles) one way
Time: 15 minutes
Difficulty: easy
Attractions: platypuses and kangaroos

This pleasant, level trail starts immediately after the first stream crossing of the main track through Carnarvon Gorge. Turning right here, follow the creek downstream past beaches and platypus-viewing platforms. Your chances of seeing a platypus are greatest at dawn and dusk, when they feed. The trail ends at the far side of the campground. Loop back to your car.

5. Boolimba Bluff

Distance: 6.5 km (4 miles) round trip
Time: 2 hours
Difficulty: difficult
Attractions: views up and down Carnarvon Gorge

This trail, much less traveled than others in the park, begins at the kiosk near the ranger station at the far side of the campground. Coterminous at first with the main track up Carnarvon Gorge, it splits off to the right after the first stream crossing. The trail climbs gradually as it laterals to the left, paralleling the creek.

At about the halfway point, you begin a very steep climb between two cliff faces. There are countless stairs here, and even some ladders to assist you in the ascent. Strategically located benches along the way permit hikers to relax and catch their breath.

Near the top of the bluff, the trail levels off and laterals to the right, through a grassy area. It then reaches a fenced overlook about 200 meters (650 feet) above the campground in the main canyon. Expansive views in all directions are enjoyed here.

Sunrise and sunset are the ideal times to undertake this trip. Return as you came.

6. Carnarvon Gorge

Distance: 19.5 km (12 miles) round trip, plus sidetrips
Time: one to two days
Difficulty: moderate
Attractions: outstanding rock art, narrow and lush gorges,
    birdlife and marsupials

This classic hike begins at the kiosk to the right of Park Headquarters, near which you leave your car. If you do it as an overnighter, you must first obtain a camping and parking permit.

You cross the creek almost immediately, the first of twenty numbered crossings. At normal water levels, all crossings are unproblematic, involving straightforward rock hopping. In the first few kilometers, you walk through relatively dry, open forest in which spotted blue gums, macrozamia, and river casuarinas (or "river oaks") predominate. The trees tend to conceal the gorge walls from view in this section. At km 3.5 (mile 2.25), about 40 minutes from the campground, you reach a side trail of about 1.5 km (1 mile) round trip to Violet and Hellhole Gorges. The former, a renowned beauty spot, contains the "Moss Garden," a cliff face festooned with greenery. But the entire grotto forms an oasis of tranquility and grace with its tiny falls, pool, and tree ferns. Hellhole Gorge has a rough trail, mostly on its right bank. Though no match for Violet Gorge scenically, it is an attractive and secluded spot with several pools and falls along the way.

Continuing to km 4 (mile 2.5), you arrive at a junction with a spur to the Amphitheater, a reputedly spectacular side gorge that has been closed in the recent past because of flood damage to a viewing platform. Visiting the Amphitheater requires climbing a ladder.

Ten minutes farther, on the right side of Carnarvon Gorge, you encounter, at km 4.75 (mile 3), the side trail to Wards Canyon and Aljon Falls. Don't miss this captivating detour. You climb steeply past Lower Aljon Falls, a very scenic cascade, then enter a shady slot canyon that shelters tree ferns as well as the rare and primitive angiopteris or king fern, with fronds that may reach 5 meters (15 feet) long. Beyond the king ferns you peer into a narrow fissure at the back of which gushes beautiful Upper Aljon Falls. The waterfall is in shade for all but about 20 minutes in the middle of the day.

By this point the walls of Carnarvon Gorge have begun to close in, permitting you to appreciate their height and form. Between crossings 10 and 11, about 5.5 km (3.5 miles) from the campground, you come to a 750 meter long (0.5 mile) spur trail ascending to the "Art Gallery," the first of two major Aboriginal rock art sites. Its drawings portray items of everyday use and handprints all "stenciled" or outlined in red or ochre pigment. Opposite the Art Gallery, enormous cliffs tower above the trail, full of the chatter of pied currawongs that have colonized the clifftops.

Beyond the Art Gallery turnoff, the gorge narrows even more and creek crossings become more frequent. At km 7.5 (mile 4.75) you reach Kurraminya Creek, a tributary on the right. You can explore it for a kilometer or more. It has some nice narrows, though to reach them you must "bush bash" for about 150 meters, as there is no trail here. Stay left of the creek at first, then cross it after you reach a place with three fallen logs. You will then discern a faint trail on the right. Follow it up until the rock terrace you are walking on pinches out, then cross to the left and follow a clear path up past a boulder. Beyond this point walking grows easier.

Back on the main trail, you reach Cathedral Cave at km 9.25 (mile 5.75). This extensive rock art panel resembles the Art Gallery, but has some unique elements, including one strange stencil of arms with hands at both ends. Just past Cathedral Cave, rocky Boowinda Gorge enters from the left. It has outstanding narrows for the first 1 km or so and affords a route to ascend Battleship Spur. To reach Big Bend campsite, cross Boowinda Creek's delta, then cross Carnarvon Creek itself. On the right bank a sign will direct you 400 meters to the campground, situated below an alcove at km 9.75 (mile 6). It has an outhouse, a pool with a resident platypus, and an air of remoteness. The campground has only 10 sites, so it should never become too crowded. You return on the same trail. But remember that light conditions in the side gorges may now be quite different from what they were a few hours before, so a second visit to some of them might prove rewarding.

BLACKDOWN TABLELAND NATIONAL PARK

Like Carnarvon, its better-known neighbor, Blackdown Tableland National Park is part of the Central Highlands Sandstone Belt. The park protects a high, remote plateau that rises over 500 meters (1650 feet) above the surrounding plains. This plateau is bounded by rugged cliffs on its eastern flank and crisscrossed by deep canyons. Sweeping vistas are enjoyed from the rim. Aborigines once roamed the area, and one of the hikes featured below allows visitors to view their rock art. Although the park does contain lush, moist pockets that harbor tree ferns and palms, the vegetation here is mainly eucalypt. Rare plant species are also found here. Trails in the park tend to be short, leading to waterfalls or lookouts.

Road access. Access to Blackdown Tableland is from the Capricorn Highway (Route 66) 2.5 hours west of Rockhampton, Queensland. The road into the park leaves the highway 11 km (6.75 miles) west of the town of Dingo, or 35 km (22 miles) east of Blackwater. It is 20 km (12.5 miles) to the park boundary, including a steep 4 km (2.5 mile) climb, and another 8 kms (5 miles) to the campground. Be warned that the road is gravel and dirt, with bone-rattling washboards. Drive slowly and carefully to avoid losing control of your vehicle. In inclement weather, the road could be hazardous and is not recommended.

Camping. Mimosa Campground, with about 30 sites, is located just off the main park road. Set in a shady, forested area, it has outhouses, fire pits, and even some picnic tables. Because cattle grazed in the park in years past, the water is not potable unless it is boiled or filtered, and it may be easier simply to bring your own supply. Camping reservations are recommended for school holidays and long weekends; write to The

to Dingo

Peregrine Lkt.

Charlevue Lkt.

Horseshoe Lkt.

Two Mile Falls

Loop Rd. (4WD)

Stony Cr. → Falls

Art Shelter

Officers Pocket

Mimosa Cr. Cpgd.

Loop Rd. (4WD)

Mimosa Cr.

0   1   2   3 km

BLACKDOWN TABLELAND N.P.

Rock Holes

Rainbow Falls

Ranger, Blackdown Tableland National Park, c/o Dingo, Qld. 4702, or call (079) 86-1964.

1. Mimosa Culture Circuit

Distance: 2 km (1.25 miles), round trip
Time: 45 minutes
Difficulty: easy
Attractions: granite formations, interpretive signs, rock art

The loop hike begins near campsite #28 at the back of Mimosa Campground. Proceeding upstream along Mimosa Creek, you visit granite "mushrooms" and balanced rocks on the way to an Aboriginal pictograph panel, which is located beneath an overhang. The panel contains red handprints created through a stenciling technique in which dye was blown from the artist's mouth. In addition, the trail acquaints hikers with a slice of the history of white settlement, as it passes by old cattle yards. Beautiful orange gum trees with their bark stripped off add to the enchantment of this hike, and boardwalks help hikers navigate wet spots along the route.

2. Officers Pocket

Distance: 2.5 km (1.5 miles) round trip
Time: 45 minutes
Difficulty: easy
Attractions: overlook

The trail starts across the main park road from the campground. It descends gently to Mimosa Creek through a forest dominated by stringy-bark trees and other eucalypti. After crossing the creek at about km 1 (mile 0.62), the trail ascends gradually, with the aid of some steps, to a fenced overlook of a high-walled sandstone gorge. Giant granite boulders along the way contribute to the allure of the hike. Backtrack to your car.

3. Rainbow Falls

Distance: 4 km (2.5 miles) round trip
Time: 1.5 hours
Difficulty: easy to Rock Holes; moderate to Rainbow Falls
Attractions: waterfall, pools with eels, erosional forms

Pick up this interesting track at the end of the park road. The trail passes through forest, arriving at an overlook on the lip of a gorge at km 1.25 (mile 0.75). It follows the rim around to the right and then forks. The right fork, which is mostly level, soon swings around to Rock Holes, above the falls, where the creekbed has eroded into fascinating and unusual shapes. There are small waterfalls here and many small but very deep pools in which to cool off, and you can walk up the stream a few hundred meters if you wish.

Back at the junction, the left fork descends on almost 250 steps to a point near the base of impressive Rainbow Falls. The track ends near pools inhabited by large freshwater eels. Beyond the trail's end, you can carefully pick your way a short distance downstream to view, on the left, a grotto with hanging gardens. Unfortunately, because of the steepness of the terrain and the slipperiness of the rock, the grotto is not accessible, and you must turn around here. Retrace your steps to the parking lot.

4. Two-Mile Falls

Distance: 3 km (1.75 miles) round trip
Time: 45 minutes
Difficulty: moderately easy
Attractions: waterfall, scenic vistas

The trip to Two-Mile Falls is one of several that begin just inside the park boundary, along the main road. From the carpark, head up the short trail to Horseshoe Lookout. A few meters before the lookout, your track branches off to the left. Hugging the cliff, it reaches Sunset Lookout in about 300 meters. Both lookouts offer expansive views of Blackdown's sandstone cliffs. The trail then descends gradually through woodlands and crosses the creek, on a bridge, to a fenced overlook. From here you can see the falls and their plunge pool. Along the way to the waterfall, the trail passes a small, picturesque grotto on the left. The creekside environment above the falls is also quite attractive, and you may see picnickers relaxing here. Return as you came.

5. Peregrine Lookout

Distance: 2.5 km (1.5 miles), round trip
Time: 45 minutes
Difficulty: moderately easy
Attractions: heathscape, scenic views

Like the hike to Two-Mile Falls, this trail commences near Horseshoe Lookout. A few meters before you reach that lookout, turn right at a junction. The trail passes through banksia and grass tree vegetation. Initially it descends a bit, but most of the way it is level. Because the trail closely parallels the rim of the escarpment all the way to Peregrine Lookout, you attain sublime views that take in both the valley 500 meters (1650 feet) below and faraway mountains. The drama of the area near the lookout is enhanced by granite boulders. Return as you came.

Chapter 7

THE FAR NORTH

Queensland's far north offers visitors a rare combination: pristine rainforests skirting the state's highest peaks and, only a few kilometers away, picture-postcard beaches, tropical islands, and the Great Barrier Reef. The Great Dividing Range rises near the tip of the remote Cape York Peninsula and hugs the coast closely for nearly 700 km (430 miles). In a few spots, like Cape Tribulation, rainforest-clad mountains slope right down into the Coral Sea. Meanwhile, the Great Barrier Reef pinches in toward the coast as it continues northward; near Cape Tribulation it lies only about 20 km (12.5 miles) offshore, within easy reach of fast tour boats. So, if you want to combine undersea adventures with rainforest hiking, you will find the perfect locale in Far North Queensland.

Here, as well, visitors to Australia will encounter the "wet tropics," preserved in World Heritage sites strung out along the coast for hundreds of kilometers. The rainforests of this region will exceed almost anyone's expectations. Visitors will discover enormous rainforest trees sustained by massive buttress roots, lianas weighing tons weaving among the forest giants, fan palms, cassowaries, tree kangaroos, and fearsome crocodiles lurking in sluggish rivers. Because the environment of the wet tropics has changed little over millions of years, it affords a sort of window that reveals the ecology of earlier ages of the earth.

However, visitors should recognize and prepare for certain vicissitudes in exploring far north Queensland. Much of the rainforest has been cleared, so you will see only the remnants protected in national parks. These offer lush, exotic beauty but relatively few hiking trails on which to savor it, at least compared to the Scenic Rim to the south. Disappointingly, this chapter will often describe trails of only a few kilometers in vast national parks, because as yet no others have been built. Hinchinbrook Island marks the great exception, with its long Thorsborne Trail, one of the continent's classic hikes.

Moreover, seasonal weather patterns affect the north much more than the south of tropical Australia. Don't come here in the wet season (December to March) unless you are willing to hazard steady rain for days on end, mud, mosquitoes, leeches, temperatures of around 35° C (95° F), and deadly box jellyfish lurking in the ocean. The Far North will please most visitors much more during the cooler months. It should remain relatively dry throughout June, July, and August, disregarding an

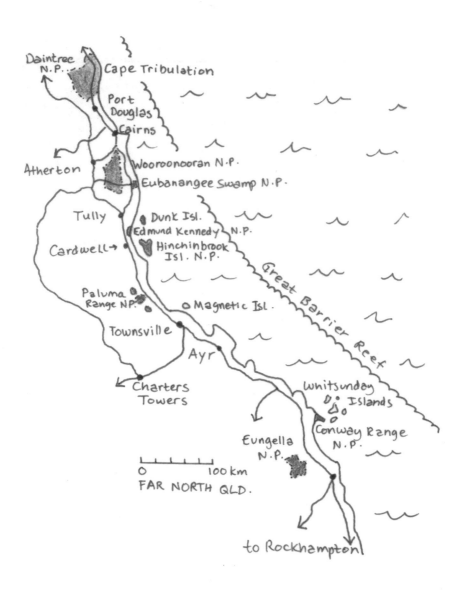

occasional showery front. Remember, too, that you cannot expect to step off the beach and swim out to the Great Barrier Reef. Even from the closest points to it, such as Port Douglas or Cape Tribulation, you must undertake a fairly long and costly boat trip to see it. But don't hesitate, for the crystal clear water and diverse marine life will make the journey worthwhile.

Finally, what I am calling the northern tropics follows Route 1 and its extension, the Cook Highway, up a long, narrow coastal strip reaching from Eungella National Park near MacKay to Daintree National Park north of Port Douglas. Allow ample time to travel the long distances on this two-lane road and to detour into nearby parks. And expect to accumulate plenty of kilometers on your rental car. Still, all cautions aside, no one should miss this wildly beautiful and exotic region. Few other countries have managed to make ancient rainforests so accessible while preserving them so assiduously as Australia.

EUNGELLA NATIONAL PARK

Eungella has arguably the finest rainforest walks in the wet tropics. It preserves a wide swath of the 1200 meter (4000 foot) high Clarke Range, in which grows some of the most luxuriant vegetation you will encounter anywhere. The piccabeen palm groves, especially, will enchant hikers. Then too, Eungella shelters some of the least shy platypuses in Australia. This is one of the few places where you can almost always spot one, though the glimpse may be fleeting. But be warned: even in the dry season this park seems prone to long spells of drizzle, fog, and chilly winds. Expect some rain and perhaps cold nights even in the normally dry, sunny winter months. In the summer, of course, rain may fall almost every day, so you should bring protection against the elements as well as against the numerous thirsty leeches that thrive on wet weather. We donated a lot of blood to them at this park.

In spite of such nuisances, Eungella has become one of the country's more popular parks, so expect company on trails and in the campgrounds.

Road access. From the Bruce Highway (Route 1) near Mackay, turn off at signs for Marian, Mirani, and/or the park itself. Follow the road through the Pioneer Valley for almost 90 km (55 miles) to reach park headquarters at the Broken River. If you want to hike in the Finch Hatton Gorge section of the park, turn off at a signposted junction just before entering the village of Finch Hatton. Drive 12 km (7.5 miles), sometimes across shallow streams and causeways, to the parking area. After really heavy rains, the road up to Finch Hatton Gorge may be impassable.

Camping. Eungella has two campgrounds, but by far the better one is Fern Flats, just past the headquarters building. It resembles an American national park campground in having individual, numbered sites, each with a picnic table. The park also provides hot showers, firewood, and barbecue grills. Immediately before crossing the Broken River bridge, you will notice another campground, really just a grassy clearing for tents. Most people would choose this one only if Fern Flats had filled up. The Finch Hatton Gorge section has no campground, but there is a low-key hostel ("backpackers' resort") on its access road.

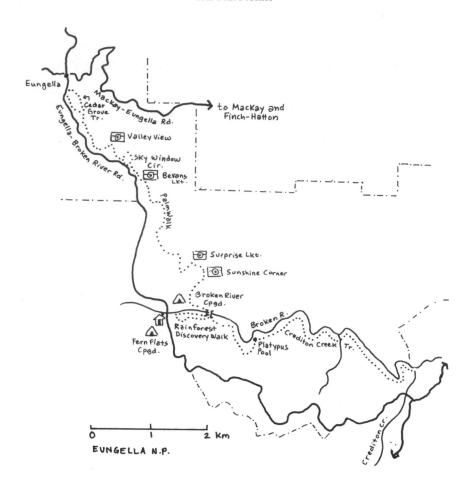

EUNGELLA N.P.

1. Palm Walk

Distance: 6.75 km (4.25 miles), plus roadwalk of 2.75 km (1.75 miles) to make a loop
Time: 3 hours
Difficulty: moderately easy
Attractions: spectacular rainforest and views of Pioneer Valley

To reach the trailhead from the Broken River bridge, drive 2.75 km (1.75 miles) down the road and park at a marked turnout. Coming from down in the valley, you would drive about 300 meters past the Sky Window turnout and look for the Palm Walk sign.

The trail meanders along a steep wall of the gorge through which flows the Broken River. Although the trail never departs very far from the road, the rainforest muffles traffic sounds so effectively that you feel miles away from all civilization. You ascend the entire way toward a rendezvous with the Broken River higher up, but the ascent is so gradual that you barely notice it. However, you do notice the exquisite rainforest trees all around you, especially the piccabeen and vine palms from which the trail takes its name. These look even more ethereal when, as is usual, drifting curtains of mist alternately obscure and reveal them.

Along the walk, you will have no trouble finding the way. There is a junction that comes at km 1 (mile 0.62) where a side trail leads back to the road. Beyond there you simply follow the trail until it finally crosses a low ridge and drops into a tributary valley leading down to and across the Broken River. En route you will enjoy occasional views down into the Pioneer Valley from cleared lookouts. The last two, Surprise Lookout and Sunshine Corner, have especially fine vistas. On the far side of the Broken River, the Palm Walk merges with the return leg of the Rainforest Discovery Walk, which takes hikers right along the river and past some excellent platypus pools. If you happen to reach this point near dusk, observe the scene quietly and you may see one of these elusive creatures. Otherwise, come back at dusk or dawn and search for them along here or from the Broken River bridge. They don't stay on the surface of the water for long, so you need to keep your eyes peeled.

After you finish the on-trail section of the hike, cross the Broken River and walk down to your car, an easy stroll along the edge of the forest.

2. Araluen Falls/Wheel of Fire Falls

> **Distance: 5 km (3 miles) round trip**
> **Time: 2 hours for both trails**
> **Difficulty: moderately easy**
> **Attractions: great rainforest, cascades and deep pools fine for swimming**

Following the road access directions given above, you begin this hike at the Finch Hatton Gorge parking area. The trail climbs moderately through tall rainforest that resounds with the calls of wampoo pigeons. After about 1 km (0.62 mile) you reach a Y intersection; the left fork heads down 400 meters (0.25 mile) to Araluen Falls, a powerful, though not extremely high, cascade.

Returning to the main trail, you now take the right fork, walking uphill, often either on stone steps or boardwalks, and passing several lovely falls. About 1 km past the fork, you arrive at Wheel of Fire Falls, with its inviting pool set amid lush rainforest. All of the falls along Finch Hatton Creek have a very large volume of water flowing over them even during the dry season; thus, you will not likely be disappointed no matter what time of year you visit. Return on the same track.

CONWAY NATIONAL PARK

Most of this huge, heavily wooded park remains inaccessible to the public. However, a few trails near the tourist town of Airlie Beach offer splendid panoramas of ocean, the Whitsunday Islands, and mainland mountains. You won't see the rainforest portions of Conway here; for that, an expensive guided tour is required. But you will enjoy a fine walk through coastal forest with superb grass tree specimens all around.

Road access. Take the Bruce Highway (Route 1) 1 km (0.62 mile) past Proserpine, then follow signs to Airlie Beach, 26 km (16 miles) away. The trail described here begins at a rough carpark about 7 km (4.25 miles) past Airlie Beach, on the road to Shute Harbor. Look for signs on the left side of the road.

Camping. The Flame Tree Caravan Park between Airlie Beach and Shute Harbor is probably the best bet. It offers a separate section for tents and a swimming pool, but, alas, no picnic tables at the individual sites. It does have sheltered outdoor kitchens though, so you can always use the tables there as well as the cooking facilities.

In the area. Most people use Airlie Beach and Shute Harbor as jumping off points for excursions out to the Whitsunday Islands. You will find a variety of island trips offered by Airlie Beach tour operators, some to uninhabited national park islands or resorts, others clear out to the Great Barrier Reef. If you have the time, by all means try to embark on one of these excursions. You can camp at designated sites on several of the Whitsunday Islands, most notably Hook, though not all have water. Otherwise, you could choose from among a variety of resort accommodations ranging from campgrounds to ultra deluxe suites.

1. Mt. Rooper

> **Distance: 6.5 km (4 miles) round trip, not including spur**
> **Time: 1.5 hours**
> **Difficulty: moderately easy**
> **Attractions: views of the Whitsunday Islands**

The Mt. Rooper Trail alone does not warrant a special trip to Airlie Beach. However, if you are planning a sojourn to the Whitsunday Islands, this hike makes a pleasant introduction to the area.

The trail begins at a makeshift, sometimes muddy parking area next to Shute Harbor. You may spot some interesting water birds in this area. The trail strikes off into the low, open forest and quickly begins a switchbacking ascent of the "mountain" (220 meters or 725 feet high). The well-graded trail makes walking easy, but the relentless ascent could fatigue some people. By all means carry enough water, because the warm

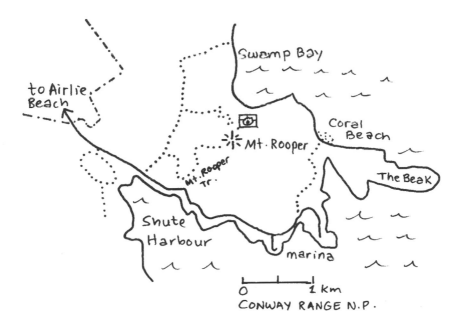

climate and sunny, open forest will wring a lot of perspiration out of you. After about 45 minutes, you will reach a platform from which views extend over much of the southern Whitsunday group. Hamilton Island should be easy to identify by its highrise resorts. With a decent map you should be able to pick out several more, including huge Whitsunday Island, Hook Island, and the Molle group.

Descending from the summit, take time to admire the idiosyncratic forms of the many grass trees growing trailside. About 2 km (1.25 miles) from the summit, you reach a spur trail to Swamp Bay, a mediocre beach with lots of coral rubble around, at least at low tide. If that holds no attractions, turn left and you will arrive back at the parking area in just a few minutes.

PALUMA RANGE NATIONAL PARK

Two formerly separate parks north of Townsville, Mt. Spec and Jourama Falls, have been consolidated into Paluma Range National Park. Both sections contain short but scenic trails. This part of Queensland is somewhat drier than lands to the north, and visitors will notice striking differences between the two sections. Low-lying Jourama Falls tumbles past open eucalypt forest that becomes desiccated and hot during the dry season. By contrast, the top of the Paluma Range, 1000 meters (3300 feet) high, receives triple the amount of precipitation as the lowlands. It boasts superb stands of rainforest, frequently mist-shrouded in summer. Both sections offer good opportunities to observe wildlife, especially around camp-grounds. The Paluma Range has been World Heritage listed since 1989.

Road Access. Detailed for each section below.

Camping. You can camp either at Big Crystal Creek Campground below the crest of the Paluma Range or at Jourama Falls. The former is very popular, so a site might need to be reserved. Call (07) 4770-8526. The Jourama Falls sites, about 20 in all, provide a few picnic tables, but no hot showers or wood. The campground lacks deep shade and could become very hot at certain times of the year.

Season. Any except summer.

In the area. The city of Townsville, located in the so-called "dry tropics" zone just south of here, maintains several trails in its popular Town Common Conservation Park. Birdwatching is a favorite activity in the common. Nearby Magnetic Island, reached via a short ferryboat ride from the Townsville docks, is also crisscrossed with hiking trails, mostly through scrubby, upland terrain. However, visitors may find the island's beaches to be more appealing, particularly in hot weather.

1. Paluma Range Lookouts

Distance: 4.25 km (2.75 miles) round trip
Time: 1.5 hours
Difficulty: moderately easy
Attractions: rainforest, extensive panoramas over the coast

Whitsunday Islands from Mt. Rooper's summit

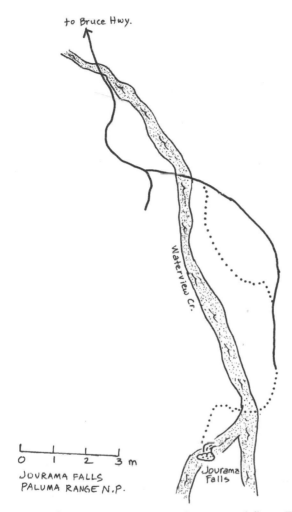

to Bruce Hwy.

Waterview Cr.

JOURAMA FALLS
PALUMA RANGE N.P.

0   1   2   3 m

Jourama
Falls

Travel Route 1, the Bruce Highway, 42 km (26 miles) south of Ingham. Turn off westward onto a secondary highway, then go left at signs for the Paluma Range onto a narrow, winding road that snakes up the mountainside. A right at this point will take you to Big Crystal Creek Campground. Don't expect to average more than about 30–35 km (20 miles) per hour on this tortuous byway. After about 18 km (11 miles) you reach the parking lot for McClellands Lookout, where the trail commences.

From a nearby picnic area the trail winds for 600 meters (650 yards) through tropical upland rainforest to Benham Lookout. This section of trail has identifying signs for tropical flora. From Benham, backtrack a bit to find the trail to Witts Lookout, which actually has upper and lower viewpoints. From both you gaze out over the flat coastal plain of northern Queensland out to the Pacific. Coastal islands, including Great Palm, Curacoa, Orpheus, and Havannah, float on the horizon far away. At the lookout you will have walked 1.5 km (1 mile) of easy trail. Studying the trail junction for Witts Lookout, you will notice another trail, continuing straight ahead into the rainforest. The latter has no sign or indication of its destination, but it leads to Cloudy Creek Falls, a delightful spot about 1.2 km (0.75 mile) past Witts. The falls has two drops and some nice, open rock where you can sit, eat a picnic lunch, and enjoy the idyllic surroundings. The last section of trail to Cloudy Creek descends quite a bit, often on stairs, and thus requires a slightly tiring return journey; hence it rates as only moderately easy.

2. *Jourama Falls*

Distance: 2.5 km (1.5 miles) round trip to main lookout
Time: 45 minutes
Difficulty: moderately easy
Attractions: a series of graceful falls, one very high

Follow the Bruce Highway 24 km (15 miles) south from Ingham, then turn off at a sign for the falls and continue 6 km (3.75 miles) farther on a fair gravel road to the campground and parking lot.

The short trail to Jourama Falls climbs steeply for much of its length, but other than that should pose few problems for walkers. It starts at the end of the road that curves past the campground. From the parking area you cross Waterview Creek and walk about 600 meters (650 yards) to a large rock pool fed by the lowest cascade in the Jourama series. Swimming keeps many hikers occupied at the pool for quite a while. Past it, the trail climbs in earnest to a lookout over several more of the cascades that make up Jourama Falls. They do not always have a great volume of water in them, but their combined drop of about 300 meters (1000 feet) should impress anyone. The setting of the falls, with much exposed rock in their gorge, has great visual appeal as well. However, in certain seasons, controlled burning blackens the landscape around Jourama Falls, which may detract from your enjoyment of the hike. Finally, note that an unmarked spur trail heads off to the right near the main lookout and eventually reaches yet another viewpoint of the falls and creek. Return as you came.

HINCHINBROOK ISLAND NATIONAL PARK

Hinchinbrook Island is separated from the mainland by a narrow channel extending north from Lucinda to Cardwell, yet it seems a world apart when you have once arrived there. Its towering peaks and ridges (Mt. Bowen, the Thumb) are shrouded in cloud for much of the day, giving it a "lost world" feel. Below the serrated ridgetops runs a trail that many consider the finest in tropical Australia: the Thorsborne Trail, named after a local conservationist who fought to preserve this magnificent island.

Indeed, the Thorsborne Trail is so popular that the QNPWS has imposed strict limits on the number of people who may hike it at any one time. Therefore, if you want to hike this track, you must plan far ahead, possibly getting reservations months in advance. And you may have to preserve some flexibility in your dates so that the park service can accommodate you under its daily permit system. Once you have reservations in place, the next step is to set up transportation to and from the island and back to your car. You can easily arrange this by acting on the information supplied below.

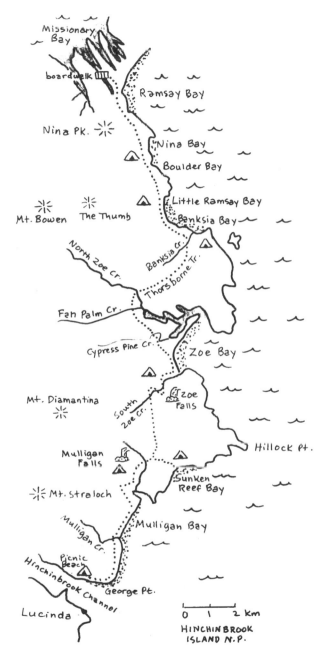

Missionary Bay
boardwalk
Ramsay Bay
Nina Pk.
Nina Bay
Boulder Bay
Mt. Bowen   The Thumb   Little Ramsay Bay
Banksia Bay
North Zoe Cr.   Banksia Cr.
Thorsborne Tr.
Fan Palm Cr.
Cypress Pine Cr.
Zoe Bay
Mt. Diamantina   South Zoe Cr.   Zoe Falls
Hillock Pt.
Mulligan Falls
Sunken Reef Bay
Mt. Straloch
Mulligan Cr.   Mulligan Bay
Picnic Beach
Hinchinbrook Channel   George Pt.
Lucinda

0   1   2 km

HINCHINBROOK
ISLAND N.P.

Road and boat access. To reach Hinchinbrook Island you must first set
up boat transportation from either Cardwell or Lucinda. Both towns are
located roughly halfway between Townsville and Innisfail. Cardwell is
directly on the Bruce Highway (Route 1), about 95 km (59 miles) south
of Innisfail. Lucinda is a small seaside village 13 km (8 miles) off Route 1

and just west of Ingham, a town 109 km (68 miles) north of Townsville. After you have obtained your camping permit, along with an official detailed map, contact the water taxi operators in either town. The Lucinda operator is:

> Trek Hinchinbrook Island
> PO Box 43
> Lucinda, QLD 4850
> Phone: (07) 4777-8307

The water taxi operators cooperate with each other. They will take care of water transportation to or from their own end of the hike and will transport you by road either to your starting point or back to your car when you have completed the hike. For example, you could leave your car in Lucinda and then be driven north to Cardwell, from which the Cardwell operator would take you to the north end of the island by boat and deposit you at the start of the Thorsborne Trail. Then, when you reached the trail's end near George Point in the south, the Lucinda operator would pick you up and return you to your car. All of this shuttling around can get expensive and complicated, but the hike is worth it.

Camping. The Thorsborne Trail has several designated sites, all with restrictions on the number of campers. You need to study the map and consult the suggestions given in this guide in order to decide how many nights to spend and exactly which sites to choose. You may want to spend more than one night at some sites just to relax and do some freelance exploring. Once you have made up your mind, contact park officials as follows:

> Queensland Department of Environment and Heritage
> Bruce Highway
> PO Box 74
> Cardwell, QLD 4816
> Phone: (07) 4066-8601

Or:

> Queensland Department of Environment and Heritage
> Canegrowers Building
> 11–13 Lannercost Street
> PO Box 1293
> Ingham, QLD 4850
> Phone: (07) 4776-1700
> Fax: (07) 4776-3770

Do not be surprised if your chosen dates and/or sites are not available. As noted earlier, flexibility may pay off in securing camping permits for the Thorsborne.

One final remark about camping on the Thorsborne Trail concerns bushrats. These pesky critters like to raid packs and steal food, so the park service has installed "ratboxes" at most of the main campsites. These metal boxes will keep your food safe during the night when rats are about.

Season. Best times would be from May through October, although the spring months often bring controlled burning.

1. Thorsborne Trail

Distance: 32 km (20 miles)
Time: 3–4 days at minimum; longer if you have time
Difficulty: moderately difficult
Attractions: magnificent coastal scenery, rainforests, swamps,
    waterfalls, deserted beaches, a truly remote and unspoiled
    wilderness

If you cross over from Cardwell to Hinchinbrook's north end, the taxi operator will usher you into the park's visitor center, where you must watch a short video on camping etiquette. Then you depart on a very scenic boat trip (with commentary) of approximately 1.5 hours. En route you will enjoy great views of Hinchinbrook's serrated peaks as well as of Goold Island and the Brook group. The boat will cross Missionary Bay, thread its way through narrow channels, and arrive at a small dock amid mangroves at about 10 A.M., which leaves you most of the day for hiking.

From the dock follow a boardwalk over to Ramsay Bay's beach, a long expanse of golden sand. Turn right and walk up the beach to a small saddle, where you will find the trail to the right of a black granite rock. Follow it on down to the middle of Blacksand Beach, behind which water is usually available except in the August to December period.

Walk south down the beach until you spot three melaleuca trees with an orange marker on them. The trail recommences here and winds inland amid coastal forest until crossing a saddle below Nina Peak. Some hikers drop packs and climb Nina Peak, a difficult proposition, especially in hot weather.

After about 1 or 2 hours you reach Nina Bay 4.5 km (2.75 miles) from the start. Nina Beach may be the loveliest of Hinchinbrook's many fine strands. It features pleasant campsites and water up a creek toward the south end of the bay. From the beach and especially the shallows just offshore, you gain amazing views of misty Mt. Bowen and the main ridge of the island. The only drawback to camping here is that, if you can spend only 3 nights on the island, you would be left with 2 days of hard slogging. An ideal plan would perhaps include a night at Nina Bay and 3 more at other campsites farther on. But assuming you intend to push on for 2.5 km (1.5 miles) to the next site, Little Ramsay Bay, simply continue down Nina Beach until you reach some boulders. Carefully follow the orange markers over to Boulder Bay. With a heavy pack this section can prove fatiguing.

From Boulder Bay's far end you head into the forest and embark on a tiring, viewless march to Little Ramsay Bay. Perseverance will be rewarded by delightful camping—except for the annoying insects—at this long, scenic beach. Views into the island's interior across a lagoon behind the beach have few peers anywhere along the Thorsborne Trail. To draw water you should skirt the lagoon on the right (north) side and look for flowing water in the first creek that enters it from the north, one that flows roughly parallel to the beach. The creek that enters from the west, the back of the lagoon, had no fresh water at all when we visited.

The second day on the Thorsborne (from a Little Ramsay Bay campsite) would logically culminate in a camp at Zoe Bay, 10.5 km (6.5 miles) or about 6 hours away. The day begins with a beachwalk southward to some rocks. At low tide you can walk right around these, while at high tide you might need to clamber over them. Cross a small beach and follow cairns or markers across a second set of rocks. You will need to ascend a small gully at one point instead of remaining on the rocks. Eventually you reach yet another beach with a lone coconut palm. Walk to its end, but this time not toward the rocks; instead, look toward the forest for an orange marker that indicates the trail's direction up a small ravine.

The trail soon tops out at a junction with a spur trail that leads down to Banksia Bay. The main trail continues on toward Zoe Bay, and the going becomes tougher. The trail climbs and then drops into the Banksia Creek drainage. It follows that creek all the way to the top of a ridge, a route that involves some rockhopping. There may be sluggish water in a small pool of Banksia Creek. Along this stretch and especially across the ridge in the Zoe Bay basin, you may encounter long stretches of blackened forest, incinerated as part of a controlled burning program to eliminate dangerous buildup of brush and scrub. The steep, rocky descent toward Zoe Bay will tax anyone with a heavy pack and may test orienteering skills as well, since markers are often hard to locate.

Eventually you glimpse the ocean and realize that you are nearing Zoe Bay. Yet it will still take several hours to reach the bay, since you swing around inland to intersect its far end. (The trail was rerouted to prevent potentially nasty encounters between hikers and a "saltie" or saltwater crocodile that was thought to inhabit a section of Zoe Bay.) But at last you leave the burn zone and enter a short stretch of rainforest and then an open melaleuca wood where an old trail departs toward the north end of Zoe Bay. Ignore this now-closed route and continue on into more rainforest, one of the finest sections of the Thorsborne.

The next 4.5 km (2.75 miles) take you behind Zoe Bay and across the drainages of North Zoe, Fan Palm, and Cypress Creeks. The rainforest along here features some enormous trees, lianas, beautiful fan palms (not seen in southern Queensland), and clear, inviting streams from which you can refill canteens. Watch carefully for markers in this often swampy section, particularly at creek crossings where it may prove difficult to locate the trail's continuation. After Cypress Pine Creek, the trail swings oceanward and brings hikers through a more open forest of melaleuca and eucalyptus, though with some boggy spots.

At long last, the trail emerges onto the beach of Zoe Bay, where you turn right (south) and walk toward the mouth of South Zoe Creek. Just before you arrive there, look for a marker indicating campsites back in the trees. You find a picnic table, toilet, and several sites adjacent to the beach. Other sites lie farther back in the forest beneath the tall rainforest canopy. These sites have fewer beach sandflies, but they lose the light sooner because of the deep shade cast by the forest. To find fresh water, you need to walk 900 meters (0.6 mile) up South Zoe Creek along the trail, the same one you will follow the next day up to Zoe Falls. But many campers walk up to the huge pool below the falls for a swim on the day they arrive, because of the possible crocodile danger in Zoe Bay itself. Camping near the falls is not permitted.

The day after camping at Zoe Beach, most people aim for a camp at Mulligan Falls or Sunken Reef Bay, both about 7.5 km (4.75 miles) away. Walk up the same trail you followed to draw water. Watch for slippery rocks at the creek crossing, and note that the trail's continuation beyond the creek starts about 20 or 30 meters upstream from the crossing point. Beyond the swimming hole, which has ropes for swinging out over the water, the trail ascends very steeply far above the falls on the south side. After much struggle, involving hand-over-hand scrambling, you reach the top of the falls and more attractive, though smaller, rock pools. You must cross the stream between two of these pools, walk up the right bank for a short way, and then recross the stream. Look for a marker indicating the crossing in the middle of the channel.

From here you begin a long but gradual ascent to 260 meters (850 feet). You will find plenty of water in South Zoe Creek and its tributaries, and even a few pools large enough for soaking feet and cooling off. The vegetation will now have changed to coastal heath, dominated by blue banksia, casuarina, and ferns. Walking this stretch will prove challenging for anyone with a backpack that rides high, as overhanging limbs constantly hinder progress. The summit of the pass to the Sweetwater and Diamantina Creek basins features a rocky "bald" that unfortunately offers little in the way of views. Past the bald, you descend—often very steeply—to an important junction. A sign indicates Sunken Reef Bay to the left and Mulligan Bay straight ahead.

If you want to visit or camp at Sunken Reef, you should first go on in the direction of Mulligan Bay for about 150 meters in order to fill up with water at Diamantina Creek, for Sunken Reef has no potable water.

The downhill walk to Sunken Reef Bay can be gruelling, especially for those with big, heavy packs, on account of overhanging limbs and gravelly, slippery slopes. But, with care, you reach the bottom of the long grade and enter a very swampy forest with a boggy creek to cross. The beach has no toilet nor even a "ratbox" to protect food; however, it is a pretty spot with few other campers around. It affords fine views out to the Palm Islands as well as of Hinchinbrook's main ridgeline. Flotsam and jetsam of every description litter the beach, and you can easily jerry-build a makeshift stool, table, or whatever you please. The only drawbacks to Sunken Reef as a campsite are the additional 2 km (1.25 miles) you must walk and the hordes of mosquitoes that descend at dusk (but then, they are everywhere).

If you go on to Mulligan Falls Campground, figure on perhaps another half hour of walking from the signed junction, first over a ridge, then down along a rather open slope with excellent views over to the jetty at Lucinda, the Palm Islands, and mainland ranges. A few more minutes bring you to a junction with trails to Mulligan Falls campground on the left and George Point (trail's end) to the right. If you want to camp here, you will enjoy the lush, tall rainforest, but you will hate the swarming insects. Below Mulligan Falls lies yet another large pool that invites swimming. It lures many more campers than the austere Sunken Reef Bay.

After a camp at either of these two spots, you will have 7.5 km (4.75 miles) left to walk to reach George Point. At first the going is very easy through beautiful rainforest. After 2.5 km (1.5 miles) you arrive at the beach of Mulligan Bay. Use the tide table that the water taxi operator gives you in order to hit the beach at low tide. The walking will be much easier then, and, above all, you will have no trouble crossing tidal Mulligan Creek. You have to beachwalk 5 km (3 miles) to George Point, and the hike seems longer than one might expect from a glance at the map. Although it may appear as though you simply need to walk to the end of the long beach to a point at its tip, in fact you need to round this point and trudge on 20 minutes more, as the beach grows ever narrower. Don't stop until you reach a sign for the George Point Campground at Picnic Beach, where you will rendezvous with your water taxi operator. Incidentally, camping here might prove a pleasant experience. It seemed to be relatively bug-free, and it even had picnic tables to sit around.

EDMUND KENNEDY NATIONAL PARK

This coastal park bears the name of an explorer who came ashore 35 km (22 miles) north of here in 1848 and then wandered south through the swampy terrain now protected in the park. Trails lead through coastal forests and mangrove swamps, often on boardwalks, and out onto a narrow but dazzling beach. Beware of crocodiles in this park, especially in the bayous and creeks; stay on bridges and don't swim or wade in estuarine waters. Also, avoid ocean swimming between October and May, when box jellyfish frequent inshore waters. Finally, bring loads of insect repellent, as mosquitoes abound. In spite of all these caveats, Edmund Kennedy can offer a delightful morning of hiking, beachwalking, and birding through tidal swamps rarely penetrated by any trails.

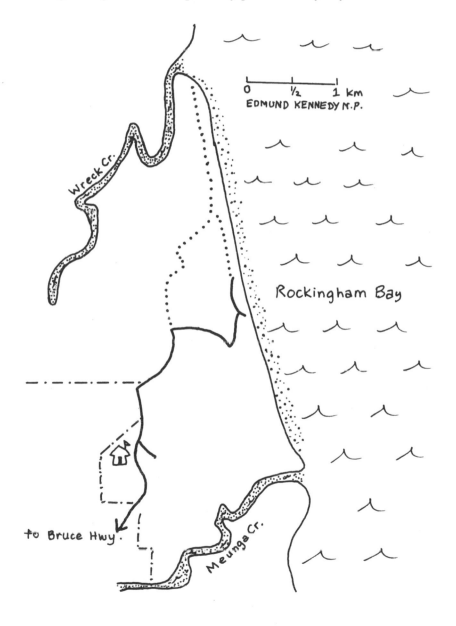

Road access. Drive about 5 km (3 miles) north from Cardwell on the Bruce Highway (Route 1), and then turn east, following the signs to the park a further 5 km (3 miles) distant.

Camping. Edmund Kennedy has a campground, but mosquitoes might spoil your stay. Consider camping farther south at Jourama Falls or maybe at a commercial campground in Cardwell or elsewhere.

1. Wreck Creek Loop

> **Distance: 4.5 km (2.75 miles) round trip**
> **Time: 1.25 hours**
> **Difficulty: easy**
> **Attractions: mangroves, beach, birdlife**

This varied walk starts at the parking/picnic area near the ocean at Rockingham Bay. From there, pick up the trail that heads off through coastal forest just behind the beach. After 600 meters (650 yards), you go straight ahead at a junction. The next 1.3 km (0.75 mile) take you across several tidal creeks that offer unusual opportunities to observe how some mangrove species send down new aerial roots and create the tangled mazelike root system characteristic of such areas. Incidentally, Australia has far more mangrove species than any other continent. Also, be on the lookout for interesting birds here, including the large Torresian pigeon, white with a black head.

At the end of the walking track, you emerge onto the beach where another 300 meters brings you near Wreck Creek. The last stretch of beach can get difficult because of all the tree hulks lying around. After a look at the creek, walk back up the beach to the picnic area if the tide is out. But do not attempt the beachwalk at high tide because of difficult crossings of tidal creeks en route; in that case, return via the trail. Even if you can't walk all the way back on the beach, plan to pause there to enjoy the spectacular views of Hinchinbrook and other islands. You may also spot some Australian oystercatchers along the beach, recognizable by their long orange bills.

2. Mangrove Walk

> **Distance: 3.5 km (2.25 miles) round trip**
> **Time: 1 hour**
> **Difficulty: easy**
> **Attractions: birdwatching, mangroves**

This trail branches off the track to Wreck Creek. Start at the parking and picnic area near the ocean at Rockingham Bay. Follow the track behind the beach through the woods for about 600 meters (650 yards). At the junction, turn left toward the boardwalks through the mangroves. Past the boardwalks, the trail winds through a melaleuca forest. Birds are plentiful, and easy to spot because the forest is not too dense. At about km 1.75 (mile 1) you reach the park road. Go left here, returning by the road to the picnic area.

WOOROONOORAN NATIONAL PARK: PALMERSTON SECTION

This new park with its tongue-twisting name actually incorporates two formerly independent national parks, of which Palmerston is the more southerly and Bellenden Ker the one farther north. Although the two sections have been made contiguous by land acquisitions, they retain a separate identity, because they lack any direct road links. Around Palmerston you will find some of the finest rainforest, most impressive waterfalls, and secluded hiking trails in all of tropical Australia. Palmerston preserves large portions of the North Johnstone River and its tributaries, a basin first opened up for Europeans by the explorations of bushman Christie Palmerston in 1882. The North Johnstone offers one of the few practicable routes in these parts from the coast over the Great Dividing Range to the Atherton Tableland, which explains why a highway runs right along it today. The only drawback to visiting the park has been a spate of recent trail closures. In 1997 few of the trails could be hiked in their entirety, but by the time you arrive, at least some should be open again.

Road access. From the Bruce Highway (Route 1), turn west onto the Palmerston Highway just north of Innisfail and travel about 34 km (21 miles) to the marked turnoff for Henrietta Creek Campground, a right turn. To reach the Tchupala Falls Trail, go back east 2.7 km (1.75 miles) to a car park along the highway.

Camping. Henrietta Creek Campground lacks some amenities, but compensates by providing secluded, private, accessible sites with tables and grills. Either bring your own water or drink the supposedly good water from the creek. No need to book ahead; just self-register when you arrive.

Season. Any. Summer in the Far North brings torrential rains which may hamper exploration but should also energize the park's many waterfalls.

1. Rock Pool

> **Distance: 800 meters (0.5 mile) round trip**
> **Time: 15 minutes**
> **Difficulty: easy**
> **Attractions: swimming hole, maybe a platypus**

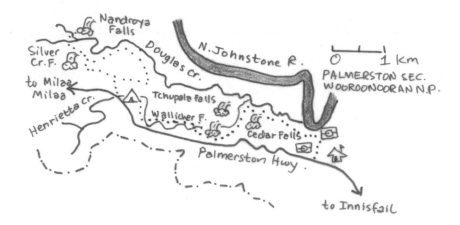

This very short, level trail begins at the end of the campground and leads through rainforest to a large, deep pool ideal for swimming. It is supposed to have platypuses in it, though I did not see any. You could also check another pool about halfway back to the campground. The trail extends another 400 meters beyond the Rock Pool to Goolagan's picnic area, where the current closure takes effect. If it were reopened for its full length, you could hike it all the way to the Wallicher/Tchupala Falls area and beyond.

2. Nandroya Falls

> **Distance: 7.25 km (4.5 miles) as a loop hike; 4.5 km (2.75 miles)
>   to falls and back on the same trail**
> **Time: 2 hours for the short version; around 3 for the loop**
> **Difficulty: easy**
> **Attractions: two falls, one exceptionally beautiful**

The Nandroya Falls hike had always been a loop until the recent closure of a section past the falls, which necessitates returning on the same trail. But few should feel disappointed, since the section of trail that remains open offers superb rainforest and creek scenery.

To find the trailhead, walk to a vehicle barrier at one end of the camping area, where the trail commences as a dirt road and swings up to the highway almost immediately. From there it turns right back into the forest, soon crossing Henrietta Creek on rocks. After about 10 minutes of walking, the trail reaches its junction with the now-closed return loop, so you have to go left here. Past this junction it ascends slightly to cross over into the Douglas Creek drainage, then descends steadily, often on stairs, to 10 meter high Silver Creek Falls. Just 10 more minutes of walking bring you to breathtaking Nandroya Falls, a 50 meter (165 foot) high

Nandroya Falls

cascade in two tiers. The bottom tier is shorter and flows down in several stages. The upper tier plunges from a nearly hidden recess in the rainforest. Below the falls a broad, chilly pool lies surrounded by impatiens. The brilliant colors of these everbloomers will delight most visitors; still, one ought to bear in mind that they are non-native plants "invading" the Australian bush and thus, in a way, weeds. As noted before, the return trip uses the same trail unless the loop section on the far side of Douglas Creek has reopened.

3. Wallicher and Tchupala Falls

Distance: 2 km (1.25 miles) round trip to Wallicher Falls; 1.25 km (0.75 mile) to the first of the Tchupala Falls

Time: 25 minutes round trip to Wallicher; 10 minutes to first Tchupala, plus additional time to see the lower Tchupala Falls

Difficulty: easy to Wallicher; moderate to visit the lower Tchupala Falls

Attractions: high volume cascades in a scenic gorge

From the car park described in the road access section follow the marked trail about 200 meters. To visit Wallicher Falls go left at the fork and continue 800 meters (0.5 mile) through rainforest. Unfortunately, the trail closely parallels the highway, so traffic noise may disturb hikers. The low but powerful falls soon come into view, and you may find some pleasant places to relax and savor the magnificent setting.

On your return to the fork, follow the signs down to Tchupala Falls, a higher and more spectacular cascade. The first fall lies only 400 meters from the junction, but one can descend on steep and sometimes wet stone stairs to see the lower Tchupalas. To scramble down and investigate all four of them would involve a considerable descent and about 45 minutes round trip. But all of these falls, thundering down into their narrow, verdant gorge, will make an unforgettable impression on anyone who takes the trouble to press on. Someday, if the trail is opened again, you will be able to continue down into the lower sections of the North Johnstone River and clamber up to Crawford's Lookout, high above the stream. Until then just return on the same steep trail to the car park.

WOOROONOORAN NATIONAL PARK: JOSEPHINE FALLS SECTION

Here, in the park's northern district, rise Queensland's two highest peaks, Bellenden Ker and Bartle Frere, forming a rampart above the flat, steamy sugarcane fields below. Their cool summits cause moist ocean winds to condense into fog as they push up the mountainsides, leaving the whole range cloud-shrouded much of the time. The higher slopes, misty and damp, have evolved a "cloud forest" ecosystem unusual for Queensland but more common in other, higher rainforests. Bellenden Ker has no trail to the top, but Bartle Frere, Queensland's highest mountain at 1622 meters

(5320 feet), does. So if you have wondered what the highest fastnesses of Australia's tropical rainforests look like, you may choose to accept the tough physical challenge of climbing Bartle Frere. If not, you could certainly walk part way up and/or saunter out to magnificent Josephine Falls. Both hikes commence from the same parking area.

Road access. From Cairns head south 66 km (41 miles) on the Bruce Highway (Route 1), turning west at the sign for Josephine Falls. A further 8 km (5 miles) of driving, including a sharp right at 6.75 km (4.25 miles), bring you to a parking lot and two trailheads.

Camping. Since the above trailhead has no campsites, hikers must either camp in the Palmerston section of the park at Henrietta Creek, or at Babinda Boulders up the road. See the previous and following descriptions for details. Another possibility would be to camp in the backcountry part way up Bartle Frere; see below for details about that option.

Season. Any for Josephine Falls, but dry season only for Bartle Frere (see note two below).

1. Josephine Falls

> **Distance: 1.5 km (1 mile) round trip**
> **Time: 20 minutes**
> **Difficulty: easy**
> **Attractions: waterfall, lookouts**

This popular, paved trail gradually ascends through jungle along a creek, with the aid of steps. Before long, it reaches several lookouts, off a small loop at the trail's end. Josephine Falls is a beautiful double waterfall having a high volume year-round, because of the huge amount of precipitation that characterizes this part of the "wet tropics." Swimming is unsafe here. Backtrack to the parking lot.

2. Mt. Bartle Frere Ascent

> **Distance: 16 km (10 miles) round trip**
> **Time: 9 to 10 hours round trip with a light daypack; longer with**
> **   overnight gear**
> **Difficulty: difficult**
> **Attractions: rainforest, cloud forest, views to the coast and**
> **   Atherton Tableland**

Mt. Bartle Frere rises to an altitude of 1622 meters (5320 feet). Since you begin the hike at about 100 meters (330 feet), the long ascent—about a vertical mile—will challenge even strong, fit hikers. Nevertheless, if you feel up to the physical ordeal, you should consider attempting this hike. You will get to glimpse some unusual environments unlike anything in

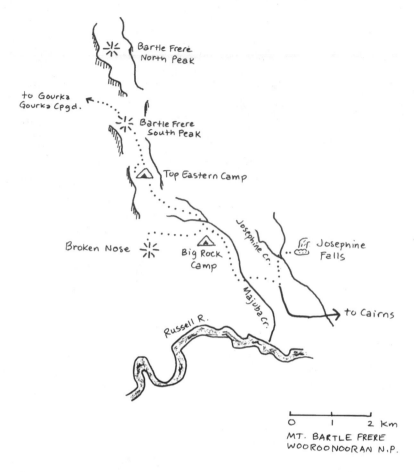

MT. BARTLE FRERE
WOOROONOORAN N.P.

other parks: cloud forest, dwarf vegetation and wildflowers near the summit, as well as extensive talus slopes. Moreover, the Bartle Frere hike has endless vistas, provided the clouds part.

Do not even consider this hike in rainy weather. The steep trail would become nightmarishly slick, and the boulders would no longer offer stable landing points for leaps.

The hike breaks down into four distinct sections. The first, from the trailhead to what the park calls Big Rock Camp, should not overtax anyone. You ascend only 300 meters (1000 feet) over perhaps 2.5 km (1.5 miles). The heat and humidity may make hikers perspire, but the trail never becomes terribly strenuous; instead, it rises gradually with many ups and downs for creek crossings en route. Notice the damage in this stretch from previous "cyclones" (i.e., hurricanes) that show up as areas of dense, low vegetation overgrown with lawyer vines and other opportunistic climbers. After about 1 km (0.62 miles) the trail will steepen a bit as it mounts onto a ridge between two major creeks, Majuba and Kowadji.

At times, the ridge narrows nearly to knife-edge proportions, so you have to inch your way over sprawling buttress roots of rainforest giants. This part of the hike affords only occasional, obscured glimpses of the gorges below, but plenty of towering rainforest to admire. Look too for the great number and variety of fruits littering the trail—food for myriad rainforest birds.

Once you reach Big Rock Camp, after perhaps one hour and fifteen minutes, be sure to fill up your canteens. You will find no more water until you return to this spot, unless you make a detour near the summit. Notice a sign here indicating that the trail splits, with one branch heading to Broken Nose (3 hours) and the other to Bartle Frere Summit (4 hours). Broken Nose, at 962 meters (3155 feet), would make an easier alternative hike for anyone not keen on continuing up Bartle Frere.

If you are going on to the summit, cross the creek and prepare for the second and toughest segment of the hike. You must ascend from about 400 meters (1300 feet) to 1100 meters (3600 feet) in the next 2.5 km (1.5 miles). To gain that much elevation so quickly, the trail becomes cruelly steep, in places so precipitous that you will climb by hanging onto roots and saplings. Few hikers will have energy for anything but the task at hand here, so depictions of scenic charm would be pointless. The most demanding section comes close to the top. Called "the landslide," it forces you to ascend a roughly 60° dirt chute by the aid of protruding roots. Along this second segment, the orange markers—ribbons, blazes, triangles, arrows—grow more numerous as the trail becomes less distinct and makes sudden, unexpected turns. Watch carefully for them, as losing the trail on this steep section could be hazardous.

Above the landslide, and after a few more horrendously steep slopes, the trail's gradient eases and turns rightward. At this point, a bit less than two hours from Big Rock, you embark on the third segment of the trip: Bartle Frere's South Ridge. A gentler ascent than the previous one, it takes you up about 500 meters (1600 feet) in roughly 2 km (1.25 miles). Though far from easy, the ridge segment offers enchanting hiking through the first true cloud forest you encounter on the journey. The mist closes in as you climb, creating an eerie atmosphere of subdued light and silence, broken only by the loud calls of unseen birds. Now palms and ferns predominate, while the often moss-covered trees grow less tall than at lower elevations. The cloud forest is the haunt of the golden bowerbird, a striking and rare species that inhabits only Far North Queensland forests above 900 meters (3000 feet). High on a ridge, but still in forest, you may notice a small, unofficial camping area to the left of the trail.

Fifty minutes from the beginning of South Ridge, the trail emerges from the forest into a zone of grasses and dwarf vegetation. Look for a sign stating: "Water 300 m." The spur trail to the water leads downhill and comes out at a small clearing the park service calls "Top Eastern Camp." Located at 1400 meters (4600 feet), this campsite attracts the many hikers who prefer to do the Bartle Frere climb in two days, but as a water source it would involve a tiring descent and reascent to fill up your canteen. To camp at Top Eastern requires a permit from the ranger's office located in Miriwinni, right near the Bruce Highway turnoff to Bartle Frere and Josephine Falls.

Beyond the water sign, you commence the fourth, and quite challenging, segment of the journey. The trail heads for a talus slope ahead and takes you among its enormous black granite boulders Your task is to "connect the dots" of the numerous orange markers on rocks and dwarf trees to make your way up the slope. Progress can be slow as you must leap from boulder to boulder like a mountain goat, often over yawn-

Mt. Bartle Frere

ing gaps and onto narrow footholds. Otherwise you need to descend one boulder laboriously, only to clamber atop the next one, sometimes by stemming. This business can get tedious and could be dangerous. One misstep could cost you an ankle sprain. Unfortunately, the top of the boulder field is a false summit. Thus, heartbreakingly, you must march down to a small saddle and then climb back up to the true summit, mostly through heath and dwarf forest. About 40 minutes after you leave the cloud forest you will stand on the "Top of Queensland" and, weather permitting, gaze out over miles of coastline to the east and westward over the emerald valley of the Mulgrave River and the Atherton Tableland. Since it is covered by pygmy forest, the summit itself lacks the premier views. A bit farther back on the trail you may encounter fewer obstructions and grander vistas.

Note that the Bartle Frere trail actually continues over the summit and down to the west, eventually reaching a camping area called "Gourka Gourka" accessed from Malanda on the Atherton Tableland. This end of the trail begins higher, at 600 meters (2000 feet), but it's the same length, so it must be generally less steep. However, the park service describes it as "undeveloped" and warns of its difficulty.

The return walk to your car holds few surprises. Following the orange markers can get tricky in places, especially on the boulder-covered slope where you won't see any for several hundred meters. But orient yourself to the water sign mentioned earlier; it will guarantee that you are on the right track. There are also a few places in the dwarf forest where you might lose it. Just hold to the rule that you should not move on until spotting at least one marker toward which to walk. Farther down, I lost the trail at a point about 10 minutes past "the landslide" when I went straight down a slope instead of making a 90° left turn. Luckily, I was able to retrace my steps and return to the last orange marker before my blunder. Physically, the return trek may prove nearly as taxing as the ascent, since the very steep terrain strains knees and forces many cautious, hand-over-hand descents on protruding roots. Indeed, unlike most mountain climbs, the Bartle Frere hike takes almost as long for the return trip as it does outbound—nearly 4 hours. All in all, Bartle Frere is one of the harder hikes most people will ever attempt, and surely not a family trip, but very rewarding nonetheless.

THE BOULDERS WILDLAND PARK

Within Wooroonooran National Park nestles an enclave administered by the city of Cairns. It protects for recreation the lower reaches of one of the loveliest streams in the range, Babinda Creek. Here visitors may camp, swim, hike, picnic, or stay in a rustic, privately owned lodge. The reserve derives its name from a collection of huge granite boulders that crop out along the stream below Mt. Bartle Frere. The creek, the rocks, and the steep, jungle-covered foothills surrounding them create stunning tableaux. Aside from its great natural beauty, the Boulders has lessons to teach. It harbors an amazing variety of tropical rainforest trees, rarely arranged in large groves, as one finds them in temperate zones, but instead intermingled in such a way that individual specimens grow widely dispersed. That is the prevailing pattern in Australia's tropical forest, and you can learn about it here on a self-guiding nature trail. As a bonus, the large and brilliant blue Ulysses butterfly frequents the picnic and parking area. Don't miss this beguiling rainforest gem, but do take care around Babinda Creek, as many people have drowned there.

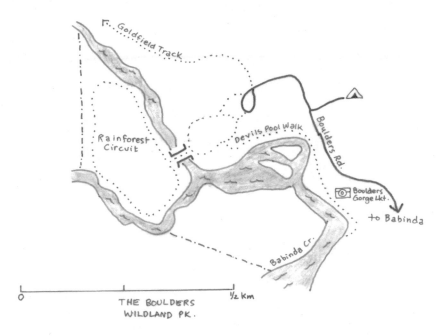

THE BOULDERS
WILDLAND PK.

Road access. From the town of Babinda between Innisfail and Cairns follow signs west about 6 km (3.75 miles) to the Boulders.

Camping. The campground here is convenient, but surprisingly, has little shade and rather barren, small sites. However, barring caravan parks, it's the only place to camp for miles.

Season. Any, but spring brings a plague of biting flies.

In the area. If you are passing through Cairns, don't miss the impressive Tjapukai aboriginal cultural center just north of the city, near the turnoff to the resort town of Kuranda in the Atherton Tableland. Aboriginal legends, history, food, crafts, and music are featured in this wonderful facility.

1. Wonga Track Rainforest Circuit

> **Distance: 850 meters (0.5 mile) round trip**
> **Time: 15 minutes**
> **Difficulty: easy**
> **Attractions: nature study**

This short track begins past the parking area. It crosses a suspension bridge near the main swimming hole and then commences its loop. Staying close to the creek bank, the trail allows for leisurely inspection of rainforest plants and gives access to rock gardens upstream before looping back across the bridge to return to the picnic ground.

2. Devils Pool Walk

Distance: 1.25 km (0.75 mile) round trip
Time: 30 minutes
Difficulty: easy
Attractions: a chance to see the renowned Babinda Boulders

From the swimming hole near the picnic and parking area, the trail, which is partially paved and partially boardwalked, follows the left bank of Babinda Creek past awesome boulders, small cascades, pools, caves, and "waterslides" (which are dangerous and should be avoided by swimmers). There is some elevation change along the trail, usually involving stairs. After 470 meters (0.3 mile) you arrive at Devils Lookout; another 130 meters takes you to Boulders Gorge Lookout, where the trail ends. Backtrack to your car.

EUBENANGEE SWAMP NATIONAL PARK

Eubenangee Swamp is an important wildlife habitat near the coast. Although it has only one trail at present, visitors will appreciate the vast numbers, and diverse species, of birds that are attracted to the wetlands around the Alice River. The swamp itself is quite beautiful, particularly in the morning mist.

Road access. North of Innisfail, turn east off the Bruce Highway (Route 1) at Miriwinni. Drive toward Bramston Beach for 9 km (5.5 miles), and then turn right onto the Cartwright Road, following signs for Eubanangee Swamp.

Camping. There is no camping here, but you can camp at nearby Babinda Boulders Park, as described above.

Season. Any. Bird migration times would be ideal.

1. Eubanangee Swamp Trail

Distance: 3 km (2 miles) round trip
Time: 45 minutes
Difficulty: easy
Attractions: birdwatching, scenic views

This partial loop trail follows the bank of the Alice River, which is inhabited by estuarine crocodiles. Then it ascends a hill through a meadow on a wide, mowed track and bends to the left. From here, you gaze down on swamps and ponds, which are magnets for pelicans, egrets, darters, and all sorts of birdlife. You also enjoy excellent views of Mt. Bartle Frere, Queensland's highest peak. Soon the trail descends the hill and returns to the parking area.

Mission Beach/Clump Mountain National Park

The land around the small seaside town of Mission Beach has only one national park (Clump Mountain), but state forests and gorgeous beaches provide many other first-rate hiking opportunities. In fact, when you consider its proximity to the Great Barrier Reef and Dunk Island National Park, Mission Beach could easily become a 3- or 4-day destination. The rainforests here grow luxuriantly because of the heavy rainfall (nearby Tully has the highest precipitation total of any Australian town). Furthermore, the rare cassowary roams the forests near Mission Beach and can sometimes be spotted by those visitors who turn up at the right times and places. Coastal walks and views around Mission Beach rival even Cape Tribulation's, as hills in both places drop right down to the beach and the Coral Sea. As well, from Mission Beach vantage points, verdant Dunk Island floats enticingly on the seaward horizon. The walks around this area are all fairly short and easy, but immensely enjoyable.

Road access. From the Bruce Highway (Route 1), turn off to Mission Beach from either of two points, one just north of Tully and the other near El Arish. Both are clearly marked. Specific directions for the various hikes are included with their descriptions.

Camping. The Mission Beach area has no public or national park campgrounds. You can stay at any of several commercial campgrounds or opt for a motel or hostel, of which the Tree Top Backpacker Resort may be the best.

Season. Any but summer, when rain can pelt down for days on end.

In the area. If you would like to combine hiking and underwater exploration, Mission Beach is a good choice. Boats leave for the Great Barrier Reef from Clump Point jetty every day. Inquire about prices, travel time to the reef (an important factor), and sea conditions when you arrive.

1. Bicton Hill Loop

> **Distance: 4 km (2.5 miles) round trip**
> **Time: 1.5 hours**
> **Difficulty: moderately easy**
> **Attractions: rainforest, views to the Coral Sea, birdlife**

To reach the trailhead, drive north on the Mission Beach–Bingil Bay Road. Pass Clump Point jetty, whence boats leave for Dunk Island, then drive by Narragon Beach. Just beyond the beach the road gets tortuous. Look sharp to your left for a clearing not far past the jetty and beach. Stop here

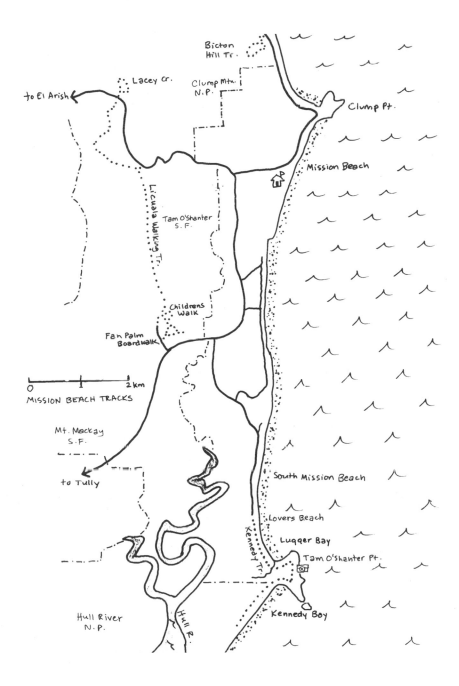

Bicton Hill Tr.

to El Arish

Lacey Cr.

Clump Mtn. N.P.

Clump Pt.

Mission Beach

Licuala Walking Tr.

Tam O'Shanter S.F.

Childrens Walk

Fan Palm Boardwalk

0   2 km
MISSION BEACH TRACKS

Mt. Mackay S.F.

to Tully

South Mission Beach

Lovers Beach

Lugger Bay

Kennedy Tr.

Tam O'Shanter Pt.

Kennedy Bay

Hull River N.P.

Hull R.

and look for a national park sign, possibly still stating Kurrimine National Park, its former name.

The park sign indicates the trailhead which leads immediately into the forest. After about 600 meters (650 yards) of walking through second growth rainforest, you will encounter a pleasant rest stop and a signed junction at which you can go either right (1.4 km/0.9 mile) or left (1.3 km/0.8 mile) to the top of Bicton Hill. The leftward option leads into a more mature and impressive rainforest and finally to the summit, from which you can enjoy a panorama of coastal islands including Dunk, Bedarra, Orpheus, and other, smaller islets. The return walk, along the other branch of the trail, takes you through exceptionally beautiful rainforest dominated by palms, ponderous lianas, and a great diversity of tropical hardwoods, many identified on small signposts. On the trail watch for the signature insect of Mission Beach, the huge, electric blue Ulysses butterfly, as well as some hefty goannas.

2. Kennedy Walking Track

Distance: 7 km (4.25 miles) round trip
Time: 2 or 3 hours
Difficulty: moderately easy
Attractions: variety of landscapes and seaward views

This track offers one of the finest beach walk experiences around. There are excellent views of Hinchinbrook, Dunk, and Bedarra Islands as well as many smaller cays, and the beaches themselves are pristine.

Start the hike at the South Mission Beach boat ramp, where you park. Initially, the well-marked track is level with the beach, behind a line of trees but with frequent ocean views. A few ups and downs, on stairs, bring you to pocket-sized Lovers Beach. The trail continues in the same fashion to Lugger Bay, at 1.25 km (0.75 mile). This broad, long beach makes an ideal stop for sunbathing or a snack because of the picnic tables provided. Swimming requires patience because of the long walk out to deeper water.

Temporarily, the trail ceases, so you simply follow the crescent of beach around to the far end, at Mije Creek. Beware of estuarine crocodiles here. The trail resumes, crossing the creek on a boardwalk and slipping behind a stand of mangroves on the way to Tam O'Shanter Point lookout at 2.5 km (1.5 miles). Immediately before reaching the lookout, you climb a flight of stairs. The lookout has a picnic shelter and possibly water.

From here, the trail continues to climb, on stairs, to its high point, about 40 meters above sea level. Soon it descends to small, rocky Turtle Bay (yes, there are turtles here). You will need to do some boulder-hopping in this area. The trail crosses another mangrove flat to arrive at 400 meter-long Kennedy Beach, another wide, sandy strand. At its far end there are toilets, water, and picnic tables. If you wish, you can continue past here for 1.5 km (1 mile) on the "Kennedy Extension," which visits secluded coves at Hull Heads, the mouth of the Hull River. Return the way you came.

3. Lacey Creek Forest Circuit

Distance: 1.2 km (0.75 mile) round trip
Time: 20 minutes
Difficulty: easy
Attractions: cassowaries, exhibits, rainforest

The trailhead for this short but interesting loop is located off the north side of the road from El Arish to Mission Beach. Near the parking area are toilets, picnic tables, barbecues, an interpretive kiosk, and an arboretum. Cassowaries frequent the area, but even if you don't see them, you will enjoy strolling through this picturesque creekside environment. The well-constructed trail crosses Lacey Creek a few times and has boardwalks and observation decks from which you can appreciate the beauty of the dense tropical rainforest.

4. Rainforest Walking Track

Distance: 4.5 km (2.75 miles) one way
Time: 1.5 hours, one way
Difficulty: easy
Attractions: well-preserved rainforest and a chance of spotting cassowaries

This non-loop hike has two possible starting points, both along the El Arish/Mission Beach Road. One is opposite the Lacey Creek Nature Trail (see above) and is 7.75 km (4.75 miles) one way. The other, referred to here as the main trail, begins at a carpark a few kilometers up the road toward Mission Beach and is 4.5 km (2.75 miles) one way. Since the stretch from Lacey Creek to the main stem of the walking track parallels the road, it can be omitted without much loss. It intersects the main trail about 200 meters (225 yards) from the carpark. At the end of the hike, you will have to double back to your car unless you have arranged a shuttle. The track terminates at the parking lot of Licuala State Forest Park, on the Tully–Mission Beach Road.

The trail is almost dead-level for its entire distance. It runs alongside a small creek over much of its length, though because the rainforest here is so dense, the creek is difficult to see except when the trail crosses it on bridges. The vegetation includes fan palms, lawyer vines, climbing pandanus, and occasional tree ferns. Near the trail's conclusion grows a "monster" strangler fig.

With luck you may see cassowaries here: large, rare birds with dark plumage, prominent crests, and wattles. You are guaranteed to see their droppings, especially on the first half of the trail, near the creek. The area is also home to numerous goannas. Birdlife abounds.

5. Rainforest Circuit Walk

> **Distance: 1.25 km (0.75 mile) round trip**
> **Time: 20 minutes**
> **Difficulty: easy**
> **Attractions: fan palms, informative signs about rainforest ecology**

Licuala State Forest Park in Tam O'Shanter State Reserve contains some short trails that are well worth your time. The trailhead for the Rainforest Circuit Walk is located off the Tully–Mission Beach Road, at the end of a one kilometer long gravel road. The turnoff, which leads north off the Tully–Mission Beach Road, is clearly marked.

This delightful, level stroll through a fan palm forest is another potential cassowary-sighting venue. Fan palms grow here in their greatest concentration south of Daintree National Park, because of the area's exceptionally high rainfall. For wet season visitors, the trail includes a 500 meter long boardwalk. Useful interpretive signs contribute to visitors' knowledge of the local flora and fauna.

6. Childrens Walk

> **Distance: 350 meters round trip**
> **Time: 10 minutes**
> **Difficulty: easy**
> **Attractions: cassowaries for kids**

This loop in Licuala State Forest Park branches off the Rainforest Walk, described above. Passing through a fan palm forest, you follow cement cassowary "tracks" on a path to a "nest" filled with large blue "eggs." The walk is fun for kids, and its beautiful vegetation makes it attractive to adults as well.

DUNK ISLAND NATIONAL PARK

Hundreds of islands dot the waters off Far North Queensland's coast, many designated as national parks. But Dunk is one of the few that combines easy access, excellent trails, and world class scenery. It belongs to the group of mountainous islands that, during the last ice age, were joined to the Australian mainland, but have since been cut off by rising sea levels. Like nearby mainland areas, Dunk receives ample rain, enough to support a thriving forest on the higher slopes. It has been developed somewhat for tourism, but only in a few places near the north end. Most of the island remains in a pristine state. However, because the resort supports a regular ferry service across the 4.5 km (2.75 mile) channel separating Dunk from the mainland, getting there is easy. On the island itself, you will find some low-key services (a store, bar, phone, etc.) clustered around the ferry terminal; however, just a few hundred meters beyond them, you regain the serene beauty of Dunk's shady rainforests and coral-girt beaches. Wildlife abounds, including Dunk's famous blue Ulysses butterfly, tropical birds, and goannas. Dunk has a languid charm that once lured beachcomber/author E. J. Banfield to live there, and today it attracts artists to a small colony just past the airport. Don't miss the hike and the island.

Road access. Take the main Mission Beach road north to Clump Point jetty. From there, ferries depart (by last report) at 8:45 A.M. and 10:30 A.M. It would be a good idea to reserve space in advance. Local accommodations can arrange this for you as well as transport you to and from Clump Point. The trip should cost about Au. $20 round trip.

Camping. Dunk Island has an excellent national park campground managed by the resort. Because of its popularity you definitely should book a site well ahead of time if you hope to camp on Dunk itself. Call the resort at (07) 4068-7220.

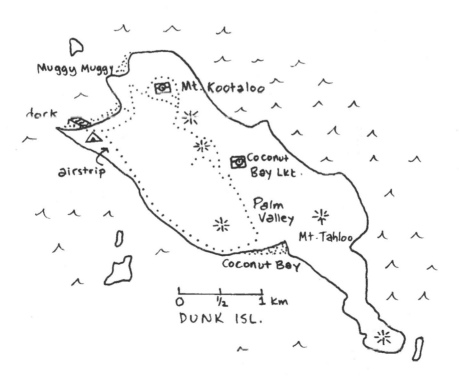

1. Dunk Island Circuit Track

Distance: 11 km (6.75 miles) round trip
Time: 2.5 or 3 hours
Difficulty: moderately easy
**Attractions: primeval rainforest, views to Coral Sea and land-
    ward, an isolated beach**

Once you disembark from the ferry, look for the campground just across
a resort road. Take this road to the left, noting the sign for "walking
tracks." Follow signs through the resort and you will be routed around
the airstrip and onto a dirt road. Walk down this road until reaching a
strange area that resembles a bus stop. There, the only sign in evidence
reads "Bruce Arthur's." Follow the direction of this sign, which leads to
the home of a local artist, behind the fence that encloses the "bus stop."
You will then walk along a farm field and eventually enter a forest, in
which signs will appear for Coconut Beach. In a few minutes more, your
trail will pass right by this beach with its terrific views off to the south,
taking in Bedarra, Palm, and—much farther away—Hinchinbrook Islands. The walk out to Coconut Beach takes about 45 minutes at a brisk
pace. The water offshore is exceptionally clear, and coral fringes the beach,
so snorkeling might prove rewarding here, at least at high tide when
water covers the reef.

At the end of Coconut Beach, the trail veers inland, and a sign advertises that Mt. Kootaloo Lookout is 5.4 km (3.25 miles) away. The trail
now enters a well-preserved, towering rainforest in Palm Valley, climbing gently and then more steeply as it passes by an arch-like fig tree.
Before long, the trail takes you high enough so that you can occasionally
see out to the Pacific and later to the mainland through the trees. There
is a trail to a lookout at Mt. Kut-tay, but it was closed as of this writing.
Past that spur the trail climbs and passes another junction with a trail
that leads down to the resort. Continue on the right branch toward Mt.
Kootaloo, and follow signs to the lookout at a second junction as well.

When you finally arrive at the lookout, perhaps 1.25 hours from Coconut Beach, you are rewarded with magnificent vistas. All of Mission
Beach, its hinterland ranges, and a long stretch of coast down toward
Tully, plus many islands, lie spread out below you. On the return walk
to the resort, you will arrive back at a junction you passed earlier; go left
here toward the resort, not toward Coconut Beach. You will descend
rather quickly, crossing a swinging bridge and Banfield's grave before
arriving in the sybaritic haunts of Dunk Island Resort. You need to locate the main road back to the jetty and decide whether to return on one
of the boats to the mainland or camp at the national park campground
(assuming you can get a spot). The Mt. Kootaloo Loop is certainly not a
wilderness hike, but it has some exhilarating moments and lovely scenery for the last 8 km (5 miles).

DAINTREE NATIONAL PARK:
MOSSMAN GORGE SECTION

For most visitors to tropical Australia, Daintree marks the end of the line. This vast park (over 70,000 hectares or 172,000 acres in total) protects, in almost virgin wilderness, some of the last, best rainforest in the country. Beyond Daintree, motorists begin the journey up the Cape York Peninsula, which still remains predominantly 4-WD country. The Mossman Gorge section preserves some high and very wet tablelands that drain into the Mossman and Daintree rivers. Unfortunately, very little of this spectacular park has been so far rendered accessible to hikers (excepting those willing to bushwhack with map and compass). The small segment of Mossman Gorge that has been opened up therefore attracts tourists like a magnet. They have few other places north of Cairns to see really world-class rainforest. Thus, no one should expect solitude in Mossman Gorge. But visitors should go there anyway, for the forest has some truly exceptional tropical hardwoods, vines, and epiphytes.

Road access. From Cairns or Port Douglas drive north on the Mossman–Daintree road until you reach the town of Mossman. Turn left at the sign for Mossman Gorge and continue about 5 km (3 miles) to road's end.

Camping. Mossman Gorge has no campground, so options are limited. Consider commercial caravan parks in Mossman or other nearby towns. Otherwise, make the gorge a stopover on your way to or from Cape Tribulation where camping is permitted (see next section).

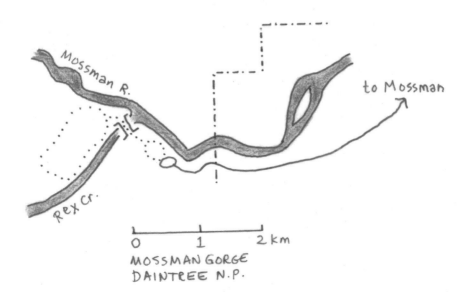

MOSSMAN GORGE
DAINTREE N.P.

Season. Any, although, as elsewhere in the Far North, summer can mean torrential rain, heat, and bugs.

In the area. River trips on the Daintree River offer opportunities to spot numerous birds and even a crocodile or two. These depart either from the vicinity of the Cape Tribulation ferry landing on the Daintree River or from a point on the Mossman to Daintree Road about 4 km (2.5 miles) beyond the turnoff to the Cape Tribulation ferry.

1. Mossman Gorge

Distance: 2.5 km (1.5 miles) round trip
Time: 1 hour
Difficulty: easy
Attractions: a rainforest in which human hikers are dwarfed,
and a popular swimming hole

From the carpark, often jam-packed, follow the trail 800 meters (0.5 mile) to the start of the actual loop walk, which begins just past Rex Creek suspension bridge. The trail winds through a rainforest remarkable for its many enormous, ancient trees. One strangler fig has buttress roots running hundreds of feet across the forest. As you return to the carpark, you might want to detour to the park's popular swimming hole, set amid boulders. You never actually see the gorge for which the park is named, only just the boulder-lined creek.

DAINTREE NATIONAL PARK:
CAPE TRIBULATION SECTION

Traveling to Cape Tribulation has gotten easier than it used to be. Still, crossing the Daintree River on the old cable ferry initiates a psychological break with the developed, touristy world to the south. Back in the 1970s, hippies, beachcombers, seekers after solitude, and back-to-the-land proponents arrived here in small numbers. Eventually, they clashed with the pro-development Queensland government over its plan to extend the existing primitive dirt road to Cape Tribulation on up across the Bloomfield River. As so often happens in Australia, the developers won the battle, but lost the war. They got their road, but the "enviros" got a national park. That park has recently been joined to Daintree to create, as noted already, one of the largest rainforest reserves in tropical Australia.

It is not easy to describe the ambience of this extraordinary place to North Americans, except perhaps to evoke Big Sur in California as it used to be or perhaps the eastern end of Maui, Hawaii. It's still an extravagantly beautiful, laid-back place with small stores, houses, and inns

Directions and distances, Cape Tribulation

tucked away in the forest. As yet, few hiking trails have been constructed around Cape Tribulation. But you can walk the beaches for miles, wondering at the fog-shrouded peaks that drop right down to the Coral Sea.

You should visit "Cape Trib," and soon, because the tour bus industry has discovered it.

Road access. From Cairns drive 104 km (65 miles) north on the Cook Highway, keeping watch for signs to the Daintree River ferry and Cape Tribulation after you pass through Mossman. Once you have crossed the river, you have another 34 km (21 miles) to Cape Tribulation itself. The Marrdja Botanical Walk turnoff will be just after the Noah Creek crossing, roughly 20 km (12.5 miles) past the ferry. The other short hike described here begins right at the Cape's parking area.

The Cape Tribulation road has not yet been paved all the way. Particularly as you drive farther north, you will encounter some bumpy stretches of dirt or gravel, though nothing an ordinary 2-WD car couldn't handle. However, some rental car agencies in Cairns will not allow customers to drive their rental vehicles to Cape Tribulation, and they have spies around the ferry to report on any car renters who try it anyway. So be sure you clarify this issue with your rental agency; if you decide to visit Cape Tribulation, you need to find an agency that will not object.

Camping. The national park service provides a nice, simple campground at Noah Beach, just past the Marrdja turnoff. Cassowaries still roam Cape Tribulation and are especially active around Noah Creek; be sure to look for them if you spend a night here. Since campfires are prohibited, you will need a stove for cooking.

You can also camp at Pilgrim Sands, a private campground and rustic resort right by a lovely beach (which, however, disappears at high tide). You can camp in the thick of the rainforest, shaded by exotic-looking fan palms, and yet you enjoy amenities like grills and hot showers. Pilgrim Sands is a few minutes past Cape Tribulation parking area; the turnoff, to the right, is difficult to spot, so drive slowly.

Season. Any but summer, when rains could wash out roads.

In the area. Cape Tribulation has one other great advantage besides its seclusion, scenery, and rainforest ambience: it lies very close to the Great Barrier Reef, which you can therefore reach quickly and fairly cheaply. Costs for a full-day trip, including a two-tank scuba dive, can be as low as Au. $80, surely one of the best deals you will find in tropical Australia. But since the water is shallow and clear, you can see almost as much with mask and snorkel as by diving. Whichever you choose, the Barrier Reef will not disappoint you.

1. Cape Tribulation Beach

> **Distance: 2.5 km (1.5 miles) one way**
> **Time: 45 minutes one way**
> **Difficulty: easy**
> **Attractions: one of Australia's most beautiful beaches**

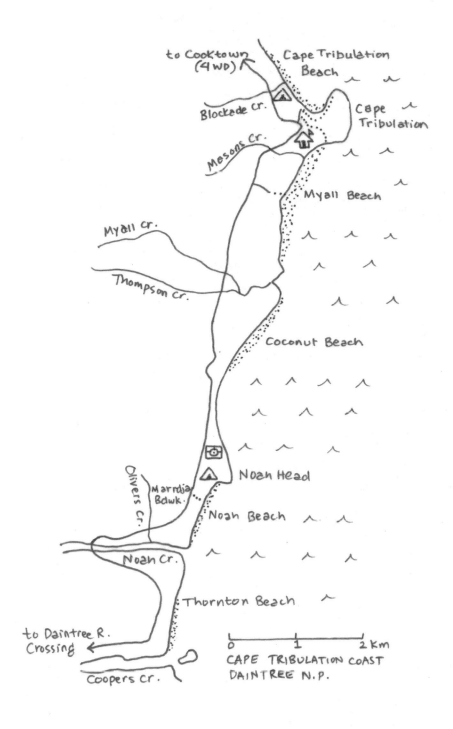

to Cooktown
(4WD)

Cape Tribulation
Beach

Blockade Cr.

Cape
Tribulation

Mesons Cr.

Myall Beach

Myall Cr.

Thompson Cr.

Coconut Beach

Olivers Cr.

Noah Head

Marrdja
Bdwk.

Noah Beach

Noah Cr.

Thornton Beach

to Daintree R.
Crossing

Coopers Cr.

0   1   2 km

CAPE TRIBULATION COAST
DAINTREE N.P.

Cape Tribulation

This easy stroll begins at the main parking lot right at Cape Tribulation. The trail crosses the cape's low saddle and winds through rainforest to the beach. From there walk south until, about three-fourths of the way down the beach, you notice a break in the trees. A boardwalk here will take you back to the main road, where you can enjoy a bite to eat before walking back as you came.

2. Marrdja Botanical Walk (Boardwalk)

> **Distance: 800 meters (0.5 mile) round trip**
> **Time: 30 minutes**
> **Difficulty: easy**
> **Attractions: a great place to learn about Cape Tribulation's**
>   **forests**

This popular trail visits both the rainforest and mangrove ecosystems along Oliver Creek near where it joins Noah Creek. The latter is habitat for endangered cassowaries as well as 26 species of rare plants. Boardwalked for most of the way, the trail winds past a remarkable variety of rainforest trees, many with name placards. A spur takes walkers across a mangrove flat that has numerous interesting bird species about. The walk features two viewing platforms along the way and eventually forms a partial loop before returning to the parking lot.

FURTHER READING

Armstrong, Mark. *Queensland: A Lonely Planet Australia Guide.* Hawthorn, Vic.: Lonely Planet Publications, 1996.

Blanch, Rob, and Vince Kean. *Bushwalking in the Mt. Warning Region: North East New South Wales; South East Queensland.* Alexandria: Kingsclear Books, 1995.

Cohen, Sharon, and Gerry Ellis. *The Outdoor Traveler's Guide to Australia.* New York: Stewart, Tabori and Chang, 1988.

Gaber, Claudia, and Stephen Clark. *Noosa's Natural Heritage: A Walker's Guide to Tracks and Trails.* Noosa: Noosa Council Enterprise Group, 1996.

Hill, Tyrone T. *Fifty Walks in North Queensland.* Melbourne: Hill of Content Publishing, 1994.

———. *One Hundred Walks in New South Wales.* Melbourne: Hill of Content Publishing, 1994.

Lackner, Thomas W. *Discovering Binna Burra on Foot.* Sydney: Envirobooks, 1989.

———. *Discovering Green Mountains on Foot.* Sydney: Envirobooks, 1989.

McKilligan, Neil M., and Ian Savage. *Bushwalks in the Toowoomba Region.* Toowoomba: USQ Press, 1993.

Rankin, Robert. *Secrets of the Scenic Rim: A Guide to the Bushwalks.* Toowong, QLD: Rankin Publishers, 1992.

Seabrook, Cheryl. *The Conondales: Bushwalking and Recreation.* Kenilworth, QLD: Conondale Range Committee, 1992.

Sinclair, John. *Discovering Cooloola: A Complete Guide and Map.* n.p.: Pacific Maps, n.d.

———. *Discovering Fraser Island.* n.p.: Pacific Maps, 1987.

INDEX

About the Author

Lew Hinchman discovered his avocation as an outdoor enthusiast over 25 years ago while he was a graduate student at Cornell University. He began by hiking the gorges of New York State's Finger Lakes region, but he soon found himself unable to resist the call of the American West. He, his wife Sandy, and their son Bryce have hiked all over Utah's high deserts as well as the Rockies, Sierra Nevada, and the Cascade Ranges. They have also floated many of the West's wild and scenic rivers. One outcome of all that outdoor exploration was Sandy Hinchman's best selling guidebook, *Hiking the Southwest's Canyon Country* (Mountaineers Books). More recently they have branched out into international destinations such as the islands of the Caribbean, Belize, Mexico, and finally Australia. Lew collected material for this guidebook during a year-long stay there. Based in southern Queensland, he and his family walked hundreds of miles of trails all over the country, but they found the tropical and subtropical regions the most enchanting. This guidebook presents the best of what they discovered. Lew is Professor of Government at Clarkson University, Potsdam, New York, and has published several scholarly books and numerous articles on philosophy, political theory, and environmental rights.